La~~y~~an's
BIBLE
Commentary

Genesis thru Numbers

Volume
1

Contributing Editors:
ROBERT L. DEFFINBAUGH, Th.M
KEITH KRELL, M.DIV.
DR. STEPHEN LESTON

Consulting Editor:
DR. TREMPER LONGMAN

BARBOUR
PUBLISHING

© 2009 by Barbour Publishing

ISBN 978-1-62029-771-1

Member of the
Evangelical Christian
Publishers Association

Printed in the United States of America.

TABLE OF CONTENTS

GENESIS

INTRODUCTION TO GENESIS

The first eleven chapters of Genesis trace events such as Creation, the Fall, the flood, and the establishing of the nations. The accounts of four great people complete the book in chapters 12–50: Abraham, Isaac, Jacob, and Joseph.

Genesis comes from the Greek word *geneseos*, meaning "origin, source, generation, or beginning." *Geneseos* is a translation of the Hebrew word *toledot* ("generations").

AUTHOR

Although Genesis does not directly name its author, Jesus and the writers of scripture clearly believed that Moses was the author of the Pentateuch (the first five books of the Bible, often referred to in the New Testament as "the Law," Mark 10:5; Luke 24:44).

OCCASION

Genesis spans more time than any other book in the Bible. In fact, it covers more than all the other sixty-five books of the Bible put together (approximately 2,400 years). The total duration is from the time of creation to the time when the Israelites arrive in Egypt and grow into a nation (about 1800 BC). The date of Genesis is sometime after the Exodus, during the fifteenth century BC.

THEMES

God's choice of a nation through which He would bless all nations is a theme throughout Genesis. It is the passing on of blessings from one generation to another.

HISTORICAL CONTEXT

The setting of Genesis divides neatly into three geographical areas:
1) The Fertile Crescent (1–11)
2) Canaan (12–36)
3) Egypt (37–50)

The setting of the first eleven chapters changes rapidly and spans more than 2,000 years and 1,500 miles. The middle section of Genesis spans about 200 years and moves from the Fertile Crescent to the land of Canaan. The final setting in Genesis is found in Egypt, where God transports the seventy souls.

CONTRIBUTION TO THE BIBLE

The story of Genesis is built around eleven accounts:

1) Introduction to the Generations, 1:1–2:3
2) Heaven and Earth, 2:4–4:26
3) Adam, 5:1–6:8
4) Noah, 6:9–9:29
5) Sons of Noah, 10:1–11:9
6) Shem, 11:10–26
7) Terah, 11:27–25:11
8) Ishmael, 25:12–18
9) Isaac, 25:19–35:29
10) Esau, 36:1–37:1
11) Jacob and Sons, 37:2–50:26

OUTLINE

GENESIS 1:1−2:25

CREATION

Setting Up the Section

The initial recipients of this story are the Israelites of Moses' day. Because it is written to the people of God, not as an apologetic to convince those who do not believe, Genesis is much more of a declaration than a defense. These chapters are not intended to give an account of the Creation that would answer all of the scientific problems and phenomenon. Rather, there is an air of mystery that permeates these two chapters, and within that mystery is the fact that God created this world and it exists within His control.

The Summary of Creation:

God Formed the Earth	God Filled the Earth
Day 1: Light (1:3–5)	Day 4: Lights (1:14–19)
Day 2: Air (1:6–8)	Day 5: Birds (1:20–23)
Day 2: Water (1:6–8)	Day 5: Fish (1:20–23)
Day 3: Land (1:9–13)	Day 6: Animals (1:24–31)
Day 3: Plants (1:9–13)	Day 6: Man (1:24–31)

THE DAYS OF CREATION

There are two purposes in the opening of Genesis (1:1):

1) To identify God as the Creator
2) To explain the origin of the world

The Genesis account does not imply that absolutely nothing existed or had happened before this. The separate creation of angels and other heavenly beings is already assumed (1:26).

The first three words ("In the beginning") translate a single Hebrew word, *bereshit*. This word does not necessarily connote a brief period of time, though the creation event is described in terms of days in later verses.

The next keyword is *God*, a rendering from the Hebrew word *Elohim*, a plural noun. This implies that God is plural, even as God is singular.

The Hebrew word translated *created* is used throughout the Bible, only with God as its subject. This word stresses the newness and perfection of that being made.

The last four words in verse 1 describe the entire universe. The Hebrew language had no word for universe, so instead the author uses the phrase "heavens and earth." This figure of speech refers to everything in creation (sun, moon, stars, plants, rocks, rivers, mountains, and so on).

Some understand a gap of an indeterminate period of time between Genesis 1:1 and 1:2. The construction of the verses in the original languages, though, does not support a consecutive statement (this happened, then that happened) but rather something included in verse 1.

In the Old Testament, the word often translated *deep* refers to the ocean, which the ancient world regarded as a symbol of chaos and evil. In the Pentateuch (Genesis through Deuteronomy) it has the connotation of a wasteland.

The word *earth* can be translated "land" as well. In this context, *land* is preferred. To the original readers of Genesis, the term *earth* did not connote a planet. The development of science did not yet support an understanding of the universe as we know it today. Earth typically refers to a specific section of land, such as the land of Egypt (45:8), the dry ground (1:10), or the land promised to Abraham (15:18).

Verse 2 describes the earth as yet unfashioned and uninhabited. When read from a New Testament perspective, it also provides the first reference to the Holy Spirit in the Bible. Many believe it gives us an idea of the constant action of the Spirit.

On day one, light appears through the darkness (1:3). The word *light* can be interpreted several ways, and the sun is not listed as a creation until the fourth day. Nevertheless, like the sun, this light distinguishes day from night (1:4–5).

Regarding the word *day*, several interpretations have been suggested:

1) The extended geological ages prior to human presence on earth
2) Twenty-four-hour periods in which God reveals (but not necessarily initiates) His creative acts
3) A simple literary device to present the creation in a framework understandable to readers
4) Literal twenty-four-hour days of divine activity

When this same word is used elsewhere in the Old Testament, it refers to twenty-four-hour periods of time. However, those that disagree with this view hold that these are days of God's activity, not human work, and it is therefore unlikely that they are supposed to be literal twenty-four-hour periods of time. Indeed, the Hebrew word for *day* covers a variety of periods: the hours of daylight (29:7), a twenty-four-hour day (7:4), or an indefinite period (35:3). All these differences indicate that verses 1:1–2:3 serve as an overture to the rest of the book, and that it may not be intended to be taken as literally as what follows.

The expanse, or space, that God speaks into being on day two is a reference to the sky (1:6, 8; see also 1:8; 7:11–12). The water above is a reference to clouds, and the water below is a reference to the water of the earth (1:7).

On the third day, God carries out two distinct acts: He separates land from seas, just as He earlier separates light from darkness (1:3) and waters from waters (1:6), and He creates plant life. The distinct varieties of plants (1:11–12) bear witness to God's organizing power.

In contrast with day two, God's acts of creation on day three are called good. They are good because both are accomplished for humanity's benefit. The third day shows the provision of dry land, on which humanity can live, and plants to sustain life (1:29–30).

On the fourth day, the lights that God had created are given a purpose, namely, to separate day from night and serve as signs for seasons and days and years (1:14).

Critical Observation

The moon is called (only here) the lesser light, and the sun is called (also only here) the greater light for a reason. Among Israel's neighbors, their pagan contemporaries, the sun and moon were designations for deities. Even today in astrology people use stars and planets for guidance, but here they are simply referred to as lights. They were appointed to regulate the fundamental rhythms of human life by defining day and night and the seasons of the year.

On the fifth day God populates the land with many kinds of living creatures (birds and fish). This is the first time God blesses something in the Bible. The word is used more than eighty times in Genesis, where it usually speaks of fertility.

Living creatures created on the sixth day are categorized in three groups. In today's language, these three groups would probably best be described as domesticated animals, small creatures, and what we would consider game or wild animals. The idea of creeping animals has more to do with their style of movement than modern scientific categories like that of reptiles.

There are parallels in the six days of creation which provide a flow to the account:

Preparation Phrase	Day 1	Day 2	Day 3	Day 4	Day 5	Day 6
"God said, 'Let there be' "	1:3	1:6	1:9	1:14	1:20	1:24
"And it was so"	1:3	1:7	1:9	1:15	---	1:24
"God saw that it was good"	1:4	---	1:12	1:18	1:21	1:25
"God called"	1:5	1:8	1:10	---	---	---
"There was evening and there was morning, the ___ day"	1:5	1:8	1:13	1:19	1:23	1:31

The plural pronouns in verse 26 are seen by many as a hint of the Trinity, but also as a reference to the complete fullness of God. The idea that humanity is created in God's image has far-reaching implications: A relationship can exist between God and humanity, and men and women can reflect God's nature. As part of that reflection, people rule over nature. The idea of ruling carries with it the connotation of responsible management rather than dictatorial control or exploitation.

Verse 27 is in the form of poetry. While some translations use the word *man*, this is a reference to all of humanity, not simply to Adam. God created humanity, both male and female.

Critical Observation

Understanding the importance of God's blessing in verse 28 is essential. Throughout the remainder of the book of Genesis, the blessing remains a central theme. *Blessing* denotes all that fosters human fertility and assists in achieving dominion. Interpreters have generally recognized "be fruitful and multiply" as commands to Adam and Eve (and later to Noah; see 9:1) as the heads of the human race, not simply as individuals. That is, God has not charged every human being with begetting children.

Humanity is supposed to subdue the earth. While the word translated *subdue* means "bring under bondage," it doesn't mean to destroy or ruin. As with the idea of ruling in verse 26, this is a requirement to act as manager with God-given authority.

Many interpret verses 29–30 to mean that both people and animals were vegetarian prior to the flood, and that it is not until after the fall of humanity, and perhaps after the flood, that meat is given as food (9:3–4). Keep in mind, however, that this writing in

Genesis is not primarily concerned with whether people were originally vegetarian but with the fact that God provided them with food.

According to verse 31, God evaluates only this day's work as very good.

It is likely that, in 2:1-3, the author intends for the reader to understand the account of the seventh day in light of the "image of God" theme of the sixth day. We are expected to copy our Creator.

Verses 2-3 make it clear that the seventh day is set apart from the first six by not only stating specifically that God sanctified it as holy, but that God did not work. This theme is repeated three times in these three verses.

q 2:4-25

MAN AND WOMAN

Genesis 2:4-25 begins a descriptive account, with humanity as the central theme. This section is not meant to be chronological. Genesis 2:7 is simply an elaboration of 1:27. The two accounts look at a similar series of events from two distinct points of view. Genesis 1 simply notes that God created male and female, adding a few remarks about their relationship to the rest of creation. The first chapter emphasizes man as one *created with* authority; Genesis 2 emphasizes man as one *under* authority.

The phrase "the heavens and the earth" (2:4) is a figure of speech that refers to the entire universe. In the second part of the verse, though, the phrase is reversed. When this happens, the phrase takes on a more literal meaning: the land and sky.

Verses 5-6 are a flashback to conditions before Genesis 1:26. This is the setting of the stage. The land is set up and poised for humanity to enter the scene.

The word translated *formed* in verse 7 describes the activity of a potter, forming vessels out of clay—ground and water. The fact that God forms man out of dust reflects man's lowly origin (see also 3:19). The Hebrew word for *man* (Adam) sounds like, and may be related to, the Hebrew word for *ground*.

It's significant to note that God creates humanity with hands, not just words. He does not simply speak people into existence as He does with the lights of the universe; God breathes life into man. Since Adam's life came from God's breath, he is a combination of dust and divinity.

The description of Adam as living is the same term that is used of animal life in Genesis 1:24. In this phrase, we see how humans and animals are similar, but this breath of life makes humans distinct from all other creatures.

Critical Observation

In 2:8–9, God's care is made evident by His provision of a garden paradise with two trees—the Tree of Life and the Tree of the Knowledge of Good and Evil. Verses 10–14 describe the boundaries of this garden. Of the four rivers mentioned, the Pishon and Gihon are unknown in the modern world (though the land of Havilah is probably an area of southwestern Arabia). The Tigris and Euphrates are now in Babylonia. The name *Eden* means "delight, pleasure." This rather extensive description sets the stage for Adam and Eve's expulsion from the garden in 3:24. It also probably signifies to the Israelites an anticipation of the promised land. Two of these rivers are exactly the ones that God uses to explain to Abraham where the promised land will be (15:18).

The Hebrew word translated *put* (2:15) connotes more than simple placement, but rather rest and safety, as well as dedication in God's presence. The man's caring for the garden is actually the idea of serving. It's a word that is translated *worship* elsewhere in the Old Testament.

It is interesting that God seems to tell Adam, alone, that the fruit of the Tree of the Knowledge of Good and Evil must not be eaten. It is important to note that there is a positive aspect to this command: God gives man the enjoyment of all of the luscious trees in the garden, and all of God's creation is pronounced "good." The tree is not a sinister tree in and of itself. The temptation to eat from the Tree of the Knowledge of Good and Evil is the temptation to seek wisdom without reference to the Word of God.

Verses 18–25 are considered the apex of the first two chapters. Everything up until this point is called good, but now the Lord says it is not good.

Adam naming the animals means that he is studying their nature (2:19–20). Names in the ancient world were descriptions. The text does not necessarily mean that Adam named every individual animal; he apparently gives names to the different kinds God brings before him. This exercise demonstrates Adam's authority over the animals.

Demystifying Genesis

The word translated *helper* (and sometimes *companion*) does not mean a servant (2:20). In fact, following His ascension, Jesus Christ uses the Greek equivalent of this word to describe the Holy Spirit, who would help believers following the Lord's ascension (John 14:16, 26; 15:26; 16:7). It signifies the woman's essential contribution, not inadequacy. The description of this companion as suitable, or corresponding, suggests something that completes a polarity, as the North Pole corresponds to the South Pole.

The Lord meets Adam's need for companionship (2:21–22). God builds woman from one of man's ribs, which could also be simply translated *side*.

How does Adam respond? He rejoices. When Adam says the woman is bone of his bones and flesh of his flesh, he is giving the ancient equivalent of the modern marriage vow "in weakness and in strength" (2:23).

One of the meanings of the verb behind the noun *bone* is "to be strong." "Flesh," on the other hand, represents weakness in a person.

Chapter 2 closes with a description of the marriage partnership. Notice that the man is responsible for leaving his family of origin. This implies faithfulness, permanence, and loyalty as the responsibility on the part of the man. Elsewhere in the Old Testament these are covenant terms.

Take It Home

Some say that the naked condition of the man and woman, as described at the close of chapter 2, goes beyond a physical description; it also has application regarding the psychological oneness and transparency required for a marriage relationship. Physically they are naked and share their bodies with each other openly, and psychologically they are not ashamed and hide nothing from each other. They are at ease without any fear of exploitation for evil.

GENESIS 3:1–5:32

THE FALL OF HUMANITY

Setting Up the Section

This passage reveals how sin enters the world and how sin can be overcome. At the end of Genesis 2, life seems ideal—paradise. Then the events described in this section forever change the world. Fear and shame enter and judgment begins. But the seeds of redemption can be found as well.

3:1–7

THE SERPENT'S TEMPTATIONS

The word translated *serpent* is the same root as another Hebrew word that means "bronze" (3:1). The word translated *crafty*, or *shrewd*, often suggests wisdom, though here it has a clearly negative connotation.

The question asked by the serpent is the first question recorded in scripture (3:1). In this case, the question casts immediate doubt on God's command.

Instead of shunning the serpent, the woman obliges him by carrying on a conversation (3:2–3). In her reply to the serpent, she does not quote the commands exactly as they are listed in Genesis 2, but instead she lists them with subtle changes.

Original Command (2:16–17 NASB)	Eve's Reply (3:2–3 NASB)
"From any tree of the garden you may eat freely."	"From the fruit of the trees of the garden we may eat."
"But from the tree of the knowledge of good and evil you shall not eat, for in the day that you eat from it you will surely die."	"But from the fruit of the tree which is in the middle of the garden, God has said, 'You shall not eat from it or touch it, or you will die.'"

As verse 4 reveals, the first thing Satan does is deny God's judgment. To make this direct contradiction of God's Word seem reasonable, Satan invents a false motive for God (3:5). Thus, the serpent stands in direct conflict with God as He has revealed Himself.

Having set the trap, the serpent lets the woman's natural desire for food carry her into the trap (3:6). The fruit looks good to her. She will (seemingly) better herself in the taking of it. Not only does she sin, but in her distorted thinking and false sense of accomplishment, she also gives the fruit to her husband.

While Adam's companion is deceived, the scriptures have already revealed that Adam has been directly warned by God about eating this fruit. It would seem that he ate willingly, aware of the consequences.

Critical Observation

The effects described in verse 7 raise the question, why did Adam and Eve not die immediately? Genesis 5:5 reveals that Adam lived to be 930 years old.

Although God's warning may have referred to physical death, primarily in view was spiritual death, which entails the loss of fellowship with God and with one another. When the man and woman eat from the tree, they immediately change their relationship with God and with each other. From their lack of shame (at the end of chapter 2) to the moment of suddenly covering themselves (3:7), an eternal shift has occurred.

3:8–24

GOD'S JUDGMENTS

The cool time of the day (3:8) can be translated the *wind* or *spirit* of the day. Often, in the Bible, the wind is a symbol of God's presence (see 1:2). A more complete transformation could not be imagined than the one described here, as Adam and his wife attempt to hide from God. The trust of innocence is replaced by the fear of guilt.

God's question (3:9) carries the implied question of why Adam and Eve are there. It is a demand that Adam take personal responsibility for his actions. Adam's response (3:10) does not express personal responsibility, but it does acknowledge something important: Life has changed. Shame, fear, and guilt have entered paradise. (Verse 10 is the first time fear is mentioned in the Bible.) Fig leaves aren't enough to cover Adam up; spiritual vulnerability is the real issue. The only solution he can devise is denial and avoidance.

Adam answers God by making excuses for himself and playing the blame game. God then addresses the woman, and she blames the serpent (3:13). God addresses the serpent with a curse. In the Bible, to *curse* means to invoke God's judgment. Some commentators take this literally and conclude that the snake had legs before God cursed it. Others take it figuratively, as a reference to the resultant despised condition of the snake. This is confirmed by the word picture of the snake eating dust.

Critical Observation

Genesis 3:15 is one of the foundational verses of the Bible. Many see this verse as the first glimpse of the gospel of Jesus. The hostility described here certainly exists between snakes and people, but God's intention in this verse seems to include the person behind the snake (Satan) even more than the snake itself. The snake's offspring would remain in opposition to the woman's offspring. In this case, Eve's offspring points to one individual—the Messiah, Jesus, who would come forth from the Jewish people.

Verses 16–19 include God's judgments on all involved. The woman will experience suffering in having children and in her desire for her husband. Adam will suffer in his attempts to control his domain. The very dust he came from will force him to struggle to survive. Man's natural or original relationship to the ground—to rule over it—is reversed; instead of submitting to him, it now resists and eventually swallows him.

Adam expresses confidence in God's promise about his wife's offspring by finally giving her the name *Eve*, which means "living," "the mother of all living," or "she who gives life." Some see this as a kind of play on words: Not only will the human race descend from Eve, but spiritual life will come from her as well.

God provides special clothing for Adam and Eve. Instead of fig leaves, He clothes them in skins. God does for the couple what they cannot do for themselves. While some see the skins as a foreshadow of redemption, it is more likely simply the practical meeting of a need.

In verses 22–24, God says that humanity has become "like one of us." This is a reference to the newfound knowledge of good and evil. This is critical because the Tree of Life perpetuates physical life in the perfect environment of the garden. When people acquire a sin nature in the physical body, they begin the process of physical deterioration, which ultimately leads to physical death. If Adam were to eat of the Tree of Life at this time, it would perpetuate his physical life forever with the presence of the sin nature.

This passage contains a certain amount of irony, in that the human race, which has been created in God's image (1:26), seeks to be like God by eating the fruit (3:5–7) but afterward finds themselves no longer in union with God.

Demystifying Genesis

Angels called *cherubim* surround and symbolize God's presence in the Old Testament (Exodus 27:7–9; Ezekiel 10:15). They are similar to bodyguards. Genesis 3:24 pictures them defending the Tree of Life with a flaming sword to keep humanity away. This is an apt picture of the separation established between God and His creation. Humanity is completely excluded in this picture, with no resources of their own that would allow them to cross into God's paradise.

📖 4:1–24

BUILDING THE FAMILY

Chapter 4 opens with the birth of Cain and Abel (4:1–2). The name *Cain* means "to acquire" or "possess." The literal rendering of Eve's reply is, "I have gotten [or have acquired] a son, the Lord." Some suppose that she understood enough of the prophecy in 3:16–19 that she believed her son would be the one to conquer the serpent. Certainly her response expresses enthusiasm and gratitude.

Unlike Cain's name, Abel's name is not explained. However, the Hebrew word *Abel* means "vanity," or "breath." Traditionally understood, Abel's name reflects on the temporary nature of his existence.

Critical Observation

Genesis 4:3–5 describes the vocations of the brothers. Both vocations are noble; one is not better than the other. And there does not appear to be anything wrong with offering fruit as opposed to animal sacrifice. Certainly grain offerings were a legitimate part of Israel's worship practices.

There may be clues in the description of the offerings themselves as to what was the problem with Cain's offering. Abel offers the *first* of his flock (4:4; see Exodus 34:19; Deuteronomy 12:6; 14:23) and the fattest (4:4; see Numbers 18:17). Abel gives what cost him most—the firstborn and the most choice selections. On the other hand, Cain's offering is not described as his first or his best, merely as *the fruit.* This difference in quality and attitude may be the key to God's differing reactions to the offerings.

When Cain learns that God is displeased with his offering, he becomes angry (Genesis 4:5). In response to Cain's anger, God asks him questions. His questions demonstrate that He is more displeased with Cain's response than with the actual offering. It is not the style of the offering, but the substance of Cain's heart that is called into question (4:6–7).

Not all of the earliest manuscripts of Genesis include Cain's request to Abel to go out to the field, but the detail is significant. According to Jewish law, the fact that Cain leads his brother to a private place would have indicated premeditation, and thus would have incurred an even harsher punishment (4:8).

God's question to Cain in verse 9 mirrors His question to Adam in 3:9. And like his father, Cain responds with a lie and defensiveness. The fact that Cain dispassionately denies what he has done shows a lack of care and concern that parallels Adam's lack of regard for his wife (3:12).

Verses 10–16 reveal God's judgment on Cain—that Cain would be an outcast wanderer. This is the first instance in scripture where a human is cursed. When God pronounced judgment on Adam, it was the ground that actually was cursed. While in modern culture, the death penalty is considered the ultimate punishment, in this ancient world, disenfranchisement was possibly worse than death. It was a loss of roots and a loss of all that defined someone.

Cain's character is revealed in his negotiation. His concern is not his dead brother or displeasing God; his concern is self-preservation. Cain settles in the land of Nod, which means, "wandering." We do not know what ultimately happens to him.

Demystifying Genesis

We do not know what sign God gave to Cain before He expelled him. Some have supposed it was a mark of some kind on Cain himself, while others suggest a special hairstyle. One of the ancient rabbis argued that the sign was a dog that accompanied Cain on his wanderings. Others think it was some sign in the external world, such as an intensified fear of killing another human being. Whatever form it took, the mark God gave Cain was not a stigma, but rather a guarantee of safe passage (4:15)—an act of mercy on God's part.

Of course, the other mystery concerning Cain is whom he married (4:17). He had probably married a sister or possibly a niece. Marriages between close relatives would have been at first unavoidable if the whole human race came from a single pair. Marriage between siblings and close relatives was not prohibited until the Mosaic Law, instituted thousands of years later (Leviticus 18:6–18). There would have been no genetic imperfections at the beginning of the human race. Genetic defects resulted from the fall and only occurred gradually, over long periods of time.

Verses 17–18 begin a history of Cain's descendants. Verse 19 introduces Lamech as a man with two wives. Bigamy was common in the ancient Near East. It is not unheard of even among the fathers of the faith. Jacob had two wives and two concubines. Solomon, famously, had thousands of wives. These men are notable as exceptions, though, among the Israelite nation.

In verses 20–22, we see that Cain prospers even though he rebelled against God. Cain's descendants take the lead in building cities, developing music, advancing agriculture, creating weapons, and spreading civilization.

One can easily see that the lines that make up verses 23–24 are parallel and poetical. Lamech is singing a song about polygamy, murder, and revenge. Lamech wears violence as a badge of honor.

📄 4:25-26

SETH

Verses 25-26 are not events that fall chronologically after verses 17-24. Instead, at verse 25, Genesis picks up an alternate branch of Adam's family tree. Seth's birth is strategic. After God's promise that Eve's offspring would defeat the serpent, her oldest son takes the life of her youngest. That doesn't leave many offspring to champion the cause. But here is another birth, which can continue the hope of God's promise through the line of Seth, a name that means "to set," or "place."

Verse 26 reveals the beginning of the worship of the God of creation, who is the focal point of the Old Testament and the Israelite nation.

📄 5:1-32

GENEALOGY: ADAM TO NOAH

Genesis 5 begins a second genealogy (the first is Genesis 4:17-34). This fifth chapter is a list of the ten descendants of Adam to Noah. The technique of mixing narrative and genealogy is found throughout the book of Genesis. A primary purpose seems to be to show the development of the human race from Adam to Noah, and to bridge the gap in time between these two major individuals.

Verse 2 returns to the theme of God blessing man (see 1:27). Throughout the remainder of the book of Genesis, there is a recurring theme of fathers blessing their children (9:26-27; 27:27; 48:15; 49:1-28). In keeping with such a theme, the author shows, at each crucial turning point in the narrative, that God Himself renews His blessing to the next generation of sons (1:28; 5:2; 9:1; 12:3; 24:11). Seen as a whole, the picture that emerges is that of a loving parent insuring the future well-being of His children through the provision of an inherited blessing.

In the description of each generation, the same literary structure is followed:

1) The age of the father at the birth of the firstborn
2) The name of the firstborn
3) How many years the father lives after the birth of this son
4) A reference to the fathering of other children
5) The father's total life span

This genealogy covers at least 1,600 years. Within the timeline of the Bible, this chapter covers the longest period in world history. The average age of the ten people listed in this genealogy is about 900.

One of the most important elements of this genealogy is the phrase that closes the account of each person: "and then he died" (NIV). This phrase (the translation of only one Hebrew word, *muth*) occurs eight times (5:5, 8, 11, 14, 17, 20, 27, and 31) and serves as a reminder of the consequences of Adam and Eve's fall. One of the most powerful functions of this phrase is the effect the one time it does not appear—Enoch does not die.

The phrase "walked with God" (NET) is only used of two men: Enoch and Noah (5:22; 6:9). *Walk* is a biblical figure for fellowship and obedience that results in divine blessing. It describes the closest communion with God—as if walking at His side.

Rather than dying, verse 24 tells us that Enoch disappears (5:24). There are no other details. In a similar situation, the prophet Elijah is picked up by a chariot (2 Kings 2:11–12), but no such details are given here.

Even though the death motif is strong in this chapter, there is even more emphasis on God's grace. We see this in the references to life, fertility (sons and daughters), Enoch's translation from this life, and other blessings.

GENESIS 6:1–9:29

THE FLOOD

Setting Up the Section

Genesis 6–8 covers a lot of ground. These chapters document the degradation of society, Noah's great flood, and the beginnings of life beyond the flood with Noah's three sons, Shem, Ham, and Japheth.

📄 6:1–13

PRECURSORS TO THE FLOOD

Genesis 6 begins by naming two groups: the sons of God and the daughters of men. Many view this as a way of describing the descendants of Cain and the descendants of Seth (4:1–25). The assumption, then, is that the descendants of Seth are God-following people, while the descendants of Cain are not. If this is the case, then the events described in verses 1–2 represent a mingling of the godly with the ungodly, and thus a watering down of righteousness on the earth.

Other interpretations of this passage include the idea that these are marriages between angels and humans, or between aristocrats and commoners.

The verb translated in some versions of the Bible as *strive* occurs only here in the Hebrew Old Testament (6:3). Other English translations use the words *contend* (NIV), *abide* (NRSV), *remain* (NET), or *put up with* (NLT).

There are two interpretations of the 120-year time limit cited in verse 3. One possibility is that the 120 years may signify the new age limit for people. Another view is that the 120 years refer to the time remaining between this announcement of judgment and the coming of the flood.

Demystifying Genesis

The word *Nephilim* occurs only in verse 4 and in Numbers 13:33, where it refers to the sons of Anak, who were people of great stature. There is another Hebrew word that simply designates a huge man—*rapha*. This word is used for men like Og and Goliath (see Deuteronomy 3:11; 1 Chronicles 20:6). The Nephilim were a more distinct group.

Genesis 6:4 is a parenthetical piece of information. Rather than relating the Nephilim to the marrying couples in verse 2, the Nephilim are simply contemporaries of that time.

Verses 5–8 describe the wickedness of the pre-flood civilization and God's offense at the state of His creation.

The keyword in verse 5 is *intent* (NKJV), or *inclination* (NIV). This word comes from the verb that describes a potter in the act of forming and molding his vessel (Isaiah 29:16). It is the description of something that is done not by happenstance but by design. Humanity's evil is far more than a surface foolishness. This passage describes an all-consuming depravity.

God's grief as described here is a mixture of rage and bitter anguish. His regret reflects the idea of breathing or sighing deeply.

Out of that regret comes a destructive plan. God's judgment will involve an almost complete erasure of man and all accompanying creatures from existence. God's pain over sin prompts Him to blot out the wicked (Genesis 6:5–7).

Noah stands as the first good news in this chapter (6:8). The *favor* that he finds is the translation of a Hebrew word that can also be translated *grace*. It comes from a root meaning "to bend or stoop."

Verses 9–13 offer us the back story. In the midst of an evil world stands a faithful man and his three sons: Noah, Shem, Ham, and Japheth.

Noah's description is noteworthy:

- Righteousness connotes conformity. In the case of Noah, he conforms to the standard set by God.
- Blameless involves the idea of completeness. Noah conforms to the standard set by God with no essential quality missing.
- Noah's character and lifestyle stand out among the culture around him. He is not only righteous in the sight of God, but he also has a credible reputation among the people of his day.

Three times in verses 11–12, the earth is described as *corrupt*. The Hebrew word translated here is rich in meaning. It was used to describe a shirt that was stained too badly to be used or a clay pot that was marred in the production process, making it unusable. The word translated *violence* (6:11) was used of acts of robbery, taking wives by force, and murder. These two words paint a vivid portrait of the deterioration of the creation that had been described in Genesis 1, by God Himself, as very good.

Verse 13 describes God's judgment. The word translated *destroy* is the same word that is rendered by *corrupt* in verse 12. God will permanently corrupt this wicked civilization.

THE FLOOD

In 6:14–16, Noah receives detailed instructions that he is to follow in building the ark. The ingredients are cypress wood and pitch. The dimensions are as follows:

Dimensions	Noah's Ark	Approximate Equivalent
Length	450 feet	1½ American football fields
Width	75 feet	7 parking spaces
Height	45 feet	3 stories
Cubic Feet	1.5 million	550 railroad boxcars
Capacity	14,000 gross tons	*Princess of the Orient*

While the Bible doesn't give enough detail to know exactly what the ark looked like, it probably was shaped like a shallow rectangular box topped with a roof, with an 18-inch space under the roof, interrupted only by roof supports, so that light could get into the vessel from every side. This design would use space efficiently and would have been stable in the water.

Along with God's proclamation of the terrible flood that He will send is a hopeful promise of a covenant (6:17–18). This is the first use of the word *covenant*, which refers to a binding promise. This covenant will mean safety for Noah and his family, even in the midst of tragic judgment.

Demystifying Genesis

How could Noah's ark potentially hold over a billion species of animals (6:19–21)? Keep in mind that the modern concept of species is not the same as a "kind" in the Bible. There were probably only several hundred different kinds of land animals that would have to be taken into the ark. The sea animals stayed in the sea, and many species could have survived in egg form. Also, Noah could have taken younger varieties of some larger animals. And finally, the ark was a huge structure—the size of a modern ocean liner three stories high.

Verse 22 presents a theme that is repeated three more times in chapter 7—Noah's obedience to God's command (7:5, 9, 16).

Take It Home

Noah's story reminds us that it is possible to be right with God, even when surrounded by wickedness. We can stand as Noah did, righteous and blameless among our contemporaries. It just requires that we listen to God's voice and do what He says.

While chapter 6 describes two of each kind of animal entering the ark (6:19–21), the instructions in the opening verses of chapter 7 become more specific (7:1–3). Noah is to take two of every unclean animal and seven of every clean animal. The purpose of this is to become clear after the flood. Birds will be needed to scout out the earth (8:7–12), and the clean animals and birds will be offered in sacrifice to the Lord (8:20). If Noah had taken only one pair of each and then offered each of these pairs in sacrifice, these species would have become completely extinct.

Critical Observation

God does not reveal the basis for His distinction between clean and unclean animals here (7:2). Noah predated Moses, who wrote down the dietary laws regarding which animals were ceremonially clean to eat, but the understanding of clean and unclean animals was already common. Even Israel's pagan neighbors observed distinctions between clean and unclean animals, though they varied from country to country.

The account of the floodwater inundating the earth (7:6–16) is both majestic and terrible, and is reminiscent of creation. Like Genesis 1, the account of the flood is structured by a careful counting of the days (371 total days):

- 7 days of waiting for the waters to come (7:4, 10)
- 40 days of water rising (7:12, 17)
- 150 days of waters prevailing (7:24; 8:3)
- 40 days of water receding (8:6)
- 7 days of waiting for the waters to recede (8:10)
- 7 more days of waiting for the waters to recede completely (8:12)

The description of the flood in verses 17–24 is a reminder of the reality of final judgment. But even with the severity of this event, there is debate on whether the flood was global or local. For those who favor the global flood perspective, the supporting factors include these:

1) The language used in the Bible text presents a global experience, though at this time in history, human perspective was not as broad as it is today.

2) The depth of water seems to support a global flood. Mount Ararat, on which the ark came to rest, is over 17,000 feet in altitude, and the waters were over 20 feet higher than all the mountains (notice the language of 7:19).

3) God's promise of never allowing another such flood seems to indicate a worldwide event (8:21; 9:11, 15). There have been devastating local floods since then.

4) When the New Testament authors speak of the flood, they speak of it as a worldwide flood (2 Peter 3:6).

The word *remember* in the opening verses of chapter 8 is a high point of this story. God remembers both His people and the promises He made to them.

Critical Observation

During the eleventh to twelfth centuries AD, Mount Ararat became the site traditionally associated with Noah's landing. Genesis 8:4, however, does not indicate a specific peak, and refers generally to its location as the "mountains of Ararat." The search for the ark's artifacts has been both a medieval and a modern occupation, but to the skeptic, such evidence is not convincing, and to the believer, while not irrelevant, it is not necessary to faith. Modern Mount Ararat lies on the border between Turkey and Armenia and encompasses parts of Turkey, Russia, and Iran—the frontier of the ancient world. From this region Noah's descendants spread out over the earth.

The picture painted by verses 6–12—the sending of the raven and the dove—reveals the hopeful waiting of those who had, at this point, been in the ark around a year (compare 7:11–13; 8:13–15). When the land is at last dry, God calls for a procession out of the ark and commands Noah and his children to replenish the earth (8:13–17). Verses 18–19 document the disembarking.

📄 **8:20—9:29**

RESULTS OF THE FLOOD

Chapter 8 closes with Noah's sacrifice at the altar, a demonstration of his dedication and gratitude (8:20–22). This altar is the first mentioned in the Bible. As the head of the new repopulation, Noah's sacrifice represented all humanity.

Chapter 9 opens with a renewal of God's first blessing and commission to Adam (1:28; 9:1). Like Adam, Noah and his sons are blessed and are commanded to reproduce and fill the earth. The word *blessed* is a keyword in Genesis—"to confer benefit." It occurs approximately eighty times in this book.

Additional blessings are found in 9:2–4. Why does God put the fear of humanity in all creatures? Probably for the protection of both, since they are no longer at peace with one another. Humans could now use animals for food, with the restriction that they drain the animal's blood first.

Demystifying Genesis

What is the purpose of God's restriction that Noah and his sons drain the blood of the animals they use for food (9:4–5)? One reason is probably respect for life and the giver of life. In the centuries to come, as the Jewish laws were developed and documented, God's people were again forbidden to consume the blood, which was considered the life of the creature.

The last phrase of verse 5 can seem a bit confusing. The literal translation is "from the hand of a man, his brother." The point is that God would require the blood of a killer, since the person killed was a relative ("brother") of the killer. The language reflects Noah's situation (after the flood, everyone would be part of Noah's extended family), but also supports the concept of the brotherhood of humanity.

Verse 6, seen as a support for capital punishment by some, remains a controversial verse. However one makes its application in the modern world, this verse upholds the sanctity of human life and human responsibility before God to protect that life. And in the terms of this verse, the reason is more than simply preservation of the race. It is the acknowledgment of God's image borne by every person.

Verse 7 reiterates 9:1, which is itself a restatement of God's direction to Adam in Genesis 1:28.

In verses 8–17, God promises not to flood the earth again. He clearly makes this an eternal promise and marks it with the sign of the rainbow (9:12–16).

Critical Observation

God attaches significance to the rainbow as a sign of His covenant, though there may have been rainbows before this pronouncement. The Hebrew word for *rainbow* is also the word for a battle bow. The point seems to be that the bow is now put away, hung in place by the clouds, suggesting that the storm is over. As a result, whenever clouds appear over the earth and a rainbow appears, God will remember His covenant, while the rainbow reminds His people of the same thing.

In verses 18–29, the history of Noah and his family moves from rainbows (9:12–17) to shadows. The explanation in verse 18 that Ham is the father of Canaan has great relevance, because it anticipates the rest of the story. It is under Moses' leadership that the Israelites set out for the land of Canaan to reinhabit the area, so Moses' original audience would have found great significance in the identification of Ham's bloodline.

After leaving the ark, Noah takes up farming like his father, Lamech. Specifically, he plants a vineyard (5:28–29; 9:20). Eventually he gets drunk and careless. The word translated *uncovered*, the description of Noah in his tent (9:21), means "to be disgracefully exposed."

As the account explains, Ham sees his exposed father. The verb used to describe Ham's seeing Noah has such force that some say it means "he gazed with satisfaction." And when he tells his two brothers about Noah, the words used mean that he "boldly announced with delight." Ham seems to have gloated over his father's shame and to have done nothing to preserve his father's dignity.

In contrast to Ham, Shem and Japheth walk in backward and cover Noah. They honor their father and win the approval and blessing of God (9:23).

Verses 24–29 describe the aftermath of both Noah's and Ham's indiscretions. When Noah learns what has happened, he pronounces a curse on Ham's son, Canaan. It seems that Noah is prophesying that Canaan is already cursed simply because he is Ham's son. Prior to this in the Bible, only God had issued a curse against anyone or against anything (the serpent in 3:14; the ground in 3:17; 5:29; 8:21; and Cain in 4:11).

After cursing Canaan, Noah proclaims a blessing in store for Japheth—extended territory and a large number of descendants (9:26–27). The son who had protected Noah would find protection himself—in the tents of his brother, Shem, served by the family of his brother Ham.

Genesis 9 ends with a summary of Noah's subsequent life. Like his forebears, Noah lives to an advanced age (950).

GENESIS 10:1–11:32

NOAH'S DESCENDANTS

Japheth	10:1–5
Ham	10:6–20
Shem	10:21–32
Babel	11:1–9
Shem's Descendants	11:10–26
Terah	11:27–32

Setting Up the Section

Chapters 10–11 track the repopulation of the earth from Noah's sons and the separation of the nations into individual cultures.

The genealogies in Genesis 10 include reference to the separation of nations (10:5, 20, 31) that occurs at the Tower of Babel, which is described in chapter 11. This interspersed narrative (11:1–9) separates the two genealogies of Shem (10:21–31; 11:10–26), paving the way for the link between the Terah (father of Abraham) clan and Shem's lineage (11:27).

📖 10:1–5

JAPHETH

This first section is the shortest and highlights fourteen of Japheth's descendants. The Japhethites split into two groups: One group settled in India and the other group in Europe. They became the coastline peoples, the Gentiles to whom the apostle Paul spread the gospel in the New Testament.

Japheth's bloodline plays a lesser role in the theme being developed in this book, which deals more with the conflict between Ham's descendants, the Canaanites, and Shem's descendants, the Semitic people.

The occupation of the lands described in verse 5 actually takes place after the account of the tower at Babel.

Demystifying Genesis

This is a modified genealogy, and it uses the words *son* and *father* even more flexibly than do the other genealogies of Genesis 4, 5, and 11. *Son* in Genesis 10 may mean "descendant," "successor," or "nation." *Father* may mean "ancestor," "predecessor," or "founder."

This section has been called a "table of nations" because it traces the connected origins of various people groups. At this time, the nations of the world were being repopulated from the same family: the three sons of Noah.

📖 10:6–20

HAM

Ham's descendants, the Canaanites, are significant because of the part they play in the future history of Israel, particularly the events at Babel (Babylon), Mizraim (Egypt), and Canaan (10:10, 13–15). The nations connected to Ham's bloodline inhabit an area from Egypt to Mesopotamia and the west coast of Arabia. The original readers of this writing were still in conflict with Ham's descendants, and would consider this history quite relevant.

📖 10:21–32

SHEM

The descendants of Shem are the Semitic peoples who inhabit the eastern lands: modern-day Iraq, Iran, and eastern Saudi Arabia. This bloodline is mentioned last (though Shem is older) because it is the principle bloodline of the history covered in Genesis. The genealogy of Shem splits at the sons of Eber (10:25). It is from the name *Eber* that the word *Hebrew* originated. The Hebrews, of course, are later referred to as the Israelites (the bloodline descending from Abraham's grandson, Jacob) and the Jews (the people who descended from Jacob's son, Judah).

📖 11:1–9

BABEL

The story of Genesis 11 occurs before the nations scatter around the world (as described in Genesis 10).

After the flood, all people spoke the same language. Noah's descendants, rather than spreading out, settle together in Shinar, a place that eventually becomes associated with evil.

Verses 3–4 describe the first idea of what becomes the famed tower at Babel. The motivation for building a city is to make a name for themselves and to keep from scattering out. This is not an act of worship, but rather an act of pride and self-preservation.

Verses 5–6, God's response to the people's efforts, is anthropomorphic; it describes God in human terms. It simply means that God wants a good look at what people are doing on earth. God, of course, doesn't need to leave heaven to see what is happening on earth.

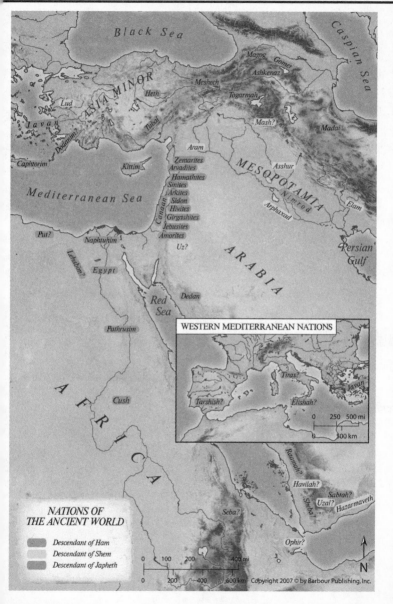

NATIONS OF
THE ANCIENT WORLD

Descendant of Ham
Descendant of Shem
Descendant of Japheth

Copyright 2007 © by Barbour Publishing, Inc.

Critical Observation

The language of Genesis 11:6 may sound as if God is worried. This verse, however, is not speaking of technology but of morality. God initiates a judgment to counter the rebellion of people who were putting their trust in their own efforts rather than His care. God is not threatened by what man might do. On the contrary, God is protecting man from himself.

Verse 7 employs the plural, "let us." God spoke of Himself in this same plural form early in Genesis in the account of creation (1:26).

As the result of the confusion of the languages, the people scatter over the whole earth rather than settle in one place. The name *Babel* means "confusion" in Hebrew and "the gate of gods" in Babylonian. This area, later known as Babylon, stands as a longtime enemy of the Israelites and holds a reputation for evil.

📖 11:10–26

SHEM'S DESCENDANTS

Genesis 11:27 begins a new division in the book of Genesis. This book covers more than 2,000 years and more than 20 generations; yet, it spends almost a third of its text on the life of this one man: Abraham, the forefather of the Israelite nation (11:27–25:18). This revisiting of the genealogy of Shem in verses 10–26 is the first step in establishing the bloodline from which Abraham descends. Verse 26 introduces Terah, the father of Abraham (at this point in history called Abram).

📖 11:27–32

TERAH

Terah, like Noah before him, has three sons, one of whom is the father of Lot (11:27–28). Lot is introduced quickly because he is a major character in the next portion of Genesis and serves as a contrast to Abram.

Though the text says only that Haran was born in Ur, Abram was probably also born there (11:28). It is generally held that Ur is located in southern Mesopotamia, near the Persian Gulf. Others, however, contend that Ur is located to the north and east of Haran.

Abram married Sarai, whose name is later changed to *Sarah*. She is his half-sister, (20:12), which is not unusual or contrary to God's will at this early date in history. It may seem strange that the details of Nahor's marriage are included here. This would have been significant information, though, to the original readers of Genesis, in that they would already be aware (since this is a historical account) that Nahor's granddaughter, Rebekah, becomes Abram's daughter-in-law.

Sarai's childlessness is a major factor in the upcoming account (11:30). Childlessness in the ancient Near East involved shame and social ridicule, and implied that the woman, or the couple, was not in the favor of the gods.

Verses 31–32 then inform us that Terah takes Abram and his family from Ur of the Chaldeans in order to settle in Canaan, but they settle in Haran instead. This may have been a matter of religion. Joshua 24:2 and 24:14–15 make it clear that Terah (and quite possibly his family) worshiped many gods. In fact, many of the names in Genesis 11:29 come right out of the cult of moon worship. Ur and Haran are both centers for this false religion, which may have been the motivation to settle there rather than moving on.

GENESIS 12:1–20:18

ABRAHAM

Abram's Call	12:1–20
Abram and Lot	13:1–14:24
Abram's Covenant	15:1–21
Ishmael	16:1–16
Abraham's Circumcision	17:1–27
Sodom and Gomorrah	18:1–19:38
Abimelech	20:1–18

Setting Up the Section

Chapter 11 describes the third time in Genesis that humanity strikes out—first in Eden, then with the flood, and finally at Babel. Beginning with chapter 12, we at last see the foundation God is laying for a solution. Through Abram, God promises a descendant who will eventually bring salvation. This is an act of grace. God is certainly a God of justice and judgment, but in His economy, grace always prevails.

📄 12:1–20

ABRAM'S CALL

In the opening verse of chapter 12, the NIV, NKJV, and KJV include the word "had," which clarifies the timeline. These translations are suggesting that 12:1 flashes back to something that happened in Ur even though 11:31 ends with Abram in Haran.

God's command to go is the translation of a term that can emphasize loneliness and isolation; ideas of parting and seclusion are often implied.

The first three verses of chapter 12 as a whole convey the inauguration of God's covenant with Abram:

1) "I will make you a great nation."
2) "I will bless you."
3) "I will make your name great."
4) "You shall be a blessing." The original Hebrew wording actually says, "Be a blessing."
5) "I will bless those who bless you."
6) "The one who curses you I will curse."
7) "And in you all the families of the earth will be blessed."

31

Since Lot voluntarily chooses to accompany Abram, he probably believes the promises as well (12:4). While the acquired people could be a reference to slaves or servants, it could also refer to converts who Abram won during his sojourn in Haran.

Abram stops at Shechem (12:6–7), a place that becomes sacred to the Israelites because, while this is God's second revelation of Himself to Abram, it is the first revelation in the promised land. Shechem is near the geographic center of Canaan (Joshua 20:7).

The Hebrew term *Moreh* means "teacher," and may indicate that the oak tree mentioned in verse 6 is an ancient shrine, or a place where Canaanite priests declare oracles.

The fact that Abram pitches his tent between Bethel and Ai probably indicates that he stays there for some time (Genesis 12:8). During his time on the mountain, Abram continues to worship by building an altar. The word translated *worship* (NET) carries the idea of not only acknowledging but also proclaiming the name of the Lord.

Verses 10–20 give us a peek into Abram's humanity as he, out of fear, asks Sarai to pretend to be his sister rather than his wife. While Sarai is indeed Abram's half-sister, this is a ruse intended to deceive, and he is trusting in his deception to protect him instead of trusting in the Lord. While he has proven himself to be a man of faith, in this case he is more afraid of the Egyptians than of God.

Medieval commentators suggest that what Abram hopes to get out of being Sarai's brother is the right to receive and deny all suitors' requests to be Sarai's husband, in this way protecting her from adultery or bigamy.

Sure enough, the Pharaoh does notice Sarai and takes her into his household, and Abram seems to benefit from the arrangement (12:15–16). The gifts he receives are provisions of wealth in Abram's day. The last two gifts, the female donkeys and the camels, tell all. Female donkeys were far more controllable and dependable for riding and, therefore, the ride of choice for the rich.

The subsequent curse on Pharaoh's household is the first example of the cursing and blessing that God promises to Abram in Genesis 12:2–3. Any misfortune in the ancient world is looked upon as an indication of divine displeasure. So when God sends great plagues, Pharaoh and his advisers may have tried to pinpoint when the troubles started. When they trace the troubles back to the time of Sarai's arrival, this leads them to Abram. The word interpreted *plagues* (12:17) in some translations is probably better translated *diseases*.

Critical Observation

Everything that Abram receives in Egypt later causes him trouble. Because of the great wealth he acquires from Pharaoh, Abram and Lot choose to separate (13:5–6). Hagar, the Egyptian maidservant who Pharaoh gives to Abram, brings division and sorrow with far-reaching consequences (16:1–16).

ABRAM AND LOT

We have no clue as to how long Abram remains in Egypt. He builds no altars in Egypt, to our knowledge, nor does he ever call on the name of the Lord. But upon leaving Egypt, he returns to his altar (13:1–4).

Verses 5–18 chronicle the downfall of Abram and Lot. Their possessions became so large that they could no longer live together (13:6–7). This point is repeated twice for emphasis. As nomadic tribesmen, they had to travel about, looking continually for pasture for their sheep and cattle. Since the land was already inhabited, there wasn't a lot of land to choose from, and the men became competitors for the best pasture. The result was a range war.

According to verse 7, the conflict between Abram and Lot is on full display before the unbelieving Canaanites and Perizzites.

Abram's approach to Lot in verses 8–9 is tender and compromising. He appeals to their kinship and offers Lot a choice. The result of Lot's choice in verses 10–13 reveals a contrast between Lot and Abram and introduces the wicked city of Sodom. Lot chooses his own benefit over Abram's, his vocation over his family, and his immediate gratification over his long-term benefit.

Lot surveys the land before him with the eyes of one weighing financial promise (13:10), while Abram surveys the land before him while receiving God's third revelation (13:14). That revelation contains three specifics:

1) God will give the land to Abram and his descendants forever (13:15).
2) Abram's heir will be his own child (13:15–16).
3) Abram's descendants will be innumerable (13:16).

These blessings are good news for Abram but far from the reality he could see. Nevertheless, God tells him to walk the land. The practice of walking through land appears to have been a symbolic, legal practice related to the idea of staking a claim on a piece of real estate. In the ancient Near East, victorious armies claimed defeated territory simply by marching through it.

Chapter 13 closes with Abram building another altar, this time in *Hebron*, a name that means "communion." It is in the region of Hebron that Abram makes his home base (18:1) and is eventually buried (25:9).

The first twelve verses of chapter 14 serve as an introduction. They describe the first war ever recorded in scripture—a war between four eastern kings and five southern kings. Shinar (Babylon, modern-day Iraq) initiates this war (14:1–2). (It is Shinar in which the first families after the flood settle, and then unfortunately attempt to build a tower at Babel.)

The Bible includes very little information about the actual battles involved, but the account is laden with geographical and political details. The territory mentioned here is quite extensive, stretching from the north and west of the Sea of Galilee, down the Jordan Valley, all the way south to the Red Sea. This war is an international power struggle to control a strategic commercial land bridge between Mesopotamia and Egypt. Whoever controls this land bridge maintains a monopoly on international trade.

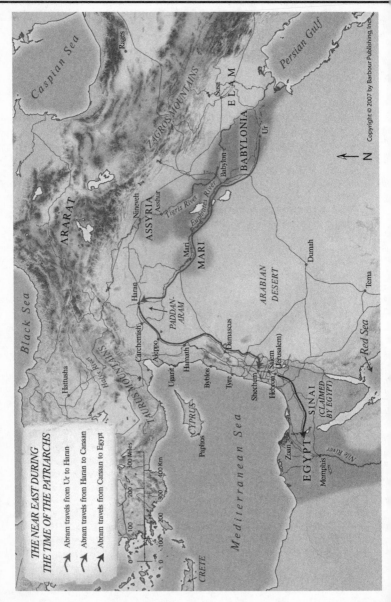

THE NEAR EAST DURING
THE TIME OF THE PATRIARCHS

↗ Abram travels from Ur to Haran
→ Abram travels from Haran to Canaan
↑ Abram travels from Canaan to Egypt

Copyright © 2007 by Barbour Publishing, Inc.

The southern kings had been subjugated for twelve years. In the thirteenth year, they attempt to throw off their shackles (14:3–4). In response, the eastern kings launch a punishing assault to end the rebellion (14:5–7). The kings of Sodom and Gomorrah, with their allies, prepare for all-out battle in the valley of Siddim, which is full of tar pits. The five southern kings think that these pits will be a natural defense, but they only meet defeat.

The events recounted are global in scope and end in the disgraceful defeat of the kings of Sodom and Gomorrah (14:10–11).

Critical Observation

Verse 13 marks the first time in the Bible that the term *Hebrew* is used—in this case of Abram, the foreigner living in Canaan.

Since Lot has separated from his uncle and moved into Sodom, he and his family are taken captive by the four eastern kings (14:12). Though Abram could have chosen to do nothing, he leads a pursuit to rescue Lot and his possessions. Abram divides his men and attacks at night. The march of Abram and his band of 318 men is one of the most remarkable forced marches in history. They travel the whole length of the Jordan River and launch a counter attack as the enemy indulges in a time of carousing and reveling in celebration of their victory (14:14–16).

This pursuit would have begun in the hill country south of Jerusalem and continued as far as Dan, the northernmost point of what came to be known as Israel. Abram traveled over 240 miles, one-way, to rescue Lot (14:16).

The king of Sodom comes to meet Abram (14:17). Abram fought his great battle for the sake of Lot and his family, but his victory also benefits the cities of Sodom and Gomorrah. A special welcoming committee had evidently been appointed, headed by the king himself, to confer upon Abram the usual reward for a conquering hero.

Melchizedek, mentioned in verse 18, is probably a title rather than a proper name. It means "King of Righteousness." Salem, of which Melchizedek is king, may be the shortened name for Jerusalem (Psalm 76:2), which at that time was occupied by the Canaanites. Melchizedek was a Canaanite, but he is called a priest of God Most High (14:18). The biblical record does not mention Melchizedek's parents, his ancestry, his birth, or his death. In that sense he is different from any other individual found in this narrative.

Melchizedek's blessing on Abram acknowledges God's work in Abram's victory. This would have been an unexpected turn of events. Though Melchizedek is certainly a Canaanite, Abram acknowledges his priestly dignity by giving him a tithe (4:19–20). (The tithe of the Mosaic Law has not been established yet.)

The story concludes with a conversation between Abram and the king of Sodom, and Abram's acknowledgement of his God and Creator. By all rights, the spoils Abram captured should belong to him, but Abram accepts none for himself. The men who fought with him, however, are rewarded their share (14:23).

This passage concludes with Abram's confessing God before people (14:22). The book of Hebrews in the New Testament applies this account to Jesus, identifying Him as a high priest in the order of Melchizedek.

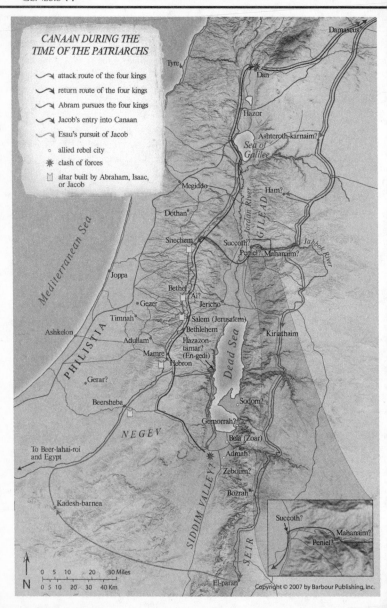

CANAAN DURING THE TIME OF THE PATRIARCHS

～ attack route of the four kings
～ return route of the four kings
～ Abram pursues the four kings
～ Jacob's entry into Canaan
～ Esau's pursuit of Jacob

○ allied rebel city
✳ clash of forces
⌂ altar built by Abraham, Isaac, or Jacob

Damascus

Tyre

Dan

Hazor

Ashteroth-karnaim?

Sea of Galilee

Ham?

GILEAD

Jordan River

Jabbok River

Megiddo

Dothan

Shechem

Succoth?

Peniel? Mahanaim?

Mediterranean Sea

Joppa

Bethel

Ai?

Jericho

Gezer

Salem (Jerusalem)

Timnah

Bethlehem

Kiriathaim

Ashkelon

Adullam

Hazazon-tamar? (En-gedi)

PHILISTIA

Mamre

Hebron

Dead Sea

Gerar?

Beersheba

Sodom?

NEGEV

Gomorrah?

Bela (Zoar)

To Beer-lahai-roi and Egypt

Admah?

Zeboiim?

SIDDIM VALLEY?

Bozrah

Kadesh-barnea

SEIR

N

0 5 10   20   30 Miles
0 5 10 20 30 40 Km

El-paran

Succoth?

Mahanaim?

Peniel?

Copyright © 2007 by Barbour Publishing, Inc.

ABRAM'S COVENANT

Though Abram turns down the reward offered by the king of Sodom, he receives a promise that God Himself will be his reward and his shield (15:1).

The shield was the primary defensive weapon of the Old Testament warrior. It was a portable fortress, a defensive wall that could be taken with the warrior into battle. It provided a barrier between the vulnerable flesh of the soldier and the dangerous impact of the enemy's weapons.

Verses 2-3 record, for the first time, Abram's response to God. Inherent in his response is the pain of having wealth and success, but no heir to pass it on to. It was a common practice in the ancient Near East for a childless couple to adopt a son, who would care for them in their old age and inherit their possessions and property. Abram suggests that he adopt his chief servant, Eliezer.

Amidst Abram's doubt and despair, God encourages him. He not only gives Abram the promise again (12:2; 13:15-16), but He confirms it by stating that Abram's descendants will be as numerous as the stars of heaven.

Critical Observation

Some consider Genesis 15:6 to be the most important verse in the Old Testament: God declares Abram righteous (clean, morally right) on the basis of Abram's faith. The idea is that God is crediting Abram's faith as righteousness. While this connection between faith and righteousness is most often considered a New Testament concept, this verse confirms that God has always desired faith from His people.

Genesis 15:7-21 recounts God's making of the covenant with Abram. The emphasis in this section shifts to the land promised by the Lord to Abram's descendants.

God encourages Abram with the fact that He had brought him out of Ur of the Chaldeans to give him the land of Canaan as his inheritance. This statement is virtually identical to the opening statement of the Sinai covenant in Exodus 20:2: "I am the LORD your God, the one who brought you out of Egypt where you were slaves" (CEV). The expression "Ur of the Chaldeans" refers back to Genesis 11:28, 31, and grounds the present covenant in a past act of divine salvation from Babylon, just as Exodus 20:2 grounds the Sinai covenant in an act of divine salvation from Egypt.

The sacrifice that God instructs Abram to make involves the same ceremonially clean animals that are used later in the sacrificial system under the Law of Moses. The use of five different kinds of sacrificial animals underlines the solemnity of the occasion.

The text implies that Abram is familiar with the ritual to take place, because God does not explicitly state what to do with the animals. His command is only to bring the animals, but Abram not only brings the animals; he also sacrifices them and lays them out as an offering (15:9-10).

In Abram's day, legal agreements were formalized by means of a very graphic covenant ceremony: the dividing of an animal sealed the covenant. The animal was cut in half and the two parties would pass between the halves while repeating the terms of the covenant. By doing so, the two parties were stating, "If I fail to fulfill my commitments to this covenant, may I suffer the same fate as this animal."

In one of the most dramatic scenes in Abram's life, he is depicted as a passive observer. In this case, though, he faces terror. This is often the response in the Bible when someone faces God's presence (15:12).

God makes a seven-fold prophecy concerning the nation of Israel (15:13–16). Abram did not live through this period of slavery, but it is the story found in the book of Exodus.

The smoking oven and flaming torch represent the presence of God. The Lord Himself passes between these pieces of animals, sealing a covenant with Abram (15:17). As He makes this covenant with Abram, God gives the geographical boundaries and the nations that will belong to Abram. The borders of this land, promised to Abram's descendants, appear to coincide with the borders of the Garden of Eden (Genesis 2:10–14). The land consists of ten nations in which God would grant Abram's descendants victory.

📖 16:1–16

ISHMAEL

Chapter 16 gives the account of Abram and his wife, Sarai, attempting to fulfill God's promise on their own.

God had promised Abram a son (12:2). But in Abram's impatience, he adopts his servant girl's son, Eliezer, so he will have an heir (15:2–3). However, God rejects Eliezer and reaffirms His promise to give Abram a son of his own (15:4). But ten years later, Abram is still waiting.

In another attempt for an heir, Sarai suggests following a custom through which Abram would have a child through Hagar, Sarai's servant. Ancient documents reveal that when a woman could not provide her husband with a child, she could give her female slave as a wife and claim the child of this union as her own.

There is an ironic reversal here. When in Egypt, Abram gave Sarai over to the Egyptian Pharaoh, and Hagar joined their entourage (12:10–20). Here in Canaan, Sarai gives Abram over to the Egyptian servant.

While Hagar is not on equal standing with Sarai, her status does change when she becomes a slave wife. If she produces the heir, she could be the primary wife in the eyes of society. According to verses 4–5, in Hagar's opinion Sarai had been demoted. The Hebrew word translated *despise* (NET) means to "treat lightly or with contempt." A contemporary rendering of Sarai's closing threat in verse 5 would be: "God will get you for this." According to verse 6, the mistreatment goes both ways as Sarai begins treating Hagar *harshly*—same word used later to describe how cruelly and unfairly the Egyptian slave masters treated Israel.

In verse 7, the angel of the Lord appears to Hagar. This is the first of this kind of appearance described in the Bible. There is debate about who this angel is; some believe him to be the preincarnate Christ. In the conversation between the two, the angel of the Lord instructs Hagar to submit not only to Sarai's authority, but to whatever mistreatment the situation involves. This requires Hagar to humble herself (16:9). Hagar's son, Ishmael, will grow up in Abraham's household because of these instructions.

It is only in association with her return and submission to Sarai that the Lord offers Hagar a blessing, the promise that she will have many descendants (16:9–12). Abram, Isaac, and Jacob are given a similar promise, but Hagar is the only woman that is given a promise like this. She is also told to name her son *Ishmael*, which means "God hears," or "God has heard."

The prophecy of verse 12 is not an insult. The wild donkey lives a solitary existence in the desert away from society. Ishmael would be free-roaming and strong. His free-roaming lifestyle will put him in conflict with those who follow social conventions. This is not a prophecy of open warfare, only of friction because of his antagonism to others' ways of life.

Verse 13 is the only place in the Bible where a person names God. Hagar names God *El Roi*—the God who sees. The name given to the well in verse 14 reflects the same thing: "The well of the living One who sees me." The text suggests that God takes up the cause of those who are oppressed.

According to verses 15–16, Hagar obeys the Lord and returns to the household. There is no mention of Sarai in these closing verses of chapter 16.

📖 17:1–27

ABRAHAM'S CIRCUMCISION

The account in Genesis 17:1–27 reveals a mixture of divine sovereignty and human responsibility. The idea of a *covenant* between God and Abram is central to this narrative (see 12:1–3).

Thirteen years have passed since the last conversations recorded between Abram and God (chapter 15). In the newest revelation, God refers to Himself as God Almighty (*El Shaddai*). The word *El* means "the strong one." This suggests that God is the One from whom Abram is to draw strength and nourishment.

This is the first time God is called by this name. So far, the primary name by which the Lord has revealed Himself is *Elohim. El Shaddai* is used exclusively in scripture relating God to His children.

The word translated *blameless* in verse 1 has the sense of wholeness when used of attitudes and is translated "without blemish" when used in the context of sacrifice (see Exodus 12:5; Leviticus 1:10).

The word translated *establish*, or *confirm*, means "to set in motion." The covenant has already been established; here God is restating it to Abram.

Abram's response, prostrating himself before God, is a typical act of worship (17:3; Leviticus 9:24; Joshua 5:14; Ezekiel 1:28).

It is at this time God changes Abram's name. *Abram* means "exalted father," a name that probably refers to God's nature more than Abram's. Here God changes Abram's name to *Abraham*, which means "father of a multitude."

God makes five "I will" statements in Genesis 17:6–8.

God also outlines the obedience He expects from Abraham; circumcision will be the sign of the covenant (17:7–14). Circumcision is an outward sign of an inward commitment.

It is to an Israelite what a wedding ring is to a bridegroom.

Abraham is to circumcise himself and every male in his household. From then on, baby boys were to be circumcised on the eighth day of life.

Demystifying Genesis

The word *circumcision* means "cutting around." It refers to a minor operation that removes the foreskin from the male organ. Only males underwent circumcision. In the patriarchal society of the ancient Near East, people considered that a girl or woman shared the condition of her father if she was single, or her husband if she was married.

Why was the circumcision to be performed on the eighth day (17:12)? We know today that on the eighth day the infant's immune system is at the optimum level for such a procedure. Important blood-clotting agents, vitamin K and prothrombin, are at their highest levels in infants on precisely the eighth day of life, making the eighth day the safest day to circumcise an infant.

Verse 14 says that an uncircumcised male will be cut off from his people. Typically, this is a reference to execution, sometimes by the Israelites but usually by God, in the form of premature death.

Sarai's name is changed as well, to Sarah (17:15–16). The names are two different forms of a word meaning "princess."

When the Lord had appeared, Abraham fell on his face, exhibiting respect and reverence (17:3). After God's promise that Sarah will bear a son, he again falls on his face, but this time to hide his laughter (17:17). When Abraham hears that God will greatly increase his descendants, he responds with respect and submission. But when he hears *how* God will carry out His plan, his respect contains a tinge of laughter.

Abraham's plea on behalf of Ishmael reveals a kind of "if only" agony. He is being asked to believe the seemingly preposterous, when a sure thing is already a part of the family.

In verses 19–22, we read God's outline of the future for both of the sons of Abraham. Abraham's son will be named *Isaac*, which means "laughter," an ironic name in light of Abraham's response (17:3, 19). God promises blessings on Ishmael as well as on Isaac. As the Hebrew people would have twelve tribes, so Ishmael's people would also have twelve families. (The list of Ishmael's twelve sons is given in Genesis 25:13–15.)

This chapter concludes with Abraham's obedience to the demand for circumcision (17:23–27). It is important to note that circumcision is not a condition of the covenant, but a sign of Abraham's participation in it.

📖 18:1–19:38

SODOM AND GOMORRAH

God's appearance to Abraham recorded in chapter 18 is apparently only a few weeks or months after the appearance recorded in chapter 17. In Genesis 17:21, God said Sarah would give birth one year later, and the account in chapter 18 gives us no indication that she is pregnant yet.

Abraham's reaction to the three visitors is typical of ancient Middle Eastern hospitality.

He hurries to serve them and bows before them (18:2–5). He also makes his best food available (18:6–8). In the ancient world, a person's hospitality was often determined by the ability to provide extravagant hospitality. Also, though Abraham has servants available to him (14:14), he is personally involved in the care of these guests.

Though many believe that one of Abraham's visitors was Jesus, preincarnate, the fact that there were three visitors should not be pressed to represent the Trinity. It's unclear whether Abraham recognized the identity of any of the men, but many scholars believe he did because he addresses one of them as "my lord."

In the next seven verses, the narrative pans to Sarah, Abraham's wife (18:9–15). The Lord affirms His promise that Sarah will have a child the following year. He even promises He will show up for the birth (17:21; 18:10).

It was customary in Abraham's day, as in some cultures today, for women to be neither seen nor heard while male guests are entertained. Yet, Sarah listens from where she is (18:10).

Verse 11 offers background information that reveals that what the guest proposes—Sarah's pregnancy—is a natural impossibility. Sarah certainly believed it to be impossible, and her laughter is not simply from being caught off guard by the idea; it reveals her unbelief (18:12).

Critical Observation

If this were the entire story, we would be tempted to say that Sarah is no example to follow. Verses 12–15 reveal a woman who doubts God and lies about it. But in the book of Hebrews, we get the rest of the story. Hebrews 11:11 reveals that Sarah does consider God faithful to keep His promises. Eventually, she finds the answer to the Lord's question, "Is anything too hard for the LORD?" (18:14 NIV).

After feeding his guests, Abraham walks with them awhile (18:16). It is during this time that Abraham learns about Sodom, and the theme of the account takes a turn from faith and fellowship to judgment.

Critical Observation

The Lord chose to disclose His intentions toward Sodom and Gomorrah because He had chosen Abraham to be a channel of blessing to all the nations of the earth, and because of Abraham's relationship with God. The Bible certainly doesn't represent Abraham as a perfect man, yet his faith in God put him in relationship with God; Isaiah 41:8 even refers to Abraham as His friend. Therefore, God trusted him with this information about Sodom and Gomorrah.

Verses 20–21 reveal God's basic plan for Sodom and Gomorrah. The word translated *outcry* in verse 20 is used to describe cries of the oppressed and brutalized. In this case, the term may have two meanings: (1) It may mean the outcry against Sodom caused by its injustice and violence, or (2) the cry of its rebellion against God (19:13).

The Lord speaks of personally observing sin (18:21). The Hebrew text here could be rendered, "I will go down personally and see if their sin is made complete."

Abraham's conversation with the Lord recorded in verses 22–33 is a prayer-negotiation for the righteous people of Sodom and Gomorrah. This is the first time in the scriptures so far that a man has initiated a conversation with God.

Keep in mind that these wicked cities are where Abraham's nephew Lot has settled. Abraham's primary purpose seems to be to secure justice (or deliverance) for the righteous minority in their wicked cities. Secondarily, he wants God to spare the cities. This interpretation finds support in Abraham's appeal to the justice of God rather than to His mercy (18:23–25).

Why does Abraham stop at the number ten? He probably felt there were at least ten righteous people in Sodom.

Take It Home

Why does God allow Abraham to intercede for Sodom? Some of the answers to that question may be seen in these last verses of chapter 18. God is a God of mercy as well as of judgment; He takes no pleasure in destroying the wicked. This narrative also shows us the power righteous people can have, and the value of intercession on the behalf of others. Abraham stands as an example of someone who desires mercy for others just as he has received mercy.

After this negotiation, two angels approach Lot at the gate of Sodom. The city gate is where the civic leaders met to finalize legal and business transactions. It is a place of prominence and influence. The implication is Lot had achieved not only his goals but also his social and political ambitions.

While there is no indication that Lot recognizes these visitors as angels, as Abraham does, he treats them with hospitality (19:1–3). The phrase "urged them persistently" (NET) is a translation of the Hebrew verb meaning "to press; to insist." This word ironically foreshadows the hostile actions of the men of Sodom, where they pressed hard against Lot and came near to break the door (19:9).

Verses 4–9 provide a chilling testament to the wickedness of both the Sodomites and even Lot himself, as the Sodomites demand to be given access to the guests and Lot offers his daughters instead. Though there is some debate on this account, the verb traditionally translated *know* in verse 5 is most often translated *sexual intercourse* in more modern-language Bibles. This idea seems to be confirmed by Lot's offer of his virgin daughters to the men. These citizens of Sodom meant to do harm.

Lot's offering of his daughters is unfathomable to a modern society. We understand it a little more when we consider the low place of women in the pre-Christian world and the high standing of any guest in terms of Middle Eastern hospitality.

The word used to describe the blindness the men of Sodom experienced (19:11) is a rare word that may indicate "a dazzled state," or a combination of partial blindness and a kind of mental bewilderment. Yet, despite their physical blindness, these men and boys persist to the point of weariness in their effort to satisfy their sexual cravings.

When the guests explain to Lot the fate of the city, the word translated *destroy* is the same word used twice in Genesis 6:13 of the judgment of the flood (19:13).

Lot has lost such credibility with his sons-in-law that they treat his message as a joke. Ironically, the Hebrew word that is translated *joking* (NIV) is the same root from which the name *Isaac* is derived, meaning "laughter."

The angels warn Lot by telling him there are great consequences for sin, but he delays responding to God. Lot is so attached to his present world of family, friends, power, and material things that he just cannot bear the thought of leaving it all behind (19:15–16; 1 John 2:15–17).

Even as the angels are rescuing Lot from the cities, he is fighting for his own self-preservation. Rather than trusting these messengers, he fights to stay within his comfort level (Genesis 19:18–22).

The destruction of the cities is described in verses 23–29. Archaeologists believe that today these cities are buried under the Dead Sea. As for Lot's wife, the Hebrew verb translated *looked back* signifies an intense gaze, not a passing glance, even though their rescuers had warned them to keep moving ahead (19:17, 26).

The follow-up account in verses 30–38 is remarkably similar to the story of the last days of Noah after his rescue from the flood (9:20–27). In Noah's case, he became drunk with wine and uncovered himself in the presence of his children. In both narratives, the act has grave consequences. Thus, at the close of the two great narratives of divine judgment—the flood and the destruction of Sodom—those who are saved from God's wrath subsequently fall into a form of sin reminiscent of those who die in the judgment. This is a common theme in the prophetic literature (Isaiah 56–66; Malachi 1). The mention of the Ammonites and Moabites is significant since these neighboring nations are mentioned in the nation of Israel's later journey to occupy the promised land.

📖 20:1–18

ABIMELECH

The account described in Genesis 20 is quite similar to another account, described in Genesis 12:10–20, where Abraham and Sarah devise a scheme to avoid potential problems with the Pharaoh in Egypt. There are some scholars who find these similarities so striking that they wonder if this is the same account recorded a second time.

As with the similar event in chapter 12, the information Abraham gives is factual. Sarah is his half-sister. Even if factual, though, he is concealing the whole truth that Sarah is also his wife. This, combined with the conversation recorded in verses 4–6 between God and Abimelech, leaves readers with the impression that Abimelech is more righteous than Abraham. In fact, according to verse 6, the Lord Himself preserved Abimelech from falling because of Abraham's deceit.

Abraham even blames God for his vulnerable condition, complaining that God made him wander away from home (20:13). The implication is that if God had not told him to leave his father's house, he would have never ended up in Abimelech's kingdom. If he had never arrived in Abimelech's kingdom, he would have never lied.

To make matters worse, the last part of verse 13 reveals that Abraham pushes Sarah into his deception.

Verses 17–18 reveal that the women in Abimelech's household are unable to have children because Sarah had become a part of the household. God heals them, yet Sarah remains childless.

GENESIS 21:1–25:18

ISAAC

Setting Up the Section

Chapters 21–25 offer the accounts of Isaac's birth and Abraham's death. This period of time is the beginning of the fulfillment of God's promise that Abraham would father a nation.

📖 21:1–34

ISAAC'S BIRTH

Verses 1–7 record the birth of Isaac. Upon the birth of Isaac, Abraham immediately obeys by calling the boy *Isaac* (17:19; 21:3). *Isaac* means "he laughs," or "may [God] smile." Abraham also obeys God by circumcising his son on the eighth day (21:4). This was God's command to Abraham and His covenant with him (see 17:7–14).

In 21:6–7, the scene shifts to Sarah, alluding to her laughter of unbelief when the Lord announced that she would give birth (18:10–15). In verses 8–9, the Egyptian Hagar again has a role in the narrative. Fourteen years earlier, Hagar had given birth to Ishmael, and for most of the intervening period, Abraham had treated Ishmael as the heir. By this point Ishmael is a teenager.

At Sarah's demand that Abraham banish Ishmael (21:10), Abraham receives a direct word from God for the sixth time since coming to the land of Canaan (21:11–13).

Take It Home

When Abraham slept with Hagar, he actually was following an accepted custom of the day. But it certainly appears in retrospect that it was an act of unbelief. God had promised an heir, and this was a way to help God's promise along. In sending Ishmael away, Abraham faced the consequences of that act of unbelief. His story stands as a reminder to trust God to fulfill His promises.

Verses 15-16 describe the plight of an ancient single mother without the support of family or friends. While Hagar does cry out to God, it is the boy's cries that God hears. This offers special meaning to the fact that *Ishmael* means "God hears" (16:11; 21:17-19).

The account closes with an example of God's sovereignty and compassion. Even though Hagar suffers, her need for support is met (21:17-21). God does not forget His promise to greatly multiply her descendants (16:10). God has compassion on Hagar's plight and becomes like a father to Ishmael.

At verse 22, Abimelech reenters the account, arriving with his enforcer, Phicol, to sign a treaty with Abraham (21:22-24). The term *Phicol* may be a title rather than a proper name. The same name is used in Genesis 26:26 of Abraham's military commander.

In contrast to Abraham's previous fear of Abimelech, he now boldly stands up to this powerful king. Abraham brings up the matter of the well that Abimelech's servants had seized from him (21:24-26). Wells were of extreme importance to seminomadic people like Abraham. The Hebrew verb translated *complained* implies that Abraham had to complain several times.

In their last conflict, it is Abimelech who models generosity, sending Abraham away with gifts (20:14-16). Here, Abraham returns the favor in a small way (21:28-30). Abraham and Abimelech also show great patience with each other.

The passage concludes with the men naming the well *Beersheba.* By granting Abraham rights to a well, Abimelech has made it possible for Abraham to live there permanently and acknowledged his legal right, at least to water.

By planting a tree, Abraham indicates his determination to stay in that region. Tamarisk trees were long-lived and evergreen. The tree is meant to be a lasting landmark to God's provision and a focal point of Abraham's worship. It serves as an appropriate symbol of the enduring grace of the faithful God (21:33).

The Hebrew phrase translated *eternal God* is only used here and carries with it a distinction for this account. This name stresses God's never-ending nature. God's promises and covenant are everlasting because God Himself is eternal. This perhaps reflects growth in Abraham's understanding of God.

Abraham now owns a small part of the land God promised him.

📄 22:1-24

AN OFFERING

In Genesis 22, we come to one of the greatest crisis chapters in the Bible—the crisis of obedience.

Notice in verse 1 that God tested Abraham. There is a vast difference between God's purpose in testing a person and Satan's purpose in testing a person. God tests to confirm and strengthen; Satan tests to corrupt and weaken.

God makes His impossible demands. The repetition of the word *son* and *only son* reiterates the severe nature of this test. This same term can refer to an infant (Exodus 2:6) or a young man (1 Chronicles 12:28). Abraham obeys God's commands immediately and unquestioningly (Genesis 22:3-4).

The name of the land, *Moriah,* means "where the Lord provides," or "where the Lord appears." It was a three-day journey from Beersheba to Moriah, about fifty miles (22:2-4).

In the biblical world, three days was a typical period of preparation for something important (for example, Genesis 42:17–18; Exodus 19:10–11; Numbers 31:19; Esther 5:1; Hosea 6:2; Matthew 12:40; 1 Corinthians 15:4).

This site is the location where the temple was later built (2 Chronicles 3:1).

In Genesis 22:5–8, we see that Abraham's obedience is based on faith. He believes God will provide the sacrifice. The word *worship* in verse 5 means "to bow oneself close to the ground."

In 22:9–10, we see that Abraham's obedience is thorough and complete. Keep in mind, though, that Abraham could not have offered Isaac without Isaac's consent and cooperation. Isaac, as the bearer of the wood, is the stronger of the two. As a young man he is also the faster of the two. Clearly, he is strong enough and big enough to resist or subdue his father.

Verses 11–12 don't imply that God is just now learning that Abraham fears Him. God is omniscient. The angel of the Lord is saying to Abraham, "By your faithful actions I experientially know that you fear God." The language is accommodated to the human understanding, uttered, as it were, from a human point of view.

Critical Observation

Verse 15 is the final recorded instance of God speaking to Abraham. God spoke directly to Abraham eight times (12:1, 7; 13:14; 15:1; 17:1; 18:1; 21:12; 22:1, 15).

Abraham's obedience is rewarded in three ways. First, God provides the very thing He demands from Abraham (22:13–14). Fittingly, Abraham names this place "The Lord will provide." Second, God provides assurances of His promises (22:15–19). It is unusual for God to speak with an oath. Abraham's supreme act of obedience draws forth God's supreme assurance of blessing. Finally, God provides for future needs (22:20–24). The narrative closes with the happy news that Abraham's brother Nahor has become the father of twelve sons. They will later become the ancestors of twelve Aramean tribes. Most of the other names in this genealogy are the ancestors of cities and tribes around Israel. They are precisely the peoples who are to be blessed through Abraham's offspring. The central purpose of this list is to introduce the future bride of Isaac, Rebekah (22:23).

Take It Home

Remember, total obedience is not only measured by what you give God; God also takes into account what you keep for yourself. Can God get close to the most important things in your life—your possessions, business, plans and dreams, and relationships? Are you willing to let go (Luke 14:26–27)? Sometimes the supreme test of our faith will be a matter of putting obedience to God above something we have lived for all of our lives. Sometimes it will involve something that might seem foolish and ridiculous to everyone else. Are you willing to be sacrificially obedient to God in every area of your life?

SARAH'S DEATH

The first two verses of Genesis 23 record Sarah's death, and the next eighteen verses have to do with the purchase of the plot where Sarah is buried. The focus of this story is that Sarah is buried in Canaan (23:2, 19), and that Abraham goes to great lengths and cost to make this a certainty. This demonstrates how Abraham's actions reflect a faith for the future.

As commentators over the centuries have noted, Sarah is the only woman in the Bible whose age is revealed (23:1). Sarah is also the only woman whose name God changes (17:15).

Sarah dies in Hebron, the center of the land of promise (23:2). Kiriah Arba was its original name, named after Arba, the greatest man of the Anakites, a frightening group of warriors (Joshua 14:15).

Abraham mourns and weeps, indicating that, in addition to crying, he goes through the traditional mourning customs of his day: tearing clothes, cutting his beard, spreading dust on his head, and fasting. This is all done in the presence of the dead body. The Israelites had a very elaborate and intense process that they went through when someone died (23:2). This is the first record of a man's tears in the Bible.

In verses 3–5, some English translations (ESV, NIV, NRSV) render the Hebrew term *Heth* as *Hittites* (also in Genesis 23:5, 7, 10, 16, 18, 20), but this gives the impression that these people are the Hittites of Anatolia. However, there is no known connection between these sons of Heth, who are apparently a Canaanite group and the Hittites of Anatolia. The sons of Heth call Abraham a mighty prince. Apparently, Abraham's influence and reputation has spread (21:22–23).

Demystifying Genesis

The ancient Israelites placed great importance in the location of their own and family members' burial sites. It was normally important to be buried in one's homeland. Verses 20–24 remind us that Abraham and Sarah's family roots were in Ur (11:31). Despite the importance of burial location, family roots, and Abraham's current alien status, he insists on burying Sarah in Canaan, even though doing so is costly. Why? Because Abraham is not looking backward to where he came from, nor is he looking at his present situation—living in a tent because he does not possess even one acre of the promised land. Abraham is looking forward.

In Abraham's day, bargaining was done from a seated position. When Abraham stands, it signals something important. Abraham has a specific grave in mind. Abraham, in faith, wishes to stake his claim in the promised land by buying a cave used traditionally as a tomb. The sons of Heth are currently in control of this area of Canaan, so Abraham makes the request of them (23:7-11).

Critical Observation

Even though Ephron offers to give Abraham the land free of charge, he still places value on the "gift" that he offers. It is extortion, pure and simple. All Abraham wants is the cave, but Ephron adds the field. More real estate, more money! Ephron is certainly not being generous to a grieving man. In fact, the price and terms of the sale indicate that Ephron is greedy and unfair.

This cave of Macphelah is very well attested to archaeologically. Abraham was buried there, Sarah was buried there, and their children were buried there. Currently a mosque stands on the burial site.

Sarah's grave is the first mentioned in scripture. Later, Abraham is buried there (25:8–9), and so are Isaac, Jacob, Rebekah, and Leah (49:30–33; 50:13). The crucial element in this chapter is not Sarah's death, but Abraham's acquisition of land from outsiders.

📖 24:1–67

ISAAC'S MARRIAGE

Genesis 24 contains a great love story. The Lord, who never speaks in this chapter, is nevertheless the main character. He is mentioned seventeen times (24:1).

The threefold description in verse 2 leads many to the conclusion that this servant is Eliezer, who is mentioned in Genesis 15:2, and whose name means "God of help" or "helper."

The oath Abraham makes with his servant seems a little bizarre, as does the servant's placing his hand under Abraham's thigh. Yet this is customary in Abraham's day (see also 47:29).

Abraham's mind-set seems to be that it is better to have no wife than to have a Canaanite wife. In the Old Testament period, the family is the most important educational unit (Deuteronomy 6:6–7; Proverbs 1:8).

A point of tension arises when the servant asks if Isaac can go to the land to meet his future wife (Genesis 24:5). It's a legitimate question. What Abraham is seeking to do requires blind faith from any woman; leave home to marry a man sight unseen. Nevertheless, twice Abraham warns his servant not to take Isaac back to Ur (24:6, 8). Abraham knows God has called him out of Ur and has promised him abundant descendants and land, so he is willing to trust the Lord in whatever He chooses to do.

Verse 10 begins a new section. The description of the servant's travels actually encompasses hundreds of miles and several months, as the servant assembles a caravan and makes his way to Mesopotamia. The city of Nahor could refer to a city by that name, or could simply mean that Abraham's brother Nahor lives there. The servant's arrival at the proper place is all a part of the divine blessing. God's hand is in the events of this story.

Although a number of English translations understand the servant's prayer as a request for success in the task (24:12 NASB, NIV, NRSV), many feel that it is more likely that the servant is requesting an omen or sign from God (24:14). Culturally, it was a normal act of hospitality to provide water to thirsty travelers. But providing water for ten thirsty camels was going far beyond what would normally be expected (24:13-14). In praying this prayer, the servant actually stacks the deck against finding someone. It would take a remarkable woman to volunteer for this lowly and backbreaking task.

Verses 15-21 record Rebekah's appearance and her family connections; they also record that she does exactly what the servant had prayed, exhibiting a servant's heart by going beyond his request and watering his camels.

Critical Observation

A typical ancient well was a large, deep hole in the earth with steps leading down to the spring water. Each drawing of water required substantial effort. Camels can consume up to twenty-five gallons of water in ten minutes, and the servant had ten camels with him. One more fact: A typical water jar held about three gallons of water. All of this together means Rebekah made many descents into the well. Her labors could have taken well over an hour.

Verses 22-27 point out the obvious: God is behind the scenes but directing the acts. God sovereignly works through the circumstances of those who are acting in faith.

Rebekah returns home and shares everything with her family (24:28-33). The servant's urgency is evident since he considers his master's business more important than the food his hosts place before him.

Critical Observation

A third tension-filled episode occurs in 24:34-49, as the servant seeks to obtain the approval of Rebekah's family. Genesis 24, as a whole, is an excellent example of the ancient storyteller's art. In those days people enjoyed repetition—in fact, they preferred it—as they listened to tales or read them. Far from being signs of inept editing or dual authorship, the servant's repetition of the details that leads up to his search are probably deliberately employed as effective literary devices.

In 24:50-54, the tension is resolved by the family's approval. Again, the servant responds appropriately by bowing to the ground in worship and gratitude. The gifts the servant offers (24:53) may have been the bride price, which would finalize the agreement.

Abraham's servant does not want to delay his leaving, which presents a difficult choice for Rebekah. She would leave her family and everything familiar and go away with a man whom she had just met in order to marry another man whom she had never seen (24:55-61). Rebekah's courageous willingness seems to be another testimony to God's leadership in this situation.

The scene now switches to where Isaac lives and meditates. This is a place where God has previously answered the prayer of Hagar, Sarah's handmaiden, after she became pregnant with Abraham's son, Ishmael (16:14; 24:62). Since Ishmael and Isaac are pitted against each other, this is an ironic twist in the account.

A final episode of tension is found in 24:62–67. The question is: How will Isaac and Rebekah respond to each other? After a play-by-play of their initial encounter, verse 67 says Isaac loves Rebekah.

Ultimately, this entire story is about God's faithfulness. He protects and guides the servant on his journey, and He brings Rebekah, along with just the right servant-spirit, at just the right time. From our historical perspective centuries later, we can see how God used the remarkable obedience of a few family members to accomplish His purposes.

📖 25:1–18

ABRAHAM'S DEATH

Before he dies, Abraham passes on his legacy: the promises he received from God. According to verses 2–4, the six sons that Abraham has with Keturah become the descendants of several Far East tribes.

Abraham wills everything he owns to Isaac, because he is the legal firstborn. But while he is alive, he honors his other sons with gifts (25:5–6).

Genesis 25:7–11 relates the account of Abraham's death. The reference to a full life carries the idea of a sense of satisfaction.

Demystifying Genesis

In the Old Testament, those who have already died are regarded as still existing. The event of being "gathered to one's people" is always distinguished from the act of burial, which is described separately (35:29; 49:29, 31, 33). In many cases, only one ancestor was in the tomb (1 Kings 11:43; 22:40), or there were none at all (Deuteronomy 31:16; 1 Kings 2:10; 16:28; 2 Kings 21:18), so the idea of being gathered to one's people or joining one's ancestors does not mean being laid in the family sepulcher.

Abraham is buried in the field that he purchased from Ephron the Hittite (Genesis 23:1–20; 25:9–10), once again affirming that he believed God would grant the land to Abraham's descendants.

Isaac dwelt near Beer-Lahai-Roi, which means "well of the living One who sees me" (25:11). Here, God delivers Hagar (see 16:14), and Isaac has come to meditate as he awaits Rebekah (24:62). Isaac later prays again, this time for his barren wife (25:21).

Critical Observation

In between the major sections of Genesis dealing with Abraham (11:27–25:11), Jacob (25:19–35:29), and Joseph (37:2–50:20), there are smaller sections dealing with Ishmael (25:12–18) and Esau (36:1–37:1). Genesis 25:12–18 looks briefly at Ishmael before continuing the story.

In this small passage about Ishmael, there is reference to God's promise that twelve princes will be born to Ishmael (17:20). God had pronounced that Ishmael would live in hostility toward his brothers (16:12). The description in verse 18 of Ishmael's descendants seems to confirm that pattern.

Like his father, Abraham, Ishmael is also gathered to his people, indicating that he is a believer in God and shares in the spiritual blessings of all who die in the faith (25:17).

GENESIS 25:19–36:43

ISAAC'S FAMILY

Twins: Esau and Jacob	25:19–34
Isaac and Abimelech	26:1–35
Jacob's Blessing	27:1–28:9
Jacob's Departure	28:10–30:43
Jacob's Return	31:1–35:29
Esau	36:1–43

Setting Up the Section

The entire book of Genesis emphasizes the sovereignty of God and the wisdom of His "delays." Chapters 26–36 trace this sovereignty through the generation following Isaac. The struggles that Jacob and Esau face, as described in retrospect in Genesis, reveal God's plan rising to the surface against the odds.

📖 25:19–34

TWINS: ESAU AND JACOB

Just as Sarah before her, and Rachel after her, (29:31; 30:1–2), Rebekah seems unable to provide the male heir that was so important to this ancient culture—despite the promise God made to Abraham, Isaac's father, to give him a nation of descendants. At this point, twenty years have passed since Isaac and Rebekah married. Isaac is approaching sixty.

The word used to describe Isaac's prayer does not connote a simple formality of prayer; instead, it implies a fervent plea (25:21). Out of that plea, Rebekah becomes pregnant with twins (25:22). Jewish legends say the twins, eventually named Jacob and Esau, tried to kill each other in the womb. According to some of the legends, every time Rebekah went near an idol's altar, Esau would get excited in the womb, and when she went near a place where the Lord was worshiped, Jacob would get excited.

More than legend, though, the words describing the struggle of the twins in Rebekah's womb carry the idea that they smashed themselves inside her. In retrospect, this struggle of the children foreshadows the fact that these twins would father conflicting nations. And, we learn in verse 23, the older son will serve the younger.

Critical Observation

This idea of the younger serving the older appears in several places in scripture:

- The offering of Cain, the older brother, is rejected, whereas the offering of the younger brother, Abel, is accepted (4:1–5).

- The line of Seth, the younger brother of Cain, is the chosen line (4:26–5:8).

- Isaac is chosen over his older brother, Ishmael (17:18–19).

- Rachel is chosen over her older sister, Leah (29:18).

- Joseph, the younger brother, is chosen over all the rest of Jacob's sons (37:3).

The intention behind each of these reversals is the recurring theme of God's sovereign plan of grace. The blessings given to these younger sons and daughters are not the natural rights of the firstborn. Instead, they are blessings associated with the call of God.

At last the twins are born. Esau's name means "hairy one"; Jacob's name means "God will protect." The Hebrew word for *Jacob* is similar to "heel," reminiscent of Jacob grasping Esau's heel during the birth. From this comes the nickname "heel holder," which has a connotation of a wrestling term, but also indicates a scoundrel. While Esau's name reflects his appearance, Jacob's name later comes to reflect his character.

There's a contrast right at the beginning between these two twins—one is outdoorsy while the other prefers a more orderly life (25:27). According to verse 28, Isaac and Rebekah each have a favorite. The verb translated *love* is indicative of favor, choice, and preference.

Isaac knows God's desire to pass on the physical and spiritual blessing of the inheritance to Jacob, but he fails to obey God's will.

Verses 29–34 recount the well-known story of Esau's trading his birthright for some stew. In the original Hebrew, there is a bit more texture revealed in this account than in modern English. Esau's so-called request is actually a forceful demand. Not only does Esau demand food, but he demands to devour it. The word translated *swallow*, or better yet, *gulp down*, is a word that normally describes the feeding of cattle.

Jacob's counterdemand, on the other hand, suggests that he has long premeditated his act and is exploiting his brother's weakness.

Demystifying Genesis

What is the birthright, and why does Jacob want it so badly (25:32–33)? Deuteronomy 21:17 and 1 Chronicles 5:1–2 tell us the birthright involves both a material and a spiritual blessing. The son of the birthright receives a double portion of the inheritance, and he also becomes head of the family and the spiritual leader upon the passing of the father (Genesis 43:33). And, in the case of this family, the birthright determines who will inherit the covenant God made with Abraham—the covenant of a land, a nation, and the Messiah.

ISAAC AND ABIMELECH

Genesis 26 is the only chapter of Genesis devoted exclusively to Isaac. While he is mentioned in other chapters, he is not the focus of attention. Here Isaac's life is summed up in the events described, all of which have a striking parallel in the life of his father, Abraham.

Isaac travels to Gerar to escape a famine (26:1–6). Gerar is the same place Abraham and Sarah went after the destruction of Sodom and Gomorrah (20:1). It was in the land of the Philistines. While in Gerar, or perhaps even before, Isaac decides to go down to Egypt just as his father had done (12:10–20).

When the Lord appears to Isaac to instruct him not to go to Egypt, He uses the same covenant language that He had used with Abraham (12:1–3; 13:14–17; 15:18–21; 17:6–8, 16; 22:17–18).

In verse 5, the word *because* seems to suggest that Abraham received the covenant as a result of works, yet nothing could be further from the truth. Granted, for Abraham and Isaac to enjoy the practical benefits of the covenant, obedience was imperative, but the covenant would be upheld despite their unfaithfulness.

The charge that Abraham kept was the office of patriarch and leader of God's people. The commandment included the mandate to leave Ur and to separate from family and land. The statutes include the rite of circumcision, and the laws refer to the practice of righteousness. Together, these terms reveal Abraham's wholehearted obedience.

· Critical Observation

Chronologically, Genesis 26 precedes Genesis 25:21–34. For another example of this, see Genesis 10–11 (table of nations and tower of Babel). If Isaac and Rebekah had Jacob and Esau by this point, the fact that they were husband and wife would have been obvious. Here, the promised seed is with Isaac and Rebekah, but no child has yet been born.

Verses 7–11 continue the parallel between Isaac's and Abraham's lives: Isaac lies about Rebekah's identity out of a fear for his own survival. The Abimelech mentioned in verse 8 is probably the son, or even the grandson, of the Abimelech who ruled over Gerar in Abraham's time (20:2).

The parallel between Isaac's life and that of his father is again evident in this account of the disputes over the wells (26:12–22). Due to their growth, Abraham and Isaac need much room for their flocks, as well as a source of water. Prosperity had brought contention between Lot's herdsmen and those of Abraham (13:5), just as it has between Isaac's herdsmen and the herdsmen of Gerar. Isaac, like his father, chooses to keep the peace by giving preference to the other party.

The names of the wells in verses 20–22 reflect the situations. *Esek* means "argument" in Hebrew, a reminder of the conflict its discovery created. *Sitnah* comes from a Hebrew verbal root meaning "to oppose; to be an adversary," and signals that the digging of this well causes opposition from the Philistines. *Rehoboth* comes from a verbal root meaning "to make room," and reminds all how God has made room for them. Since he finally has a well that is uncontested, Isaac might logically have decided to stay there. Instead, he moves on to Beersheba (26:23).

We read in 26:23–25 that God appears to Isaac in Beersheba (His second revelation), calming Isaac's fears and reviewing the promises He had given previously (26:2–5). Isaac's response is to build an altar, worship the Lord, and settle down there. These verses seem to confirm the fact that Isaac's decision to move out of Philistine territory pleased God.

This account in Isaac's life closes with good news in verses 26–33. Abimelech again testifies to God's blessing of Isaac and gives God glory.

Critical Observation

Like many biblical passages, the next section of scripture has bookends. Two reports of Esau's pagan marriages (26:34–35 and 28:6–9) frame the major account regarding Isaac (27:1–28:5). These Esau accounts provide a kind of prologue and epilogue. The main account then centers on Isaac's giving the blessing to Jacob.

Genesis 26:34–35 is best read as an introduction to Genesis 27. Esau marries at age forty, just as his father Isaac did (25:20). Esau, however, marries two Hittite women from the land of Canaan (36:2).

Abraham had warned his servant not to take a wife for Isaac from among the wicked Canaanites, who would not give up their gods for their husbands (24:3). Thus, the servant finds Rebekah from the country and family of Abraham (chapter 24). Note that Isaac seems to have had no hand in Esau's wife-taking, though Esau is, at one point, his favorite son, according to Genesis 25:28. Compare this with Isaac's own experience with his father, Abraham, who sent a servant five hundred miles to get a suitable wife for Isaac (24:1).

📖 27:1–28:9

JACOB'S BLESSING

This lengthy passage is like a theatrical play in five scenes, though these scenes are broken down differently by different commentators.

• Act One: Isaac Asks Esau for a Meal (27:1–4)

In the willfulness of his old age, Isaac is determined to pass on the blessing to Esau, despite what the Lord has said (25:23) and what the boys have shown with their lives. The fact that he attempts to make this transaction—which should have been a family event—without the knowledge of his wife, Rebekah, and his son, Jacob, compounds his sin.

Isaac's insistence on a good meal before the blessing recalls Esau's own trading of the birthright for a pot of stew, and thus casts Isaac in a similar role to that of Esau (25:27–34).

Critical Observation

The words *my son* and *here I am*, which also appear along with the words *my father* in Genesis 27:18, set this story up as a parody of Genesis 22:1–19, where the same words are used. In the Genesis 22 story, both Abraham and his young son, Isaac, employ the words *here I am* to convey trusting availability. Abraham obeys God, and Isaac obeys Abraham. Here Isaac takes the role of God but orders an unholy dish of food instead of a holy sacrifice. Esau is the obedient son in Isaac's ill-conceived plan, which blows up in both of their faces.

- **Act Two: Rebekah's Scheme (27:5–17)**

In 27:5–10, the story intensifies. The word used to describe Rebekah's listening suggests that this is a habit, a pattern of behavior, not happenstance. Her behavior gives us an idea of the level of mistrust and poor communication in the family.

Critical Observation

The plan is carried out with garments and the skins of goats. Jacob himself would later be deceived when his sons dip the garment of Joseph, his favorite son, in the blood of a goat to make him think Joseph has been killed (27:16; 37:31–33).

Rebekah, not Jacob, is the mastermind behind the plot to outwit Isaac and obtain his blessing for Jacob, a plot that seems to reveal some forethought. She volunteers to absorb any curse that Jacob will incur (25:13). This would be impossible, of course, but it reveals her sense of urgency.

- **Act Three: Jacob's Esau Imitation (27:18–29)**

The relationship between Jacob and Esau is like a boxing match. The first round occurs at birth (25:21–28), and the second round is over the birthright (25:29–34). Here we have the third round of Jacob's battle with Esau. In all three rounds, Jacob manipulates his brother.

In this scenario, who is deceiving whom? On one hand, Jacob is definitely deceiving his father, Isaac. However, Isaac—because he thinks Jacob is really Esau—thinks he is deceiving Jacob by giving the blessing to Esau. Both intend to deceive the other, yet only Jacob succeeds. Even through this act of deception, God's will is done, and the family blessing continues through Jacob.

Jacob has already received the blessing of the promised land through the birthright that he obtained. In Genesis 27:28, Isaac blesses Jacob with fruitfulness in the promised land (Deuteronomy 7:13). The dew of heaven provides irrigation. The fatness of the earth is rain. Grain and new wine evoke the image of a banquet, overflowing with joy (Psalm 4:7).

Isaac also blesses Jacob with dominion over the nations and his family. The people and nations refer specifically to the Gentile people and nations. He is also granted dominion over Rebekah's descendants through Esau, who would also become Gentiles. The curses and blessings equate to God's protection and are particularly linked to dominion (Numbers 24:9).

- ### Act Four: Esau's Horror and Revenge (27:30–45)

When Esau discovers the ruse, he is enraged. Once the blessing was given, it had the force of a legal contract and could not be revoked.

The two losses that Rebekah feared may have been Isaac's death and then Jacob's death at the hand of Esau, or Jacob's death at the hand of Esau, then Esau's necessary departure.

- ### Act Five: Jacob's Departure (27:46–28:9)

When Rebekah fears for Jacob's life, she manipulates Isaac into sending Jacob away. In effect, she gives Isaac a cover story. Her real goal is to protect him, not to find him a wife. Isaac agrees, calling Jacob to his side, repeating the Abrahamic blessing, and sending him off to Haran to find a wife.

In one sense, the plot to receive the blessing from Isaac is a great success. However, in another sense, it is a terrible failure. Jacob receives the blessing, but he has to leave the inheritance with Esau.

The best move that Esau could think of reveals his character. Given that he has already displeased his parents by marrying Hittite brides, he disappoints them further by marrying an Ishmaelite to bring into the family. The families of Isaac and Ishmael have been in contention since Isaac received Abraham's blessing rather than Ishmael (17:18–20; 25:14–18).

📖 28:10–30:43

JACOB'S OTHER LIFE

Jacob's journey retraces the steps of his grandfather, Abraham, who came from Haran to the promised land many years before. It is natural that Jacob's mother, Rebekah, would think of Haran when she cast about for a safe haven for her wayward younger son. The trek from Beersheba to Haran was far enough that Esau wouldn't follow Jacob there. Yet there was family at Haran, so Jacob wouldn't be alone.

The two most significant events in the life of Jacob are the visitations from God, both while he is sleeping. The first visitation happens in a dream. Angels are taking messages from earth up to heaven, and messages from heaven down to earth, on some kind of stairway, though the Hebrew word for *ladder* is used here (28:13–15).

The stairway is reminiscent of the tower of Babel, in which rebel humanity attempted to build a tower that reached into heaven (11:4). The ladder in Jacob's dream, by contrast, brought heaven to earth.

Jacob wakes up amazed by his experience, sure that the God of his fathers is the source of it (28:16–17). He had received the blessing passed down from his grandfather, Abraham. Why does Jacob raise a pillar and not just build an altar like his grandfather, Abraham? Perhaps it is a connection with the stairway in his dream. Nevertheless, Jacob is acknowledging God. Pouring oil on the pillar constitutes an act of consecration. The pillar becomes a monument marking the place and the event. The name given to the place means "house of God."

Jacob's vow is understood by some to be another form of his scheming nature

(28:20–22). Others suggest that he is simply making a commitment, acknowledging the need for God's help in order to keep that commitment.

After many days of traveling, Jacob arrives in Haran. He plans to stay there a few months, find a wife, and then return home to Beersheba. Little does he know that Haran will be his home for twenty long years.

The phrase describing Jacob's journey carries the suggestion that Jacob has a new lease on life now that God has promised him the blessing he had so desperately tried to gain by his own efforts.

In Haran, Jacob meets Rachel and her family. She is attractive and is a shepherdess in her own right, a sign of wealth in this era (29:9, 17).

According to verse 11, after Jacob meets Rachel, he kisses her. Most likely, he kisses her on both cheeks, a traditional greeting. However, it is worth adding that this appears to be the only case in the Bible of a man kissing a woman who is not his mother or wife. So it is possible that this was more than just a "holy" kiss.

According to verses 12–15, Jacob works for Rachel's father, Laban, for over a month before they negotiate any payment for Jacob's labor.

Verses 16–17 introduce Laban's other daughter, Leah. In Hebrew, *Leah* means "cow," and *Rachel* means "ewe lamb." There is some mystery regarding Leah's eyes. A few English translations understand Leah's eyes to be her best quality, so they translate the Hebrew word for "soft" (*rak*) as *lovely* (NRSV), *pretty* (NLT), or *delicate* (NKJV). However, most scholars suggest that Leah's eyes are a detriment in some way. The point is, she does not measure up to her gorgeous sister.

In 29:18–20, we learn that Jacob offers to work for seven years to earn the right to marry Rachel. Verse 20 is often misunderstood. It doesn't necessarily mean that the time passed quickly. More likely it means that the price seems insignificant when compared to what he is getting in return.

Finally, the wedding ceremony takes place (29:21–25), but Jacob wakes up with the wrong sister. According to contemporary Western customs, no man could be fooled in this way. The most likely explanation is that when Laban brings his daughter, Leah, to Jacob, it is late and dark, and she is veiled from head to toe. It seems that the wedding feast hosted by Laban is an intentional ploy to dull Jacob's senses with wine (29:22). We are not given information as to Rachel's and Leah's roles or even perspectives on the situation, but Genesis 30 leads one to conclude that sisterly jealousy is part of this deception. Laban's explanation that he must see his firstborn daughter marry first seems ironically appropriate in this story. Jacob had dishonored the principle of the firstborn by cheating his brother out of the birthright and the blessing. Now, God forces him to honor the principle he had violated by marrying Leah first. The deceiver is deceived. God trains Jacob by allowing him to meet his own sins in someone else.

Jacob receives Rachel seven days after he consummated his marriage to Leah (29:28–30). Jacob marries two women in eight days.

When verse 31 refers to Leah as unloved, this does not mean that Jacob hates her, but rather that he loves her less than Rachel. Leah's becoming a mother ensures that her importance will increase in Jacob's estimation, as well as in the estimation of her family and society in general.

The name of her firstborn, *Reuben*, means "see, a son" (29:32). The name of her second born, *Simeon*, means "hear" or "listen" (29:34). The name of her third born, *Levi*, means "attached" or "associated" (29:34). Levi is an influential child. The tribe of Levi supplies the royal priesthood (Numbers 3:5–13). The name of her fourth born, Judah, means "praise." The Messiah would come through the line of Judah (29:35).

Demystifying Genesis

Is Jacob's situation a case for multiple wives? Not necessarily. It is a description of the facts as they happened. There are other men in the Bible who took more than one wife, including the notable examples of King David and King Solomon. Exodus 21:10–11 also makes provision for the first wife if a man takes another wife. There is no text that presents multiple spouses as God's preference, though it is an accepted custom in some cultures. Jacob's life story stands more as a testimony against the practice. His wives are in conflict over their shared husband throughout the account.

Chapter 30 begins with a dramatic moment: Although her husband loves her, Rachel does not consider her life worth living without children. Jacob responds in anger. In fact, the word translated *anger* here is quite graphic. It means "to breathe hard, be enraged, flare the nostrils." Jacob's anger is heated as he, in essence, says Rachel's childlessness is not his fault.

Rachel's solution is an ancient custom that allows an infertile woman to offer her female servant as a wife, then claim the child of this union as her own. This is culturally acceptable and completely legal, and, in fact, it was a solution that had been employed by Abraham and Sarah, Jacob's grandparents (16:1–3; 20:4).

When Bilhah, the servant, becomes pregnant, Rachel falsely assumes that God is pleased with her schemes. She adopts Bilhah's first two sons as her own.

Since Leah is no longer conceiving, according to 30:9–13, Leah offers her maid, Zilpah, to Jacob to increase their brood. This joining provides two sons: Gad, whose name means "fortune," and Asher, whose name means "happy."

The story shifts gears in 30:14–21. Little Reuben comes upon some mandrakes, a plant that bears bluish flowers in winter and yellowish, plum-size fruit in summer. In ancient times, mandrakes were reputed as aphrodisiacs (Song of Solomon 7:13) and for aiding in conception. The fruit was even called "love apples." Leah gives Rachel the mandrakes in exchange for nights with Jacob. Thus, Leah's fifth and sixth sons are born, and finally a daughter.

Critical Observation

Rachel, who takes the mandrakes, remains barren for three more years; Leah, who doesn't have the mandrakes, has three more kids. She has a total of seven children—the number of perfection. This is more than the other three women in this story. However, she never receives what she desires most—Jacob's love. Leah spends years trying to win her husband's approval, but it never happens. She spends the rest of her life in a loveless marriage, even though she has half of the sons who would be the fathers of half the tribes of Israel.

In this story, both women want what the other has. Leah feels that having sons for Jacob will somehow earn his love, while Rachel is as desperate for children as Sarah had been before her.

This particular portion of the story concludes in 30:22–24. After fourteen years, Rachel conceives a son named Joseph. The theme of the entire narrative is the movement from barrenness (29:31) to birth (30:22). For all the maneuverings of the sisters, it is still God who opens the womb.

After the birth of Joseph, Jacob asks to be released from Laban's authority. Unlike today, Jacob could not simply pack his bags and leave. The authority structure in this Eastern, extended family is far more complex and restrictive—as it is still today in some Eastern cultures. There is a shared ownership of Jacob's wives and children. To leave without his father-in-law's permission and blessing could lead to outright war within the family clan.

Jacob had been living with Laban in Paddan-aram for twenty years (31:38). For fourteen years, he had worked for Laban, keeping his agreement in exchange for Laban's two daughters (29:30; 31:41). Another six years elapse before Jacob finally makes the break. During that time, eleven sons and one daughter are born.

Laban is averse to Jacob's leaving, not because he loves his nephew, or son-in-law, but because he knows his prosperity is dependent on Jacob's presence.

Jacob lets Laban know rather candidly that it doesn't call for an act of divination to discover why he has experienced material prosperity. It is fairly obvious that this is the product of a combination of factors—Jacob's faithfulness and hard work and God's favor and blessing resting upon him (19:29–30).

Verses 31–33 suggest that Jacob has prepared for this moment. Why the speckled and spotted sheep and goats? It is a foolproof way to distinguish between the flocks of Laban and Jacob. It appears to favor Laban, since goats in the Middle East are generally black or dark brown (Song of Solomon 4:1), and the sheep are nearly always white (Psalm 147:16; Song of Solomon 4:2; 6:6; Daniel 7:9). It gives Jacob an opportunity to put his trust in God. And as we'll discover in Genesis 31, Jacob selects the spotted and speckled because of the Lord's instruction (31:10). Furthermore, Jacob's dream from God ensures him that the Lord will protect him from the dishonesty of Laban.

From every angle it seems a great deal for Laban, yet Laban's actions in verses 35–36 are an attempt to make sure Jacob does not get even the speckled animals.

Jacob counters with a plan from God. It was generally believed that, by placing the kind of visuals described here before the animals as they were mating, it was possible to influence the appearance of their offspring (30:37–43). Interestingly, the Hebrew words for *poplar* and *white* are puns on the name *Laban*, which means "white."

📄 31:1–35:29

JACOB'S RETURN

Jacob's plan seems to be working (30:37–43), and both Laban and his sons are unhappy about Jacob's growing herds. Essentially, Laban's sons are accusing Jacob of stealing their inheritance. From their perspective, it is disappearing right before their eyes. As a result, they become envious and bitter toward Jacob. Laban also treats Jacob differently.

The last recorded revelation that Jacob received from God was twenty years earlier, while he was still in the land of promise (28:10–22). God had promised to bring Jacob back to the land (28:15); now, at last, God gives Jacob the divine directive to return to the promised land (31:3).

Jacob lays out the facts to Rachel and Leah about Laban—the family tension and the unhealthy work environment—and God's divine providence (31:4–13). Despite Jacob's challenges, God proves Himself faithful.

Rachel and Leah agree with Jacob's assessment. Seven times in 31:4–16, Jacob and his wives mention God by name. The sisters uncharacteristically agree and submit themselves to Jacob's leadership. After all, their father Laban had stolen their inheritance, treated them like foreigners, sold them, and used up the money from their dowry.

So the trip begins. It was nearly three hundred miles from Haran to the mountains of Gilead. Jacob travels with the knowledge that Laban might be pursuing him from behind in order to kill him, and Esau, his brother, might be waiting ahead, also wanting to kill him.

Jacob and Rachel deceive Laban in their departure (31:19–21). Rachel steals his household idols while he is busy at work shearing his sheep. These idols are small figurines (probably 2–3 inches long) used in divination and to bring good luck. Why does she steal them? No exact reason is given, but it may have been simply for protection and "luck," which would have revealed some attachment to the religion of her father.

Critical Observation

It is curious that Rachel—the wife he most loved and wanted—most often turns out to be Jacob's greatest hindrance. In spite of the fact that Rachel has a growing trust in God, she is reluctant to make a complete break from her idolatrous past.

Jacob leaves without informing Laban. Jacob is doing God's will by returning to the land of promise, but he is not doing it in God's way.

Laban catches up to Jacob, a journey that takes seven days since Jacob had a three-day head start. It is interesting that God reveals Himself to Laban, a man who, thus far in this account, has not expressed the kind of faith we associate with messages from God (31:22–55). God will accomplish His purposes in whatever way is necessary.

After an uneventful search in which Rachel sits on the idols to hide them, Jacob unleashes twenty years of pent-up frustration (31:36). In his rebuke to Laban, Jacob shows himself to be a man of faith (31:31–42).

This part of the story concludes in 31:43–55. Jacob takes a stone and sets it up as a pillar (31:45). This may have been in the form of a heap of stones that functioned both as a table for the meal and as a memorial of the event. Standing stones sometimes marked supposed dwelling places of the gods (28:17–18) or graves (2 Samuel 18:17). In this case, it seals a treaty.

It seems Jacob gives two names to this place of agreement. *Galeed*, meaning "witness heap," is the name from which the name Gilead came. *Mizpah*, meaning "the witness or watchtower" (Genesis 31:47–48), recalls that both of these men said the Lord would be the watchman between them. Both names signify what had taken place between Jacob and Laban.

Laban has two deities in mind, as the Hebrew plural verb translated *judge* indicates. Jacob worships the God of his fathers; Laban swears by the pagan god his fathers worshiped (31:53).

Verse 55 is the last mention of Laban in the Bible.

Jacob leaves Laban and goes on to Canaan. He does this in obedience to God's command (31:3). The angels that meet him join Jacob's company of travelers for his protection. This is the reason for the name *Mahanaim* ("double host" or "double camp"). These angels were apparently intended to reassure Jacob of God's protective presence (32:1–2).

Genesis 32:2–21 describes Jacob's preparations for meeting Esau. At the news that Esau has four hundred men with him, Jacob becomes afraid. Esau may have had a large army because he had had to subjugate the Horite (Hurrian) population of Seir (32:6). His soldiers probably consisted of his own servants, plus the Canaanite and Ishmaelite relations of his wives.

After Jacob cares for the physical concerns of the journey, he turns to the spiritual concerns, offering up the first recorded prayer and the only extended prayer in Genesis (32:9–12). At the end of the prayer, he offers back to God the only thing he has—God's promise to his family.

Jacob's wording in his instructions to his servants (32:7–18) is important. He first humbles himself by calling himself Esau's servant. He also calls Esau "lord." Jacob seems to want to impress Esau with his greatness.

Demystifying Genesis

Why does Jacob send such an impressive gift to Esau? As a bribe or payoff for his sin of deception and theft? Possibly, but it could also have been an act of restitution and reconciliation. It also could have been for the practical reason that he wants Esau to know he is wealthy (verses 14–15 list over 550 animals given as gifts) and is not returning for the inheritance.

Hebrew narrative style often includes a summary statement of the whole passage, followed by a more detailed report of the event. In this case, verse 22 provides a summary statement while verse 23 begins the detailed account.

It is when Jacob is alone, having done everything he could to secure his own safety, that God comes to him. God has arranged the circumstances so that He could get Jacob alone at a moment when he felt completely helpless. God comes to Jacob as a wrestler to teach him how to fight like a man.

Why does he touch Jacob's thigh? Because the thigh is the largest and strongest muscle connection of the body. The man is deliberately crippling Jacob at the point of his greatest strength (32:24–30).

The new name Jacob receives, *Israel*, means either "God strives," or "he who strives with God." If the latter interpretation is the one intended by the wrestler who blesses Jacob, then the name fits well with Jacob's character as one who, throughout his life, struggles with God (32:28).

The name given to this place, *Peniel*, means "the face of God" (32:30).

Genesis 33 is a pivotal chapter in Jacob's life—facing Esau after twenty years. Jacob has every reason to believe that twenty years has not diminished Esau's anger, as he sees Esau marching toward him with four hundred men.

By going ahead of his family to meet Esau, Jacob shows that he has overcome the fear that had formerly dominated the old Jacob. He also shows valor in protecting his family. Bowing to the ground before Esau demonstrates humility. This is ancient court protocol for approaching a lord or king (33:3, 6–7).

In Esau's culture, men walked; they didn't run. By running to Jacob (33:4–5), Esau is breaking the cultural norms and humbling himself. His kiss seems to be an indication of forgiveness (33:4–5).

The fact that Esau refuses Jacob's herds as gifts is significant. Esau is not the taker that Jacob has been.

Jacob's comparison of seeing Esau to seeing God's face (33:10) may seem like flattery or overstatement. It could also have been recognition on Jacob's part of God's character in the life of his brother.

The word translated *gift* is the word "blessing." When Esau finally accepts Jacob's gift, he gives Jacob the opportunity to feel forgiven.

Jacob claims to be going to Seir, but he goes to Succoth instead (33:12–17).

Succoth is to the north and the west; in other words, it is in the exact opposite direction from Esau. Perhaps Jacob did not want to face his father, or perhaps reconciling with Esau was a different matter than living side-by-side. It could have also been a practical concern regarding pastures for the herds.

Critical Observation

As a result of Jacob's choice to settle away from his brother, he never saw his father again. The next time we find Jacob and Esau together in scripture is twenty-seven years later at the graveside of their father, Isaac (35:29).

Jacob settles near the city of Shechem (33:18), even though God had commanded him to settle in Bethel (28:21; 31:3, 13). This may have been fear-based. In spite of Esau's warm greeting, Jacob probably didn't trust him. Nevertheless, he builds his first altar, as Abraham had also done at Shechem, when he had first entered Canaan (12:6–7).

This is the first instance in which an altar is named (33:20; see also 35:7; Exodus 17:15; Judges 6:24). *El-Elohe-Israel* means "the mighty God is the God of Israel." Jacob uses his own new name, Israel (Genesis 32:29). Here he acknowledges God as *the* God, his own God.

In Genesis 34, we come to a horrific account. This story serves to warn us of the high price of compromise. The tragedies that take place in this chapter are the result of Jacob's failure to be obedient to God's command to return to Bethel.

Dinah is in her early teens and is Jacob's only daughter—his daughter by Leah, the wife he did not love (30:21). Dinah's name means "justice." The Hebrew word translated *went out* in 34:1 bears a sense of impropriety.

The account can be a bit confusing in that the place is called Shechem, and the man Dinah encounters is also named Shechem. He is the son of Hamor, who is the leader of that part of the world. As Hamor's son, Shechem could have whatever he wanted.

Jacob seems far less affected by the news of Dinah's assault than her brothers (30:5–7).

In verse 7, the name *Israel* is used here for the first time as a reference to God's chosen people. The family of Jacob had a special relationship to God by divine calling, reflected in the name *Israel* (prince with God).

Neither Hamor nor Shechem offers an apology. Apparently, they assume that the offense is no big deal. Hamor offers an alliance between the two peoples to include intermarriage, trade, and land deals (34:8–12).

As was customary in their culture, Jacob's sons take an active part in approving their sister's marriage (34:13; see 24:50). They were correct in opposing the end in view: the mixing of the chosen seed with the seed of the Canaanites. Yet they were wrong in adopting the means they selected to achieve their end (34:13–17); thus, the description "Jacob's sons" rather than "Dinah's brothers." The sons are following in their deceitful father's footsteps (34:13).

Regarding the proposal made by Jacob's sons, the men of the city become convinced on financial grounds. While Shechem has fallen in love with Dinah, to these men circumcision seems a small price to pay if it results in a huge financial windfall from the alliance (34:13–24).

The slaughter described in verses 25–29 outrages Jacob on an unexpected level. He seems to think only of his lowered standing among the local inhabitants. His selfish response (34:30–31) reflects his focus on himself.

It is interesting that Simeon and Levi refer to Dinah as their sister rather than Jacob's daughter, which would have been appropriate in addressing Jacob. This could imply that Jacob had not showed enough concern for Dinah, so her blood brothers felt compelled to act in her defense.

Chapter 35 opens with God's renewed command to Jacob to go to Bethel. It is at Bethel that Jacob has his first real encounter with God and is told about God's plan to bless him. It is also at Bethel that Jacob first builds an altar of worship to the Lord.

Jacob's instructions to his entourage to wash and change their clothes are the kind of instructions that often signify spiritual preparation for a new beginning (35:1-5).

The inclusion of the phrase "the sons of Jacob" suggests that the other cities fear Jacob's boys (35:5; Deuteronomy 11:25) because of what they had done to the people of Shechem. Yet, it also seems evident that, as Jacob obeys the Lord, the Lord protects Jacob and his family by causing a fear to fall on the surrounding cities.

Jacob faithfully fulfills his vow to God at Luz (Genesis 35:7-15), which he renames Bethel, or "house of God." The insertion of the story of Deborah's death and burial probably is an indirect reference to Jacob's mother, Rebekah, and perhaps an allusion to her death (35:8).

At Bethel, the Lord reconfirms His covenant with Jacob, again affirming Jacob's new name (already pronounced by the angel; see 32:24-28) and promising him many descendants and land (35:9-12). God's promise of land was first given to Abraham and then to Isaac, and here it is renewed with Jacob.

Jacob solemnizes this occasion by setting up a second pillar (28:18; 35:13-15) that perpetuates the memory of God's faithfulness for the benefit of his descendants. He not only sets the stone apart by pouring oil on it, as he had done thirty years earlier, but he also makes an offering to God and reaffirms the name Bethel.

Rachel's death is recorded in verses 16-20. She, who had so longed for a child, dies bearing her second son. She gives him the name *Ben-oni*, which can mean "son of my sorrow"; but the name that Jacob gives is *Benjamin*, which means "the son of the right hand."

The tower of Eder (or Migdal Eder) mentioned in verse 21 is simply a watchtower built to help shepherds protect their flocks from robbers (2 Kings 18:8; 2 Chronicles 26:10; 27:4). Since the time of Jerome, the early church father who lived in Bethlehem, tradition has held that Eder lay very close to Bethlehem.

Verse 22 mentions Reuben, now an adult. He was the son that brought the mandrakes to Rachel, hence playing some small part in the all too brief restoration of his mother's conjugal rights (Genesis 30:14).

A *concubine*, as Bilhah is described in verse 22, was sometimes a slave with whom her owner had sexual relations. She enjoyed some of the privileges of a wife, and people sometimes called her a wife in patriarchal times, but she was not a wife in the full sense of the term.

Reuben's relations with Bilhah are a power move as much as anything else. In that culture, a man who wanted to assert his superiority over another man might do so by having sexual relations with that man's wife or concubine. It may have included a play for asserting his mother's role as "first wife." With the death of Rachel, who had been Jacob's favorite, Bilhah, Rachel's servant, may have been able to move into a favored role. Reuben's actions make Bilhah detestable to Jacob; thus Leah has a better chance for power in the household.

While Reuben's actions may have been on behalf of his mother, they are an affront to his father as the head of the family. In the end, though, according to 1 Chronicles 5:1-2, Reuben's actions cost him.

Chapter 35 closes with a list of Jacob's sons and the account of his father Isaac's death. The use of Israel rather than Jacob in verse 22 may suggest that, here, the patriarch responds rightly (not the old Jacob but the new) to this situation.

Benjamin is not born in Paddan-aram but near Bethlehem (35:16–18). Therefore, the statement that Jacob's twelve sons were born in Paddan-aram (35:26) must be understood as a general one.

With the record of Jacob entering into his father's inheritance, the history of Isaac's life concludes. Isaac lives for twelve years after Jacob's relocation to Hebron. He shares Jacob's grief over the apparent death of Joseph, but dies shortly before Joseph's promotion in Egypt. He is buried in the cave of Machpelah, near Hebron (49:29–31).

📖 36:1–43

ESAU

Chapter 36 is the account of Esau, Jacob's twin, and his descendants. The name *Esau* means "red." This is a reference and reminder of Esau's foolish decision to trade the birthright and blessing of his father, Isaac, for a pot of red stew (25:30).

Esau takes his wives from the Canaanites, even though this was considered a religious mixed marriage and was strictly forbidden by his family. But Esau, in open defiance, takes wives from the idolatrous Hittites and brings them to his tents within the camp, where they make life miserable for Esau's parents, Isaac and Rebekah (26:35). He later adds a third wife from the descendants of Ishmael (28:9).

Demystifying Genesis

The names of Esau's wives present a problem, in that the names given in earlier chapters do not correspond with the names listed here. In 26:34, it is said that Esau marries Judith and Basemath. Genesis 28:9 reports that he adds Mahalath. But in 36:2–3, the names are different, though the fathers associated with them are the same. The wives probably took different names, either when they moved from Canaan to Edom, or because of changes over time (a common practice; Esau became known as Edom over the incident with the red stew which he traded for his birthright).

Since infertility has been a large theme in the stories of Abraham's family, it is significant that there is no mention of infertility when it comes to Esau's line.

The dividing of territory between Esau and Jacob described in verses 6–8 is reminiscent of the episode between Abraham and Lot in 13:1–13. There are two reasons for Esau's move: (1) There isn't sufficient water and pasture for both Esau's and Jacob's flocks and herds, and (2) Esau has finally come to accept that the promised land of Canaan is to be passed on to Jacob.

Critical Observation

Esau's name is also Edom, thus the reference to his descendants as Edomites. These people are important neighbors to Israel, though not always agreeable ones. Even so, God commands special treatment for the Edomites among Israel.

Esau and his descendants are men of great political power (36:8–43). They are called chiefs (36:15) and kings (36:31). These men reign as kings in Edom before any king reigns in Israel.

Some have hailed verse 31 as an indication that Genesis must have been written after the beginning of the monarchy, some three hundred years after Moses. But in the previous chapter, God prophesied to Jacob that kings would come forth from him (35:11), a promise that had also been made to Abraham (17:6, 16). Put into that context, the information contained here would not have been an unreasonable forecast for Moses to make.

Esau's sons, who walked away from God, had the distinction of being kings long before Jacob's sons to whom it was promised. While Esau's sons and grandsons become rulers, Jacob's sons remain lowly shepherds for generations (47:3).

GENESIS 37:1–50:26

JACOB'S SONS

Joseph's Journey to Egypt	37:1–36
Judah	38:1–30
Joseph's Success in Egypt	39:1–41:57
Joseph's Brothers in Egypt	42:1–47:31
Jacob's Blessings	48:1–49:33
Jacob's and Joseph's Final Days	50:1–26

Setting Up the Section

For the final time, Genesis introduces a new series of generations. This marks the final section in the book of Genesis. The storyline of the last fourteen chapters focuses on Jacob's sons. Of those twelve sons, most of the focus is on Joseph. This whole section reveals how God's plan for His people triumphs over human frailties to guide and strengthen those who follow Him.

📖 37:1–36

JOSEPH'S JOURNEY TO EGYPT

Chapter 36 reveals that Esau's descendants are mighty chieftains; in contrast, by Moses' day (over four hundred years later), Israel is still a fledgling nation of slaves, recently escaped from Egypt, owning no land of their own. Edom, on the other hand, is an established kingdom that has the power to refuse Israel passage over their land.

While the last fourteen chapters of Genesis include Jacob, the storyline focuses on Jacob's sons. And of his twelve sons, special interest is spent on Joseph, who is mentioned twice as much as Jacob. This means a quarter of the book of Genesis is devoted to Joseph.

Elsewhere, the word *report* is used in the negative sense of an untrue report (37:2; Proverbs 10:18). This may imply some exaggeration or inaccuracies on Joseph's part, which would have added fire to the rivalry between him and his brothers.

Jacob's favoritism, signified by the special tunic he gives his favorite son, is no help. The tunic was probably a long robe extending all the way down to the wrists and ankles, as opposed to the ordinary, shorter one with no sleeves that working men wore.

While it's not clear exactly what the tunic looked like, the idea that it is a coat of many colors comes from the Greek translation of the Old Testament. The tunic sets Joseph apart as the favored one.

Critical Observation

Favoritism and rivalry have a long history in Jacob's family. Jacob's father, Isaac, preferred Esau. His mother, Rebekah, claimed Jacob as a favorite. In Jacob's own family, his preference for Rachel set up resentment between not only Rachel and her sister (also Jacob's wife) Leah, but probably between their children as well.

Verses 5–11 recount two of Joseph's dreams. Dreams in this narrative concerning Joseph always come in pairs (chapters 40–41). One dream seems to confirm that the other is not a fluke or a one-time event.

Joseph's first dream involves sheaves, which subtly points to his future role in overseeing all of Egypt's grain distribution. Amazingly, twenty-three years later, in fulfillment of Joseph's dream, all eleven of his brothers prostrate themselves in submission to Joseph on at least five different occasions (42:6–7; 43:26, 28; 44:14–16; 50:18). Joseph's second dream is far more graphic. It involves celestial imagery bowing down to him. Joseph probably reveals part faith and part foolishness in sharing these dreams with this already contentious family.

Later, according to verses 12–14, Joseph is sent to check on his brothers. It is not uncommon for shepherds to lead their flocks many miles from home in search of pasture. Shechem was about fifty miles north of Hebron. Jacob owned land there.

When he doesn't find his brothers at Shechem, Joseph goes to Dothan, a location fifteen miles north of Shechem. In verse 18, when Joseph finds his brothers, there is a shift in perspective. Suddenly the story is told from his brothers' point of view.

Reuben, who advocates for Joseph's life, is the firstborn and the decision-maker in the family (27:21–24). He is apparently not part of the family group that was plotting to kill Joseph. That group consisted probably of Dan, Naphtali, Gad, and Asher—the four sons against whom Joseph brought a bad report (37:2).

Verses 23–28 record how the brothers capture Joseph and subsequently sell him to the Midianite merchants for twenty pieces of silver. Slave-trading was common in Egypt. The price agreed on for Joseph was the same price that was later specified for a slave between the ages of five and twenty years under the Mosaic economy (Leviticus 27:5).

When Reuben returns to find Joseph gone, he knows that as the oldest, he will have to answer to his father for whatever has happened (Genesis 37:29–32). Thus evolves the brothers' scheme. Notice that the brothers never actually say Joseph is dead. They simply deceive their father.

The boys live for years without ever telling their father what they had done. Had Jacob believed more strongly in God's revelations through Joseph's dreams, he might not have jumped to the conclusion that Joseph was dead, and his sorrow might not have been as great (37:33–35).

Joseph ends up in Egypt, in the home of one of the most responsible officers of Pharaoh's administration (37:36).

Take It Home

God is never defeated by anyone's deceit. Jacob deceived and was deceived. The brothers hated, envied, plotted, and lied. And when you get to the end of the chapter, God has placed Joseph exactly where he needs to be to accomplish God's purposes. All of this points to the sovereignty of God. When you and I sin and go against the will of God, we don't thwart the purpose of God; we thwart ourselves. Our job is not to work out the details. Joseph didn't. Our job is to remain pure and usable. God will work out the details. He did in the case of Joseph, and He will do it for you, too.

📖 38:1–30

JUDAH

Genesis 38 records a scandalous story from the life of Judah, Joseph's brother.

Verses 1–11 tell us that Judah leaves home and moves to Canaan. This means he is living among people that his family considered unclean. There, he marries and raises children to adulthood. When Judah's oldest son Er dies, Er's wife, Tamar, becomes a childless widow. Since carrying on the bloodline is of the highest value in this culture, the custom of the day is for Er's brother to marry Tamar and supply Er with an heir. This custom, called levirate marriage, is described in Deuteronomy 25:5–10. The word *levirate* comes from a Latin word meaning "husband's brother."

The downside of this agreement for the second brother is that the son born is considered the heir to the deceased. His birth does not increase the wealth of the younger brother at all. This is why Onan does not cooperate in providing Er with an heir.

After Onan dies, Tamar expects that the third son of Judah will provide her an heir when he is old enough, but that is never Judah's intent.

According to verses 12–19, when Tamar realizes that Judah lied to her, she plans a ruse to make him take responsibility for the situation. Sheep-shearing was a time for partying and celebration (1 Samuel 25:11, 36; 2 Samuel 13:23, 28), and the place Judah was going to shear his sheep was a place with abundant sexual temptation. This is an ideal situation for Tamar to trick Judah into having sex with her in exchange for three distinctive items: his personal seal, the cord with which it probably hung around his neck, and his staff—probably carved and one-of-a-kind.

When Judah finally hears the stories of pregnant Tamar, the so-called prostitute, he calls for her judgment by burning (Genesis 38:20–24). In the Mosaic Law, the penalty of burning was only for a priest's daughter who had become guilty of prostitution (Leviticus 21:9). The usual mode of death was by stoning (Deuteronomy 22:20–24; John 8:4–5).

Going to execute judgment on Tamar, Judah faces the woman who has his personal belongings and is pregnant with his twin sons. There is evidence that among ancient Assyrian and Hittite peoples, part of the levirate responsibility could pass to the father of the widow's husband, if there were no brothers to fulfill it. Thus Tamar was, in one sense, claiming what was due her. She had tricked Judah into fulfilling the levirate responsibility and now would bear his children.

Tamar and Judah have two sons: Perez and Zerah (38:27–30). *Perez* means "a breach" or "one who breaks through." Perez becomes the ancestor of David (Ruth 4:18–22), who in turn becomes the ancestor of Jesus Christ (Matthew 1:3). *Zerah* means "a dawning or brightness."

The struggle between the twins at birth is reminiscent of the struggle of Jacob and Esau, Judah's father and uncle (Genesis 25:24–26; 38:27–30).

📄 39:1–41:57

JOSEPH'S SUCCESS IN EGYPT

The account of Joseph's life in Egypt begins with chapter 39. The theme of this narrative is found in the statement in verse 2: The Lord is with Joseph (39:2).

After Joseph's brothers sell him into slavery, the Midianites take him down to Egypt and sell him to Potiphar (37:36). Potiphar is the chief executioner or chief of police.

Even in these less-than-ideal circumstances, Potiphar notices God's hand on Joseph (39:3).

Critical Observation

Verse 6 describes Joseph's outward appearance. The Bible rarely offers this kind of description. The only other men who are referred to in this way are David (1 Samuel 16:12) and Absalom (2 Samuel 14:25).

Verses 7–20 describe Joseph's life in Potiphar's house, and particularly his interaction with Potiphar's wife. According to verse 7, she carefully scrutinizes Joseph, and then eventually propositions him. When he refuses, she manipulates the situation to make it appear that Joseph has acted inappropriately, and so he is thrown in jail.

In this time and place, attempted rape was a capital offense. The milder punishment Joseph receives suggests that Potiphar does not believe his wife. Furthermore, the king's prison was a place for political prisoners and would hardly have been expected to accommodate foreign slaves guilty of crimes against their masters. Another very telling observation is that the prison was in the basement of Potiphar's house (40:3, 7). Joseph was thus demoted.

Verses 21–23 reveal Joseph's persistent good character. He is not enslaved by his circumstances.

While Joseph is in Potiphar's jail, God brings some influential and unexpected guests: Pharaoh's cupbearer, or butler, and baker. The cupbearer and baker are not guilty of some minor indiscretion or inadvertent offense against Pharaoh; they had greatly offended him (40:1–3).

Joseph's role is to act as a servant to these men, and in the course of serving them, he also interprets some dreams for them (40:4–11). He recognizes that their dreams are revelations from God and invites the two prisoners to relate their dreams to him. He is careful, however, to give God the glory for his interpretative gift (40:8; 41:16, 25, 28, 39).

Verses 14–19 relate Joseph's interpretations—one having a positive outcome and the other having a harrowing outcome. In some translations, Joseph is credited with saying that the baker's head would be lifted up, but that is actually a reference to a hanging. The baker would not simply suffer execution, but his corpse would be impaled and publicly exposed.

Joseph's predictions come true just as God had said (40:20–23). One of the men is reinstated by Pharaoh, and the other is executed. Between the end of chapter 40 and the beginning of chapter 41, however, two years pass without the cupbearer fulfilling his promise of remembering Joseph and his interpretative gifts.

Take It Home

Joseph is an excellent example to follow regarding life's disappointments. Nowhere in this narrative do we see Joseph feeling sorry for himself or blaming others. He simply took each situation as it came and made the best out of it. The biggest problem in life is not having problems. Our problem is thinking that having problems is a problem.

Two years after the cupbearer's return to court, Pharaoh has two dreams symbolic enough to require interpretation (41:1–7). In the first dream, seven fat cows are eaten by seven gaunt cows (41:1–4). In the second dream, seven plump ears of grain are eaten by seven thin ears (41:5–7).

The magicians that Pharaoh sends for shouldn't be confused with contemporary magicians, who wear tuxedos and pull rabbits out of hats. These were the wise, educated men of Pharaoh's kingdom. They were schooled in the sacred arts and sciences of the Egyptians. Yet they are unable to help Pharaoh (41:8).

Though it was two years before that the cupbearer (or butler) had promised to remember Joseph, it is these troubling dreams that finally make it happen (41:9–13). He summons Joseph for the Pharaoh. Notice that part of Joseph's preparations for meeting Pharaoh is to shave. The Egyptians preferred to shave all the hair off their bodies and wear wigs (41:14).

Once in Pharaoh's presence, Joseph makes it clear that he can interpret the dreams only in God's power (41:15–16). In essence, Joseph tells Pharaoh (who is considered a god in his own country) that his God is superior to and sovereign over Pharaoh and the gods of Egypt. This is quite a stand to take.

Pharaoh explains his dreams to Joseph (41:17–24), and Joseph interprets the dreams and discusses a plan of action with the great king of Egypt (41:25–36). Three times in this section, Joseph attributes the outcome of Pharaoh's dreams to God (41:25, 28, 32).

Because of these events, Joseph becomes an advisor to and an officer of the Egyptian government (41:37–45). To naturalize Joseph, Pharaoh gives him an Egyptian name (41:45; Daniel 1:7) and an Egyptian wife from an appropriate level of society. Joseph's name, *Zaphenath-paneah*, is probably Egyptian for "God speaks; He lives."

Critical Observation

Joseph's marriage to an Egyptian seems out of place. The patriarchs generally avoided marriage to Canaanites, but this was a marriage to a non-Canaanite Gentile, which was less serious.

Under the circumstances, it doesn't seem that Joseph is given much choice. Perhaps more important, it's clear from the names given to their two sons that Joseph doesn't allow his wife's pagan background to influence him away from God. It is this falling away that is the issue with mixed religious marriages in the Old Testament.

This chapter of Joseph's life closes with his preparing Egypt for the seven years of famine (41:46–49). During this time, God blesses Joseph with two sons (41:50–52). Joseph names his firstborn *Manasseh*, which means "making to forget." He names the second *Ephraim*, meaning "God has made me fruitful in the land of my affliction." If the name of Joseph's first son (Manasseh) focuses on a God who preserves, the name of Joseph's second son (Ephraim) focuses on a God who blesses. Joseph gives his boys Hebrew names that are testaments of God's faithfulness.

📖 42:1–47:31

JOSEPH'S BROTHERS IN EGYPT

In chapter 42, the scene switches to Canaan. The seven years of famine that Joseph predicted are now in full force (41:54–57). The famine has spread to Joseph's family in Canaan (42:1–2).

Demystifying Genesis

What would have kept Jacob's sons from going to Egypt until their father instructed them? For one thing, the trip was long (250–300 miles) and dangerous, and a round trip could consume six weeks' time. Even after arriving in Egypt, the brothers couldn't be certain of a friendly reception. As foreigners from Canaan, they would be vulnerable and could even be arrested and enslaved.

It's evident that Jacob is a man controlled not only by favoritism but also by fear. He has already lost his favorite wife and his favorite son. He was determined to prevent the loss of Benjamin, who was his final link to Rachel, his favored wife. It also appears that over the years since the death of his eleventh son, Joseph, Jacob may have grown suspicious of his ten older sons. This suspicion manifests itself in 42:4, where Jacob refuses to send Benjamin with his brothers into Egypt to buy food for the family.

When the brothers arrive in Egypt and are ushered into Joseph's presence, the predictions of Joseph's dreams from long ago (37:5-7) are fulfilled as his brothers bow before him.

The last time the brothers had seen Joseph, he was a seventeen-year-old boy who was in a position of weakness, being carried off into slavery by the Midianites (37:2). At this point in the story, though, Joseph is nearly forty, the governor of Egypt, wearing the royal clothing of a king; and to top it off, he is powerful and confident in his role.

The brothers are astounded at Joseph's accusation that they are spies. What spy would travel with his brothers and in a group of ten? A good spy wants to be inconspicuous.

Demystifying Genesis

Why does Joseph do this? Was it just a cruel act of vengeance—the product of twenty years of bitterness and resentment? No! The Bible is very clear that Joseph never indulges in any resentment against others who had injured him (45:5; 50:18-21). Joseph's purpose in speaking harshly and accusing his brothers of spying is not motivated by bitterness, but by a desire to covertly discover information regarding the health and well-being of his father, Jacob, and his younger brother, Benjamin. He also is testing their character—have they changed in how they care for each other?

Joseph gives his brothers a glimmer of hope when he tells them he fears God (42:18). The name he uses for God is the name of the Hebrew's God (*Elohim*). The brothers would not have expected this from the seemingly harsh Egyptian prime minister. But there is enough hope of fair treatment in those words to keep them from despairing.

According to verse 24, Joseph's pent-up emotions simply had to come out, so he leaves the room and weeps privately. This is the first of six such experiences. Joseph also weeps when he sees his brother Benjamin (43:29-30), when he reveals himself to his brothers (45:2), when he meets his father in Egypt (46:29), when his father dies (50:1), and when he assures his brothers that they are truly forgiven (50:17).

The scripture does not say why Joseph chooses to imprison Simeon rather than any of the other brothers (42:24). Perhaps the reason is in the brothers' discussion of their guilt in having sold Joseph into slavery. In that discussion, Joseph learns for the first time that Reuben, the oldest son of the family, had kept the other brothers from killing Joseph. If Joseph had intended to imprison the oldest brother, he may have had a change of heart. Simeon, being the second oldest, would have been the one responsible for their collective wickedness.

There's a good chance that Simeon had been the ringleader in throwing Joseph into the pit, where his intention was to kill him. Simeon had been the leader in the slaughter of the Shechemites. In Jacob's final words to his sons, he refers only to Simeon's violence and anger (49:5-7). By putting Simeon in prison, Joseph may have intended to eliminate Simeon's influence on the others on the return journey, or perhaps he hoped that the time in prison would break Simeon's hardened heart. At the very least, Joseph chooses to keep him as leverage and to see if his brothers are willing to desert Simeon as they had him.

Before his brothers leave, Joseph hides their payment for the grain in their grain sacks (42:25-28). Perhaps this is to test his brothers to see if they could still be bought with money. Joseph wanted to know if they would do to Simeon what they did to him. The brothers panic because they could be accused of stealing this money. Interestingly, Joseph's brothers never mention God until now.

When they return home, Jacob's sons share with their father what happened (42:29-36). Unfortunately, Jacob's response only serves to prolong their return, Simeon's imprisonment, and his reunion with his long-lost son.

Reuben's offer in verses 37-38 may have made sense to Reuben, but basically he is only offering to increase his father's sense of bereavement by losing two grandsons in addition to his youngest son.

Genesis 43-45 describes what happens when Joseph's brothers return to Egypt. In chapter 43, Joseph exhibits tender love; in chapter 44 he exercises tough love; and in chapter 45 he lives out God's sovereignty.

Even after some time has passed, Jacob still isn't willing to make the hard decision to send Benjamin. First he suggests they just buy a little food, in hopes that the governor in Egypt won't require Benjamin to go there with his brothers (43:2).

Fortunately, Judah steps up and lovingly puts Jacob in his place, as well as offers to be the collateral for Benjamin (43:3-10). This is the first evidence of real character we find in Judah so far in Genesis. Up until now, he has been like his father, self-centered and self-absorbed.

When Jacob finally allows the brothers to make the trip with Benjamin, he employs his gift-giving strategy of diplomacy. It is the same strategy he had employed when he was preparing to meet his brother, Esau (33:10-16). Jacob's gift-giving isn't motivated by love or friendship; it is intended to soften the heart of the Egyptian leader.

When the brothers are reunited with Simeon (43:15-25), they go from agony to ecstasy in a matter of moments. Then Joseph hosts a meal for the brothers, who years before had callously sat down to eat while he languished in a pit (37:25). We aren't told whether Joseph even acknowledges the gifts that Jacob sent.

Verse 33 marks the second occasion that the brothers bow down before Joseph. They are seated in order by age by a host who presumably is entirely ignorant of their birth order. The chances of that happening are approximately one in forty million. It must have seemed like magic.

Joseph shows respect to Benjamin as his distinguished guest by giving him larger and better servings of food than his brothers receive. Special honorees frequently received double portions, but a fivefold portion was the sign of highest privilege. With this favor,

Joseph is not only honoring Benjamin but is also testing his other brothers' feelings toward Benjamin. He may have wanted to see if they would hate him as they had hated his father's former favorite. Evidently they pass this test.

Genesis 44 reveals Joseph's effort to discover the truth—to find out whether his brothers are still the selfish, godless, wicked men who sold him into slavery twenty years earlier. A silver cup like the one he had placed in Benjamin's sack is, of course, valuable. But Joseph's decision to put silver in the bags probably also stems from his personal recollection that his brothers had sold him into slavery for twenty pieces of silver. Now he is testing them.

When the accusation of theft is made, the brothers are no doubt indignant because they are confident in their righteousness. But when the silver cup is discovered in Benjamin's sack, they are broken and show evidence that they had become a family (44:3–9).

In verses 5 and 15, divination is mentioned. This practice of determining information from the movements of liquids was not a practice of the Israelites. But even in the Egyptian culture of this time, a cup was not a standard tool for divination. If you read closely, Joseph does not actually claim to practice divination.

Genesis 44:18–34 is the longest and most moving speech in the book of Genesis. Fourteen times in this speech, Judah mentions his father, Jacob. Jacob would eventually crown Judah with kingship (49:10), because he demonstrates that he has become fit to rule according to God's ideal of kingship—that the king serves the people, not vice versa. Judah is transformed from one who sold his brother as a slave to one who is willing to be the slave for his brother.

In 45:1–15, this account comes to a resolution. Joseph reveals his identity. The response of the brothers to Joseph's revelation of his identity is a term translated *dismayed* or *dumbfounded*. This is a term used of paralyzing fear as felt by those involved in war (Exodus 15:15; Judges 20:41; 1 Samuel 28:21; Psalm 48:5). But after a threefold expression of Joseph's goodwill toward his siblings (weeping, explaining, and embracing), his brothers are finally able to talk to him.

Critical Observation

Throughout the course of Joseph's life, he has discerned God's providential control of events. Four times he states that God, not his brothers, is behind what has happened (45:5, 7–9).

Upon parting, Joseph's admonition to his brothers not to quarrel on their journey is a bit unclear (45:24). Probably he means just that; not to become involved in arguing and recriminations over the past. The brothers had already quarreled over their sin against Joseph (42:21–22). Joseph may have known that as soon as these men left his presence they would be tempted to assign blame to one another.

Take It Home

How is Joseph able to forgive his brothers? First, he sees his situation from an eternal perspective (50:19–20). Then he prepares in advance to forgive. Finally, he receives their confession and repentance for their sins.

Whom do you need to forgive? Do you want restitution? Can you let someone who offended you off the hook in the way that Joseph did? Will you see that God's sovereignty allows you to forgive others for whatever sin they have committed against you?

Jacob is stunned to receive news that his favorite son, Joseph, is alive. At the age of 130, he prepares the family to leave Canaan and head out to join Joseph in Egypt. Jacob's sacrifices at Beersheba (46:1) are not burnt offerings, but offerings of thanks that Joseph is alive, and perhaps also vows to God. The fact that the names *Israel* and *Jacob* are used interchangeably in verses 46–47 indicates that the earlier negative connotations of the name Jacob have faded (31:11; 32:28; 35:10).

Demystifying Genesis

Why sacrifices at Beersheba? Beersheba was at the southernmost boundary of Israel. In essence, it was the point of no return. Furthermore, Beersheba was a significant place to Jacob's family. This is where Abraham had dug a well, planted a tamarisk tree, and called on the name of the Lord (21:30–33). Abraham even lived in Beersheba after offering Isaac on Mount Moriah (22:19). Isaac also lived in Beersheba (26:23, 32–33) and built an altar there (26:24–25). It is perhaps at this altar where Jacob presents his sacrifices.

God appears once more to Jacob (46:2–4), as He had to Jacob's grandfather, Abraham (22:11). God identifies Himself in virtually the same way as when He spoke to Jacob during his vision of the stairway up into heaven (28:13). He also offers the fourth and final "do not be afraid" consolation recorded in Genesis (see 15:1; 21:17; 26:24).

After hearing directly from the Lord, Jacob and his family leave Beersheba and travel to Egypt (46:5–7).

To the first readers of this book, the names in verses 8–27 mean something. This is a list of every tribe (and every major family group within that tribe) that later formed the nation of Israel. Every Hebrew knew his family ancestry. The division of labor, the organization of the army, and the parceling of the land all were done according to tribe. This list of names reminds original readers of their identity as God's people in fulfilling His purposes; in the four hundred or so years from Jacob's time to Moses', the number of Israelites had mushroomed from seventy to more than two million!

In verses 28–30, the fact that Jacob chooses Judah to be the guide indicates that he trusts his son, which suggests that the men had told their father everything and were in his good graces again. Now Jacob can see the hand of God in all that has happened. In spite of his past failures, Judah now proves he is faithful, and his descendants are eventually named the royal tribe (49:8-12).

The reunion between Jacob and Joseph recalls Jacob's former meeting with Esau (32:3). In both situations, after a long period of separation, Jacob sends a party ahead to meet the relative. Previously, Jacob had said that the loss of his sons would bring him to his grave in mourning (37:35; 42:38). But finding Joseph alive enables his father to find a measure of peace.

Critical Observation

Joseph encourages his family to be completely honest with Pharaoh when asked about their occupation so that he would send them to live in Goshen (46:34). Goshen had some of the best pastureland in all of Egypt. It would be a place to keep the Hebrews isolated and insulated from the culture and religion of Egypt, since the Egyptians considered sheep unclean and Hebrews detestable (43:32).

One of the greatest dangers to the covenant promises of God was intermarriage between the Hebrews and the Egyptians, because intermarriage would inevitably lead to spiritual compromise and the worship of the false gods of the Egyptians.

Joseph explains to Pharaoh the needs of his family (47:1-6). He even introduces five of his brothers to Pharaoh. After the brothers answer Pharaoh's questions, they ask his permission to live in Goshen. Pharaoh agrees to their request and even offers any capable brothers a job—to be put in charge of Pharaoh's livestock.

Jacob's blessing of Pharaoh (47:7) is unusual in that it implies Jacob is superior, even though Pharaoh is a man of immense worldly power and influence. The precise meaning of the Hebrew verb translated *blessed* is difficult in this passage, because the content of Jacob's blessing is not given. The expression could simply mean that he greets Pharaoh, but that seems insufficient. Jacob probably praises Pharaoh, for the verb is used this way for praising God. It is also possible that he pronounces a formal prayer of blessing, asking God to reward Pharaoh for his kindness.

Verses 13-27 demonstrate the fulfillment of Jacob's blessing on Pharaoh (46:31-47:10). Joseph is able to save Egypt and its neighbors from a severe famine and alleviate the desperate plight of the Egyptians. God blesses Pharaoh because he has blessed the Israelites with the best of Egypt.

According to verse 22, Joseph gives preferential treatment to the Egyptian priests. More than a sign of religious support, this concession is probably due to the powerful lobby that the priests have with Pharaoh.

The tax described in verse 24 is not out of line with what was common in that day in the ancient Near East. It was lower than the average 33.3 percent.

The account of Jacob begins to draw to a close in verse 28. Jacob enjoys the blessings of God for seventeen more years—ironically, the same number of years he enjoyed Joseph until Joseph was sold into slavery to Egypt by his older brothers (37:2).

Why does Jacob insist on being buried in Canaan (47:29-31)? It isn't because he has already invested in a family plot. Knowing that the day of his departure is drawing near, Jacob makes his death a testimony to his faith and a stimulus to the faith and obedience of his descendants. This would serve as a reminder to his descendants that Egypt was not home, but only a place to sojourn until God brought them back to their true home, Canaan, the land of promise (Hebrews 11:22).

📖 48:1-49:33

JACOB'S BLESSINGS

Jacob is coming to the end of his life. He has not always honored God, but is an example of a man who finishes well. Before he dies, Jacob passes the torch on to those who follow.

It is likely that in the seventeen years Jacob lived with Joseph in Egypt, he invested in Joseph's sons Manasseh and Ephraim. These sons were born during the seven years of abundance, before the first year of the famine (41:50). Jacob went down to Egypt somewhere around the end of the second year of the famine (45:6) and lived seventeen years after he arrived (47:28). Since Jacob is near death, the sons of Joseph must have been about twenty years old.

Jacob might have been losing his health, but he was not losing his memory. In verses 3-4, he shares his testimony. Twice, God had appeared to Jacob at Luz (28:10-17; 35:9-12), and in both appearances God promised him that he would become a great nation and that he would possess the land of Canaan. While it is not recorded that God specifically promises Jacob the land will be an everlasting possession (48:4), God does make that promise to Abram (17:7). This was probably orally passed on through Isaac.

Jacob effectively adopts his grandsons (48:5-6). Ephraim and Manasseh go from being Jacob's grandsons to his number one and two sons. Keep in mind that Joseph's sons are half-Egyptian. This is a large step for a full-blooded Israelite like Jacob. It is also a step that displaces Reuben and Simeon as the two oldest sons. Thus, in future lists of the twelve tribes of Israel, Ephraim and Manasseh are normally included in the place of Joseph.

Normally, the birthright would have been given to the firstborn son. But Reuben and Simeon had disqualified themselves from positions of status and leadership in Israel's family because of their sin: Reuben due to his sin of lying with Bilhah, Jacob's concubine (35:22; 49:4; 1 Chronicles 5:1-2), and Simeon due to his violent murder of the men of Shechem (Genesis 34:25). In essence, Jacob is giving Joseph the double blessing that is generally reserved for the firstborn (Reuben). In the future, Joseph's other children will be incorporated into the tribes of Ephraim and Manasseh (48:6).

Jacob's words in verse 7 are a reminder of his love for Rachel, the wife for whom he worked seven years and then seven more.

When Israel asks, "Who are these?"(48:8), the question is not an indication of Jacob's blindness but the initiation of the ceremony.

Genesis 48:13-20 is the first of many scriptural instances of the laying on of hands. By this symbolic act, a person transfers a spiritual power or gift to another. In this case, Jacob symbolically transfers a blessing from himself to Joseph's sons. Ephraim and

Manasseh do become great tribes. At one time, Ephraim was used as a synonym for the kingdom of Israel.

Jacob's blessing of Ephraim and Manasseh also carries prophetic significance and force (48:19–20). This is the fourth consecutive generation of Abraham's descendants in which the normal pattern of the firstborn assuming prominence over the secondborn is reversed: Isaac over Ishmael, Jacob over Esau, Joseph over Reuben, and Ephraim over Manasseh.

In verse 15, Jacob calls God his shepherd. This is the first mention in the Bible of God as a shepherd to His people.

Critical Observation

Jacob testifies of an angel who had redeemed him from all harm (48:16). The Angel of the Lord appears frequently in the Old Testament. He appears to Hagar when she flees from Sarai (16:7–13), wrestles with Jacob (33:22–32; Hosea 12:4), and appears to Moses in the burning bush (Exodus 3:2). Many believe this angel is a preincarnate appearance of Jesus Christ. This is further supported by the first use of the word *redeemed* in the Bible.

Jacob's prophetic promise to Joseph in Genesis 48:21–22 is a play on words. The word for *portion* means "ridge," or "shoulder (of land)," and is the same as *Shechem*, the name of a city in Manasseh's territory. The Israelites later bury Joseph at Shechem (Joshua 24:32). In Jesus' day, people spoke of Shechem (near Sychar) as territory Jacob had given to Joseph (John 4:5).

Jacob speaks as though he has taken Shechem from the Amorites by force, but no such battle is recorded (48:22). He may have viewed Simeon and Levi's slaughter of the Shechemites as his own taking of the city (34:27–29). Jacob gives Joseph Shechem, which he regards as a down payment of all that God would give his descendants as they battle the Canaanites in the future.

Like Jacob, Joseph also had remarkable faith. In giving his two sons to Jacob, he is virtually consenting to their being rejected for a future and position in Egypt. By identifying his sons with the despised shepherding people, Joseph seals them off from ascendancy. It is madness from the perspective of the Nile. But like his father, Jacob, Joseph believed the word of promise—that God was building a great people who would one day return to the land of promise.

Take It Home

The first 28 verses of Genesis 49 record Jacob's last words to his twelve sons. All twelve of Jacob's sons, regardless of their faithfulness, have a future and a blessing. But *only* the faithful sons would have an inheritance in the land. This is an example of a principle that continues even today: The actions of believers determine their future blessings in God's program.

Jacob's prophecies refer to the distant future (49:1). The double exhortation to give attention to Jacob's words stresses the importance of what he is about to say (49:2). The prophecies included here are not the spontaneous thoughts of a dying man, but the carefully prepared words of a prophetic poet.

Jacob's three oldest sons are disinherited for their unfaithfulness (49:3-7). The first-born son normally has two rights. First, he becomes the leader of the family, the new patriarch. Second, he is entitled to a double share of the inheritance. But Reuben is not to receive this blessing because he is reckless and destructive. The picture painted with these descriptive words is of water that floods its banks and goes wildly out of control. The result is an evaluation of Reuben that points to wildness and weakness, an undisciplined life. This is a reference to Reuben's misconduct in Genesis 35 (49:3-4).

True to Jacob's prophecy, the Reubenites never produce a leader of any kind for Israel. They never enter the promised land (Numbers 23). They build unauthorized places of worship (Joshua 22:10-34). The tribe produces no significant man, no judge, no king, and no prophet.

When Jacob says that Simeon and Levi are brothers (Genesis 49:5-7), it is not a statement simply about their family relationship as brothers as much as their similarity in character—they are two of a kind. Interestingly, Jacob still characterizes his sons as angry men. He doesn't say their anger *was* fierce; instead, he says it *is* fierce. These men have remained angry.

Jacob's prophecy that these tribes will be scattered is fulfilled, as the tribe of Simeon later inherits land scattered throughout Judah's territory (Joshua 19:1-9; see also 1 Chronicles 4:28-33, 39, 42). The tribe of Levi becomes priests with no inheritance, but scattered throughout the rest of the tribal lands.

Even though these first three tribes suffer loss for their sins, Jacob's prophecies about them are still a blessing. They retain a place in the chosen family and enjoy the benefits of God's promises as Jacob's heirs. Yet, they are disqualified from the reward that could have been theirs because of their failure to repent of their sin (Numbers 32:23-24; Ezekiel 18:30).

Jacob gives the seven acceptable sons responsibilities, and the two most faithful sons receive greater responsibility. True to the poetic qualities of the text, the images of the destiny of the remaining sons are, in most cases, based on wordplays of the sons' names (Genesis 49:8-27).

Judah will be preeminent among his brothers, and they will praise him. Judah's hand will be on the neck of his enemies, and his brothers will bow down to him. But leadership of his descendants will not be fully realized until the days of King David, some 640 years later (49:8).

In some translations, the word *Shiloh* appears in verse 10. There's been much discussion about the exact meaning of this word, but modern translations simply translate it as *he*. Many believe this is a reference to the Messiah, and that it functions as a confirmation that He will come through Judah's bloodline (Zechariah 10:4; Hebrews 7:14).

Zebulun is promised territory between the Mediterranean Sea and the Sea of Galilee (Genesis 49:13). It is possible that Zebulun and Issachar share some territory (Deuteronomy 33:18-19), so Zebulun could have bordered the Sea of Galilee.

Issachar will prefer an agricultural way of life rather than political supremacy among the tribes (Genesis 49:14–15). Evidently, Issachar is strong and capable, but also passive and lazy. In contrast to Judah, who subdues his enemies like a lion, Issachar submits to the Canaanites.

According to Jacob's prophecy, Dan will judge Israel (49:16–18). This prophecy comes to reality partially during Samson's era in ancient Israel (Judges 13:2). Dan's victories benefit all Israel. Yet this tribe leads Israel into idolatry (Judges 18:30–31; 1 Kings 12:26–30) and becomes known as the center of idolatry in Israel (Amos 8:14).

The tribe of Gad will become tenacious fighters and be victorious over all the foreign armies they face (Genesis 49:19; Jeremiah 49:1).

Asher will enjoy some of the most fertile land in Canaan (Genesis 49:20; Deuteronomy 33:24–25; Joshua 19:24–31).

The tribe of Naphtali will be well-known for producing eloquent speakers and beautiful literature (Genesis 49:21). The most famous of these is Deborah, who composes a beautiful poem of military triumph (Judges 5:1–31). Along with the land of Zebulun, Naphtali's territory is near the Sea of Galilee, the region where Jesus carries out much of His teaching and ministry (Matthew 4:15–16).

Joseph's blessing is especially abundant (Genesis 49:22–26). Judah receives the leadership of the tribes, but Joseph obtains the double portion of the birthright (1 Chronicles 5:2). The two tribes bearing his sons' names will see the fulfillment of the blessing, even though during his lifetime Joseph faced much opposition.

The tribe of Benjamin has a reputation for being fierce and aggressive (Judges 19–21). We have a number of examples of the tribe of Benjamin's aggressive leaders: Ehud (Judges 3:15–23), King Saul (1 Samuel 9:1; 14:47–52), and Paul the apostle (Acts 8:1–3). The tribe demonstrates a warlike character (Judges 5:14; 20:16; 1 Chronicles 8:40; 2 Chronicles 14:8; 17:17).

The rest of chapter 49 has to do with Jacob's death. In verses 29–33, a repeated phrase serves as bookends: Jacob is going to his people (Genesis 49:29, 33). This ancient expression describes Jacob's reunion with those who had preceded him in death and had exercised faith in God. Jacob's specific instructions reveal that he probably reflected on his death; he wanted to make sure that everything was in place.

📖 50:1–26

JACOB'S AND JOSEPH'S FINAL DAYS

Joseph was a man of faith and a man of sensitivity. The only tears recorded in Joseph's life are not for himself but for the plight of his brothers and the loss of his father (50:1–7).

The Egyptians show great honor to Jacob and to Joseph in their seventy days of mourning after Jacob's death. This length of time is only two days short of the length of mourning for a Pharaoh.

When Joseph goes to bury his father, all of Pharaoh's servants and elders, and all of the elders of Egypt, accompany him (50:7–8).

The location of the threshing floor at Atad is not certain (50:10). The expression "the other side of the Jordan," used in several Bible translations, could refer to the eastern or western bank. However, it is commonly used in the Old Testament for Transjordan. This would suggest that the entourage came up the Jordan Valley and crossed into the land at Jericho, just as the Israelites would in the time of Joshua.

God's promises are all connected to Canaan, but Joseph does not choose to stay there (50:14). He knows his calling concerns Egypt. He takes one look at the land of promise, which he has not seen since he was seventeen years old, and then goes back to the place where God had called him.

Joseph's brothers exhibit some negative and positive responses when their father dies (50:15–18). Initially, they respond negatively due to guilt, fear, and paranoia. They assume that Joseph has been simply biding his time out of respect for his father Jacob. But now that Jacob is gone, they are gripped with the terrifying expectation of punishment for their sins. So they falsely claim that Jacob has issued a charge for Joseph to forgive his brothers. However, Jacob never did this, because he recognized that Joseph had completely forgiven his brothers.

Positively though, the brothers own their sin against Joseph. They beg for forgiveness, bow down before Joseph, and offer themselves up as slaves (50:17–18).

In response, Joseph recognizes God as the only One who is able to judge. While not diminishing the manner in which his brothers wronged him, he recognizes God's greater purpose (50:19–21). Joseph's claim that God meant for good what his brothers meant for evil is the theme of the entire Joseph narrative.

Joseph was a man who experienced God's blessing (50:22–26). More than fifty years elapse between verses 21 and 22. During this period, God abundantly blesses Joseph with a long life, the privilege of seeing his great-great-grandchildren, and a remarkable faith. It is only fitting that the book of Genesis ends on a note of blessing, since it has been a consistent theme throughout the book.

Although God's people would spend four hundred years in Egyptian bondage, Joseph already saw the day when God would bring them back to the promised land. In light of this faith, Joseph makes his wishes known to be buried in the promised land (50:25). This is an expression of faith and confidence that God's covenant promises will come to pass. Joseph dies and is placed in a coffin in Egypt (50:26). Unlike his father, Jacob, Joseph's body isn't buried immediately. Instead, his coffin lay above ground for over four hundred years, until the people of Israel take it back to Canaan as they leave Egypt under Moses' leadership. So there it sat, in Egypt, for four hundred years, as a silent witness to Joseph's confidence that Israel was going back to the promised land, just as God had said (Exodus 13:19). Joseph's faith in God's promises to his forefathers provides a fitting climax for the book of Genesis.

EXODUS

INTRODUCTION TO EXODUS

Exodus tells the story of the birth of the nation of Israel through their deliverance from bondage in Egypt and the receiving of God's instructions, based on His covenant, for building their nation to honor Him.

AUTHOR

Though there is debate among scholars about the authorship of Exodus, Moses is considered the author by most evangelical scholars.

PURPOSE

The main purpose of the book of Exodus is to describe God's rescue of His enslaved people and His making them a nation. This book chronicles God's faithfulness to His people—in spite of their sin.

OCCASION

The book of Genesis closes with the family of Israel making a home in Egypt under the leadership of Joseph. Exodus picks up centuries later in Egypt after the family of Israel has grown into the nation of Israel. While Joseph had saved the Egyptians from starvation, his family's descendants had become slaves. Exodus follows the story of God's people from the birth of Moses, the leader of Israel during this period in their history, through their deliverance from bondage, the giving of the law, and the construction of the tabernacle in the desert.

THEMES

Exodus is rich in themes which will recur in the Old and New Testaments—the burden of bondage to sin, God's faithfulness and deliverance in spite of stubbornness, and the radical vision that He has for His people.

CONTRIBUTION TO THE BIBLE

In many ways, Exodus expands on what Genesis teaches us about God's character and His intentions for creation. We witness both His judgment in the plagues on the Egyptians and His mercy in the deliverance of the Israelites from slavery. The Exodus introduces the Law of the Lord, which will bring both blessing and suffering to the nation of Israel until it is fulfilled by the work and person of Jesus Christ. Exodus establishes how Israel is going to be set up, and much of the rest of the Old Testament recounts their struggle to meet God's requirements. The book also describes God dwelling with His people in the tabernacle, which is ultimately an image for the kingdom of heaven. It is rich in relevance to the New Testament with its many symbols of the sacrificial lamb, the holiness of God, and the fatal consequences of people's failure to keep His commandments.

EXODUS 1:1–22

PHARAOH'S FEARS AND ISRAEL'S FAITH

Setting Up the Section

There are times when God is there, but He is, at least from our perspective, silent. The period of time depicted in the first chapter of Exodus is a time when, from all appearances, God is silent. Nevertheless, God is present and His hand is at work in the lives of His children.

📖 1:1–7

LINKING THE PAST TO THE PRESENT

The beginning of Exodus links the events of Genesis to those recorded in Exodus—two books intended to be understood in relationship to each other. Genesis provides an excellent backdrop for Exodus, reminding Israel of her roots and of the basis for God's blessings, which were soon to be experienced. Exodus 1:1-6 sums up the history of Israel as a clan, as described more thoroughly in Genesis 12–50. These six verses remind us that all that is going to take place in this book is directly related to what has gone before. Verse 7 fills in a nearly 400 year gap, covering the period from the death of Joseph to the time of the Exodus.

Most importantly, this portion of the introduction to the book of Exodus (1:1–6) links the existence and rapid growth of Israel as a nation to the covenant that God made with Abraham (Genesis 12:1–3; 15:12) and reiterates to the patriarchs (Genesis 26:2–5, 24; 28:13–15). The sons of Israel and their families are seventy in number (Exodus 1:5) when they arrive in Egypt. But when the sons of Israel leave Egypt, they do so as a great nation (1:7, 12, 20; 12:37).

Demystifying Exodus

Periods of silence similar to the gap in the history of Israel (1:7) exist throughout scripture. During these periods, God is at work behind the scenes, and in ways that at the time are not immediately apparent. Verses 8–22 demonstrate that during periods of apparent silence, God is at work providentially, bringing His purposes to pass and preparing history for another of His dramatic interventions into the affairs of people.

A NEW KING'S POLICY

There is considerable disagreement among the scholars as to the identity of this new king who does not know about Joseph (1:8). Much of the problem hinges on the date of the Exodus (see intro). Keeping with an early date for the Exodus, it is most likely that the king referred to here is new in a very significant sense. He represents not only a new person, but also a new dynasty.

The fears of the Pharaoh are of interest. He fears the numerical strength of the Israelites and seeks to diminish them. He fears that they will become allies with the enemy, overcome them, and leave Egypt. Interestingly, everything Pharaoh fears comes to pass, in spite of his diligent efforts to prevent it. But Pharaoh's plans are contrary to the purposes and promises of God with regard to His people.

Pharaoh's plan is to enslave the Israelites and tighten control over them. A substantial part of this plan seems to be that of intimidation and oppression, so demoralizing and frightening to the Israelites that they will not dare to resist their masters. Yet just as Israel had greatly multiplied during the time of Joseph (Genesis 47:27), and after his death (Exodus 1:7), so they continue to multiply under the cruel hand of their taskmasters. The Egyptians came to dread the Israelites and worked them ruthlessly (1:12–13).

The Egyptian response to the phenomenal numerical growth of the Israelites is to increase the workload and intensify the harassment and cruelty imposed on them by their taskmasters (1:14). These tactics do not work, which leads to an even more evil plot directed against the people of God, as outlined in verses 15–21.

Critical Observation

The curse of God in Genesis 3 includes hard toil, which is surely the lot of Israel in Egypt. The salvation of mankind, as promised also in Genesis 3, is through the birth of a child. So, too, it is through the birth of a child (Moses, in Exodus 2) that God provides a deliverer for His people. As people strove to provide themselves with security and significance, Egypt sought to secure herself by forcing the Israelites to build cities with bricks and mortar (compare Genesis 11 with Exodus 1:14; 5:1).

PHARAOH AND THE MIDWIVES

Pharaoh's demands of the midwives are quite abominable. Not only does he propose acts of violence on the innocent, he also passes on all responsibility for the death of these Hebrew infants. He wants the midwives to solve this national dilemma of the Hebrew birthrate. But the midwives fear God more than Pharaoh, so they refuse to put the infant boys to death (1:17). Pharaoh's plan backfires.

God rewards the midwives for fearing Him by enabling them to be fruitful themselves (some scholars suggest that barren women were often made midwives). God also records names of two of these God fearing Hebrew midwives—as an example to believers throughout the centuries.

Take It Home

God cares not about your position or your prestige in life. He cares only if you fear Him and trust in His Son, Jesus Christ, for the forgiveness of your sins and eternal life. The fact that the writer of Exodus names the midwives but leaves Pharaoh unnamed is a good picture of God's value on those who obey Him. If you are His child, He knows you by name. If not, no matter what your earthly splendor or power, you are nameless to Him, and you will spend eternity apart from Him.

EXODUS 2:1–25

MOSES: ISRAEL'S DELIVERER

Moses—Out of the Water	2:1–10
Moses Flees to Safety	2:11–25

Setting Up the Section

Few stories in the Bible are more familiar than that of Moses set afloat in the waters of the Nile and his rescue by the daughter of Pharaoh. Exodus 2 shows how God's hand is at work in the history of Israel, preserving the life of one child who will become Israel's deliverer.

📖 2:1–10

MOSES—OUT OF THE WATER

We see from verse 2 that Moses is exceedingly well formed and beautiful, and that his parents perceive that God has a special purpose for their child. But Moses is not suggesting that God moved his parents to hide him because they were convinced that he was particularly special in appearance or in purpose, but rather that they saw something special about him as a child of God. Exodus 2:2 could simply be rendered, "she saw that he was good." The Hebrew word meaning "good" is frequently used by Moses in the five books of the Law, and in most it has the sense of goodness which is the result of being made (or given) by God, and of being declared good by Him. The frequent expressions in Genesis 1 and 2, "it was good," employ the same term.

The biblical perspective is that children come from God (Psalm 127). Every child is the product of divine creation (Psalm 139:13–14) and is thus "good" in the eyes of God. Moses' parents refuse to put their child to death because God created him, and because this means he (like every other child ever born) is special to God. They feared the God who created their son more than the Pharaoh who wished to kill him.

Pharaoh's daughter comes face-to-face with the implications of her father's policy of genocide (Exodus 2:6). What Pharaoh had commanded was not only unthinkable, it was undoable. She names the boy *Moses*, a name rooted in the event of her finding him as a baby at which time she drew him out of the Nile.

Critical Observation

The deliverance of Moses is significant in that it is a beautiful illustration of the truth declared in Ephesians 3:20–21. Not only was Moses spared and protected by Pharaoh's daughter's love, but his parents were allowed to keep him for a time, train him in the ways of their God, and then, in addition to all these blessings, they were paid for it. Now, in the palace of the Pharaoh whose orders were, "Throw them in the water!" there is a Hebrew boy whose name means "Taken from the water." Once again, God providentially preserved and prospered His people. Not only was Moses spared, but now there is a Hebrew living in the palace, part of the royal family. What a challenge to the limits of our faith! What a gracious God we serve!

📖 2:11–25

MOSES FLEES TO SAFETY

Verse 11 passes over nearly forty years (see Acts 7:23), taking up the story of Moses as an adult. Moses makes the critical decision to identify with his people before he goes out to observe the affliction of his brethren (as described in Hebrews 11:24–26), which informs us that the reason Moses visits his brethren is due to his decision to identify with them and even suffer with them. Thus, Moses does not lose his status as a son of Pharaoh's daughter by the killing; he gives it up before the killing. Moses' visit to his brethren backfires, in one sense, but it is used providentially to prepare him for his future calling.

Demystifying Exodus

Moses' premeditated murder (Exodus 2:12) cannot be defended. Yet while Moses' method of dealing with this problem is wrong, we see that his motivation is commendable. Moses sought to defend the oppressed. When he sought to rebuke his Hebrew brother for wrongly mistreating another Hebrew (2:13), Moses reveals, once again, the disposition of a deliverer.

Rather than taking his place as a deliverer of his people, at this point Moses flees to find himself delivering the oppressed elsewhere. At the well, Moses does not like how the women are being pushed in line by the shepherds (2:15–17). Moses enforces the policy of "ladies first," and once again delivers the oppressed. Moses can not look the other way, even when advantage is being taken of strangers.

With great economy of words, Moses briefly records that this chance encounter leads to a lengthy stay in Midian, his marriage to Zipporah, and the birth of a son, Gershom. Moses names the child Gershom because he felt like an alien in a foreign land (2:22). In Midian, a land closer to Canaan than Egypt, Moses thought of himself as an alien and a sojourner. He still thought of Egypt, not Canaan, as his homeland. One can hardly think of this time as that of great faith or purpose in Moses' life. The faith and commitment to the people of God with which verse 11 began has somehow eroded into something far less.

Verse 25 tells us that in spite of all these appearances, God is at work. Humanly speaking, it looks as though everything is working against Israel, yet this reiterates that God is very much informed, involved, and intent upon fulfilling His purposes and promises. This section ties together the agony of God's people in Egypt (described in chapter 1, but overshadowed by the personal account of Moses in chapter 2) with the deliverance about to take place in the following chapters.

Take It Home

We can easily acknowledge the fallibility of those who do not know or serve God. But having acknowledged the depravity of mankind in general, we should not forget also the fallibility of the faithful. Every detail of our lives, every incident, every failure, is employed by God providentially to further His purposes. While this should in no way make us lax in our desire to know God's will and to obey Him, it should serve to assure us that even when we fail, He does not. How do you see this to be true in your own journey? And what can you learn from Moses' experiences?

EXODUS 3:1–22

THE BURNING BUSH

Setting Up the Section

Chapter 3 introduces a significant change in the drama of the deliverance of God's people from Egypt. From God's providential dealings in the life of the nation of Israel, we move to God's direct intervention through Moses and the miracles He performs. We move from the silence of God over the past four hundred years to God's speaking directly to Moses from the bush, and later on, from the same mountain.

THE GOD OF THE BURNING BUSH

The revelation of God to Moses is the basis for Moses' obedience, as well as for the entire nation. It is also the basis for all of God's actions with regard to Egypt and to His people. In many ways, the incident of the burning bush is critical to our understanding of God.

The burning bush made not only a profound impact upon Moses and the nation of Israel, but it also continued to serve as a key event in history—the significance of which is not lost on Israel in the generations that followed. This passage of scripture is one that must have been well-known to the Jews of Jesus' day. The account of the burning bush is so central to the thinking of the Gospel writers, Mark and Luke, that they (perhaps like most men in their day) came to call this section of scripture "the bush" portion (Mark 12:26; Luke 20:37).

The bush is apparently a typical common desert bush, but the fire is far from ordinary. The closer Moses gets to the bush, the more incredible the scene becomes. Moses surely had to wonder about this phenomenon. Scholars have offered numerous "natural" explanations for the burning bush over the years, not wanting to acknowledge a full-fledged miracle. Yet we know from the biblical account that this is truly a unique intervention of God in time and space.

Demystifying Exodus

Attempts to explain the burning bush as something other than miraculous abound. Some of the most common include that it was a natural phenomenon called "St. Elmo's fire," which is a discharge of electricity that causes a kind of glow, or firebrands of light which often occur in dry lands with an abundance of storms. Others suggest that it may have been a volcanic phenomenon, or simply that this account is a myth, like other ancient accounts of burning objects that were not consumed. Still others say that it may have been a beam of sunlight piercing through a crack in the mountain, or a purely psychological experience. The author (Moses) himself, however, provides a wholly supernatural explanation——the burning bush that would not be consumed was aglow with the angel of the Lord (Genesis 16:7; 22:11; Exodus 3:2; Judges 6:11; 13:3), the preincarnate manifestation of the second person of the Godhead.

The character of the God who is calling and commissioning Moses is the basis for Moses' faith and obedience. The God of the burning bush is a holy God, an object of fear and reverence. At the time the law is given on Mount Sinai, God's holiness is the basis for Israel's conduct, which the law prescribed. But how is the holiness of God a significant factor in the Exodus? The sins of the Egyptians must be dealt with, and additionally, the possession of the land of Canaan by the Israelites (Exodus 3:8, 17) is a judgment on these peoples for their abominations in the sight of God (see Genesis 15:16; Leviticus 18:24–28).

The God of the burning bush is the covenant-making, covenant-keeping God of Abraham, Isaac, and Jacob. In verse 6, God identifies Himself to Moses in this way. He is the God who made a covenant with Abraham and reiterated it to Isaac and Jacob. There is no new plan, but simply the outworking of the old plan, revealed to Abraham in Genesis 15.

The God of the burning bush also reveals Himself to be a compassionate, imminent God who commissions people to participate in His purposes. Some of the richest revelation concerning the character of God is found in verses 11–15, where God responds to two questions raised by Moses. In essence, these questions can be summarized: "Who am I?" (3:11), and "Who are You?" (3:13). God's response to these questions serves to clarify His character even further.

Forty years before, Moses made a critical decision concerning his identity—he was an Israelite, and thus could not be known any longer as the son of Pharaoh's daughter. Moses determined that he would attempt to deliver his people, but at the time Moses had assumed authority which had not yet been given him. Moses had forty years to ponder his presumption and its consequences. Here, his question reflects caution and a desire to receive a clear commission from God.

God's answer seeks to refocus Moses' attention from looking at himself to having faith in God. What is important is not the instrument in God's hand, but the One in whose hand the instrument is being held. God promises Moses that His presence will go with him as he obeys his calling. Moses' authority is wrapped up in the presence of God, which is assured when he is obedient to God's command.

Critical Observation

It has been observed that the Great Commission of the New Testament is strikingly similar to the commission of Moses. The Great Commission begins with the statement, "All authority in heaven and on earth has been given to me" (Matthew 28:18 NIV), and ends with, "Surely I am with you always, to the very end of the age" (Matthew 28:20 NIV). Divine authority is inseparably linked with divine presence. Many of us are waiting for God to give us a sign before we are willing to step out in faith. God may well require that we act in faith before we are given a sign of His presence and His power.

Scholars have spent a great deal of effort to determine the exact meaning of the expression, "I AM WHO I AM" (3:14). Predictably, they do not all agree. As the "I AM," God is not the God who *was* anything, in the sense that He changes. Whatever He was, He continues to be, and He will be forever. God exists independently and unchangeably. Therefore, whatever God has begun to do He will bring to completion, because there are no changes which necessitate any alterations in His original plans and purposes.

How can Moses and the people of Israel be assured that God will deliver them from Egyptian bondage and lead them into the promised land? Their confidence is well placed in the God whose nature and character is that of the "I AM" in Exodus 3. Isaiah 43:1–3 references this same idea and is intended to comfort Israel and assure the nation of God's promises. Just as Israel was not swallowed up by the sea, neither will she be swallowed up by her present and future affliction. Just as the burning bush was not consumed by the fire, so Israel will not be consumed by the fires of affliction and adversity, now or forever (see Malachi 3:2–3, 5–6).

Take It Home

The basis for the call of Moses and for his obedience to that call is an assurance as to the character of God. The measure of our faith is proportionate to our grasp of the greatness and the goodness of our God. No person's faith will be any greater than his or her grasp of the greatness of God as the object of faith. For the Christian, there is no thought more comforting than the eternality of God and His unchanging character. It assures us that His purposes will be fulfilled.

📖 3:16–22

MOSES' MARCHING ORDERS

Now that God has revealed Himself, He reveals His plan for Moses and for Israel. Moses is to repeat the words which God has spoken to him from the burning bush, request a three-day "leave" for the Israelites to worship God in the desert, and finally, collect the wages that are owed to the people of God for their hard work in Egypt.

These commands are all based on the promise and the prophecy which God had previously given Abraham in Genesis 15:12–20. The real struggle now is between Moses and God, and whether he will do what God commands. As the next section reveals, Moses will learn that God's commands are not to be refused.

EXODUS 4:1–31

BEATING AROUND THE BURNING BUSH

Signs for a Reluctant Leader   4:1–17
Signs for the Exiled Israelites   4:18–31

Setting Up the Section

Moses seeks to prove that he is not the man for the task which God has given him. The essence of Moses' argument is, "Send someone else!"

📖 4:1–17

SIGNS FOR A RELUCTANT LEADER

In the past, Moses doubted his calling; now he is doubting the Word of God, for the Lord has just told him the leaders of Israel will accept him (3:18). From the words which follow this assurance, we know that Moses is not only told that the leaders of Israel will accept his leadership, but that it will all work out, just as God has said. Moses is guilty of unbelief.

God still graciously deals with the weakness of Moses by granting him the ability to perform three signs. For the Israelites, these signs are visible evidence that God did appear to Moses in the burning bush. Not only do these signs emphatically prove the existence of the God of the Hebrews, but they give evidence of His superior power.

Rather than acting on the basis of who God is, Moses retreats on the pretext that he is not a gifted communicator. This is indeed a piece of false humility. Moses does not have a speech problem, as some might suppose. According to Stephen, he is eloquent (Acts 7:21–22). Moses is not only doing a disservice to God (by refusing to believe Him and obey in faith), but to himself. Moses should not trust in his own abilities, but neither should he deny the abilities which God has given him.

God reminds Moses that, as his Creator, He fashioned him precisely as He intended, and he is therefore fully able to carry out his commission. The problem of what to say is one that the Lord will handle in due time (Exodus 4:12). While Moses is worrying about what he will say when he gets to Egypt, God is spurring him to get going. Moses is looking too far down the path. Verse 13 reveals the bottom line: Moses does not want to go. It is not that he lacks the assurance or the authority; he simply lacks the courage to act.

God is longsuffering and patient, but now He is angry. God's anger is not only reflected in a visible way, but it is evident in His answer to Moses (4:14–17). Aaron could speak fluently, so why not let him speak for Moses? As later events indicate, the presence of Aaron is a burden for Moses and at times a stumbling block for others (Exodus 32:1–5; Numbers 12:1–12).

📖 **4:18–31**

SIGNS FOR THE EXILED ISRAELITES

Jethro, who seems to be a wise and gracious man, grants Moses' request, wishing him well (4:18). It almost seems as though Moses rearranges the facts God has given when he asks for Jethro's permission to leave, so as to suggest that Moses needed to see if his own people were, in fact, alive and well. Does Moses inadvertently confuse the facts, or does he deceptively rearrange the facts so as to gain the permission of Jethro to take his family to Egypt? The text does not tell us.

Critical Observation

Here, for the first time, the nation of Israel is referred to as the firstborn son of God (4:22–23). Because Pharaoh would not release Israel, God's firstborn son, to worship Him in the desert, God would have Moses tell Pharaoh that He will kill his firstborn. The mention of Israel as Yahweh's firstborn is significant in this larger context. The firstborn son was to the Egyptians not only special, but in many respects sacred. It is therefore most interesting that the people of God are regarded as firstborn in this passage.

One's initial impression of verses 24–26 is that they are inappropriate or out of place, an idea that is not worth entertaining. This action on God's part seems so unusual and so harsh that some have even suggested the "deity" mentioned here was demonic. What does this action on Zipporah's part mean, and what is the purpose of including this story in Exodus? Many believe this enigmatic event explains Moses' deeply rooted resistance to obeying the call of God to return to Egypt to rescue the Israelites.

To the Israelite, the covenant God made with Abraham and reiterated to the patriarchs and Moses was their "gospel." Circumcision was the sign of the covenant—evidence of the parents' faith in the promise of God to Abraham that through his seed blessings would come to Israel and to the whole world (see Genesis 12:1–3). As a testimony of the parents' faith in God's covenant promise, every male in Israel was to be circumcised.

The basis of Israel's preservation (as pictured by the bush that doesn't burn) is the covenant made with Abraham by the eternal God who is, from now on (Exodus 3:15) the "I AM." The covenant was the "gospel," the promise of blessing and salvation which every Israelite was called upon to believe and whose belief was symbolized by the circumcision of his sons and all the males in his household. Moses was to go to Egypt and tell the Israelites that God was about to fulfill His promises, based upon His covenant. And yet Moses had not yet circumcised his son. And if this son is his firstborn, he has had many years in which to do so.

The conclusion of chapter 4 serves as a divine commentary on the fivefold objection of Moses to the call of God. The last verses of the chapter, which report the belief of the people and their worship of God, inform us that Moses' fears were unreal and unreasonable. All of his objections as reported in chapters 3 and 4 have no foundation and are based more on his fears than on reality.

Critical Observation

Moses, with all his fancy royal Egyptian and personal experience with God, failed to obey God in the simplest area of his life—to circumcise his son. He cannot challenge men and women to step out in obedience, based upon their faith in God's covenant promises, when he has not yet circumcised his son as an evidence of his faith. Thus, Moses' problems in relation to his public work are rooted in his personal walk. No wonder Paul writes this to Timothy: "Pay close attention to yourself and to your teaching; persevere in these things, for as you do this you will insure salvation both for yourself and for those who hear you" (1 Timothy 4:16 NASB).

The leaders portrayed in the Bible are not the giants we would like to find, but people whom God has used in spite of their weaknesses and failures. Surely we must admit that Moses, like Elijah, was a man of "like passions" (see James 5:17), a man who had the same fears and failures as we do. It is not the greatness of the man which is the key to his success, but the character of the God who calls and uses fallible people to do His will.

Take It Home

It is hard to call others to faith when one's own is deficient. The gospel is the bedrock foundation on which our personal walk and our public work is based. This is one reason why we as a church believe that the remembrance of the Lord's death is necessary on a weekly basis—and why sacraments like the Lord's Supper and baptism still have such significance. They are not just rituals, but touchstones to remind us what is essential and foundational to our faith and walk. It is unbelief that keeps us from realizing God's purposes. We must remind ourselves that the things of this life are momentary and that eternity will expose what is both lasting and enjoyable.

EXODUS 5:1–6:13

THE REALITY OF BONDAGE

Demands for Deliverance	5:1–21
God Promises Deliverance	5:22–6:13

Setting Up the Section

After Moses has met with God, he returns to Egypt where his fears that Pharaoh would resist God's demands to let the Israelites go are realized.

📖 5:1–21

DEMANDS OF DELIVERANCE

In this passage, Moses first uses God's powerful (and now popularized) phrase: "Let my people go." God desires to be alone with *His* people, but Pharaoh is annoyed by the arrogance of the request. He even says he suspects Moses is lying about receiving divine revelation. Even though Pharaoh is warned there will be consequences, he remains arrogant himself—without any fear or reverence for the God of the Israelites. His heart is already hardened to the plight of the Hebrews. In response to the Israelites' request, he further complicates their situation by demanding bricks without providing straw for them to be made.

Critical Observation

Historical records show that Egyptian serfs around this era were allowed to take time off for religious festivals and celebrations. This fact underscores how proud Pharaoh was in his dealings with the Israelites. In the ancient world, the foreman was typically held accountable and responsible for the conduct of the group of slaves in his charge. Thus the foremen were beaten for the Israelites' inability to make enough bricks and, according to the custom that all slaves could make direct petitions even to Pharaoh, they complained.

GOD PROMISES DELIVERANCE

God reiterates to Moses His commitment to deliver the Israelites from bondage in Egypt—these are the promises of the Abrahamic Covenant. Yet even the promise of deliverance does little to raise the hopes of the beleaguered people. The Hebrew word for *redeem* is the same word used in the story of Ruth, when she is redeemed by the house of Boaz. It refers to the right of family members to acquire persons or property belonging to other family members that are at risk—just as God redeems His people during their time of need in Egypt and ultimately purposes to save their souls through the work of Jesus Christ.

EXODUS 6:14–7:13

GOD'S PEOPLE: MOSES AND AARON

Setting Up the Section

God often uses genealogies to testify to His faithfulness and work across generations in space and time.

GENEALOGY OF MOSES AND AARON

Evidently the genealogy of Moses and Aaron is partially truncated since only four generations are recorded for the 400-year period during which the Israelites wander in the desert. This record introduces the team that God has chosen to lead His people, His children, out of slavery. The genealogy testifies to how intimately connected the Israelites would always be with Egypt, because scholars note that it includes Egyptian names—like Phinehas and Putiel.

AARON TO SPEAK FOR MOSES

God likens the relationship between Moses and his brother, Aaron, to the one between God and His prophet. Aaron will speak for Moses. Later on in this story, when the Israelites commit idolatry under Aaron's watch (chapter 32), Moses will discover what a frustrating and disappointing relationship this can often be! Aaron is Moses' mouthpiece in part because of Moses' own lack of faith in himself. Another significant description here is the hardening of Pharaoh's heart. Throughout the story of Israel's deliverance, both God and Pharaoh play a role in this process, which will ultimately bring great sorrow and destruction to the Egyptians through the plagues and defeat in the Red Sea.

📖 7:8–13

A SLITHERING STAFF AND A HARD HEART

The miracle of turning the staff into a snake is a demonstration of Moses and Aaron's God-given powers. Though the Egyptian sorcerers were able to imitate the miracle to a point—changing their staffs to serpents—their power was inferior to the power God gave Aaron and Moses.

The point of this supernatural ability on the part of Moses and Aaron is also to demonstrate to Pharaoh, who was considered a god himself, that Moses has been divinely appointed and anointed and is an opponent to be reckoned with. The demand increases from the request for an opportunity for communion with God to a demand for release of the Israelites from slavery. Again Pharaoh's heart is hardened. Eventually, even the sting of the plagues and the death of his firstborn cannot penetrate Pharaoh's heart to be humble before God.

EXODUS 7:14–10:29

THE FINGER OF GOD

Plague One: The Nile Turns into Blood	7:14–25
Plague Two: The Frogs	8:1–15
Plague Three: The Gnats	8:16–19
Plague Four: The Flies	8:20–32
Plague Five: Livestock Killed	9:1–7
Plague Six: Boils	9:8–12
Plague Seven: The Storm	9:13–35
Plague Eight: Locusts	10:1–20
Plague Nine: Darkness	10:21–29

Setting Up the Section

The plagues which God brings upon the Egyptians are a unique kind of tragedy—part of God's judgment of Pharaoh and his people for their oppression of the Israelites (see Genesis 15:13–14; Deuteronomy 11:1–4; Psalm 78:44–52).

📖 7:14–25

PLAGUE ONE: THE NILE TURNS INTO BLOOD

There are some tragedies in life which are simply that—part of the suffering and sadness of life. There are also tragedies which have a very positive and beneficial purpose—the tragedies of Job's life, for example, or the tragedy of the cross of Christ. The sufferings of the nation of Israel during the four hundred years of their slavery in Egypt also will, in the drama of Israel's history, prove to be beneficial.

The Nile is virtually the lifeblood of Egypt. Without the silt it provides during its times of overflow and the water it provides to sustain life, Egypt would be almost uninhabitable. The meaning of the miracle of turning the Nile to blood can best be understood in light of God's later prophecy, recorded in Ezekiel 29:2–6, where He concludes that by this miracle all of Egypt will know that He is the Lord.

This plague serves as an attack on one of the Egyptian gods. The Egyptians believed that Hapi, a god of fertility, was also the god of the Nile.

📖 8:1–15

PLAGUE TWO: THE FROGS

Frogs were common in Egypt, especially around the Nile River, but there had never been this many. From this account, one can visualize frogs hopping and croaking all over Egypt, and even overrunning the palace of the Pharaoh. The frogs got into the food, into the kneading troughs, and ovens. When Egypt is finally rid of the frogs, thanks to Moses, huge heaps of dead frogs are piled all over the country, creating a stench that is a plague in and of itself. God is making the Israelites' presence a real nuisance to the Egyptians. Soon, it is their groaning, not the Hebrews', that will accomplish God's purpose.

Critical Observation

Frogs were also regarded as having divine power. In the Egyptian pantheon, the goddess Heqet had the form of a woman with a frog's head. From her nostrils, it was believed, came the breath of life that animated the bodies of those created by her husband, the great god Khnum, from the dust of the earth. Therefore frogs were not to be killed.

📖 8:16–19

PLAGUE THREE: THE GNATS

It is not altogether certain what is meant by the Hebrew term translated *gnat*. The King James Version renders the term *lice*, which is also possible. Some have suggested that it was a plague of mosquitoes. It does not really matter exactly what is meant. The gnats plagued both humans and animals. The significance of this plague is that the magicians of Egypt are unable to produce these gnats themselves, which leads them to tell Pharaoh that it is the work of God (8:19). From the other places where this same expression is found (Exodus 31:18; Deuteronomy 9:10; Psalm 8:3; Luke 11:20), it seems to refer primarily to the power of God directly intervening in the affairs of men and women. Nevertheless, Pharaoh's heart is hardened, and he refuses to listen.

📖 8:20–32

PLAGUE FOUR: THE FLIES

With this plague, the second sequence of three plagues is commenced. Here, discrimination is made between the Egyptians and the Israelites. While the exact species of flies that plagues Egypt is not certain, one can assume that they are bigger and more difficult than the gnats previously set loose on the Egyptians. Because the flies are so bothersome, Pharaoh is willing to negotiate with Moses. Pharaoh's request, "Pray for me" (8:28), indicates his self-centered interests. Moses leaves, but with the warning that there must be no more deceit on Pharaoh's part regarding his promise to let Israel go. But when the flies are gone, so is Pharaoh's motivation to release Israel.

📖 9:1–7

PLAGUE FIVE: LIVESTOCK KILLED

The fifth plague is directed against the livestock of the Egyptians, but not the cattle of the Israelites. There is only speculation as to the cause of death. By whatever means, God virtually wipes out the cattle of the Egyptians. Since wealth was measured largely in terms of cattle, this was an economic disaster. The gods of Egypt were once again proven to be lifeless and useless.

📖 9:8–12

PLAGUE SIX: BOILS

There is a subtly humorous note here. The magicians are not only unable to rid the land of Egypt of the boils, they are also so afflicted themselves that they cannot even show up to stand before Moses.

📖 9:13–35

PLAGUE SEVEN: THE STORM

God often uses weather to humble people and to demonstrate His power. Remember the instance where the disciples were caught in a storm on the sea and Jesus walked on water? Describing this as the plague of hail is only partly true. In reality, the plague is the worst thunderstorm in Egypt's history (9:18), and the death and destruction that occurs is the result of both hailstones and lightning (9:24).

This plague begins the third and final trilogy of plagues. Things get considerably worse as the plagues continue to progress. These last plagues begin with the warning that unless Pharaoh releases the Israelites, God will send even more plagues against Pharaoh and Egypt (9:14). God could have legitimately and easily wiped out all of Egypt in one blow, but He does not (9:15). However if Pharaoh persists in his hardness of heart, things will get considerably worse.

In verse 16, Moses explains why God has allowed Pharaoh's stubbornness to persist. God raised Pharaoh up for the purpose of hardening his heart and thus providing the occasion for God to manifest His power to mankind.

📖 10:1–20

PLAGUE EIGHT: LOCUSTS

The previous plague of the thunderstorm had destroyed the flax and barley crops, but the wheat and spelt crops were not destroyed since they matured later (9:31). The locusts, however, would wipe out the remaining crops. This plague brings Pharaoh to a point of humility before Moses and God, but still there is no deal made between them.

PLAGUE NINE: DARKNESS

The darkness of the ninth plague is so intense that it produces dread in the hearts of the Egyptians. God often refers to His way and Himself as "the light," particularly in the incarnate Christ. Consider how striking the frightening plague of darkness must have been. Some have suggested that the darkness described here is only a partial darkness, created by a dust storm. This can hardly be the case, for the darkness described is much more intense. The three days of darkness had a tremendous emotional and psychological impact on the nation as a whole. The experience may have been something like the three-day period of blindness that Saul experienced prior to his conversion (see Acts 9:8–12).

Critical Observation

The plague of darkness struck hard at one of the chief Egyptian deities, the sun god Re, of whom Pharaoh was a representation. Re was responsible for providing sunlight, warmth, and productivity. Other gods, including Horus, were also associated with the sun. Nut, the goddess of the sky, would have been humiliated by this plague. It was God's way of demonstrating that He alone has power over any other being in His creation. The plagues were an indictment and judgment of the gods of Egypt and demonstrated God's existence and power.

The ninth plague, like the third and the sixth plagues, comes upon the Egyptians without warning, which gives them no opportunity to prepare for the disaster—physically or psychologically. Pharaoh offers to allow the Israelites to leave Egypt to worship God, but insists that the cattle must remain behind (10:24). When this offer is rejected, Pharaoh hotly warns Moses that he must leave his presence, and to return will be to his death. Moses agrees, but he has yet one more plague to proclaim before his final exit from Pharaoh's presence. This tenth plague, he threatens, will bring about the release of the Israelites.

These plagues are a prototype, a sample, of God's future judgment. They are like those which Israel will experience (Deuteronomy 28:27) if they disobey the law God is soon to give. There is much similarity between the plagues of Egypt and the plagues described in the book of Revelation, which are poured out upon the earth in the last days, preceding the return of the Lord. Thus, in Revelation we find the victorious tribulation saints singing the "song of Moses" (Revelation 15:3).

Take It Home

Obviously, not all calamities are the result of sin and evidence of God's judgment. Job's adversity was not the result of his sin, but a means of Job's growth in his walk with God. Job's affliction is also a teaching tool for Satan, who cannot fathom why a saint would continue to worship God when it's not profitable, but painful, to do so. When God is punishing men and women for sin, He is not silent about it. When He is silent at the time of the suffering of a saint, this is a test of faith, not an evidence of God's judgment. The plagues on Egypt remind us of the seriousness of sin.

God's actual judgment of sin is something false religionists seek to deny. Judgment is not easy to believe in or dwell upon. Thus the plagues against Egypt are not popular reading, but are nonetheless a vital part of divine revelation. The psalmist in Psalm 73 looks about and senses that the wicked are not suffering for their sin, but are prospering, while the righteous seem to be the ones who suffer. In this present day, it may seem that sin is profitable, while righteousness is painful. At such times we must remember that we accept the fact of God's future judgments (as we do His future rewards) by faith.

God's judgment of the Egyptians is severe, so it's instructive to consider several perspectives. God judged the gods of Egypt more than He did the Egyptians. Just as hell is the place prepared for Satan and his angels, so judgment here is for the Egyptian gods and whoever chooses to serve these gods. God's judgment may be intended to bring some of the Egyptians to a saving faith. The fact that some Egyptians leave Egypt with the Israelites (Exodus 12:38) gives substance to this possibility. Also, God's judgment upon the Egyptians is the means of delivering His people from terrible bondage. Finally, God's judgment is poured out upon His own Son on the cross of Calvary, so that all mankind might be saved. God's "severity" extended to His own Son. There was an alternative provided by God to suffering the plagues of Egypt—heeding God's warning and doing as He commanded. God's judgment could be avoided by faith and obedience.

EXODUS 11:1–13:16

THE PASSOVER AND THE PLAGUE OF THE FIRSTBORN

The Tenth Plague Foretold   11:1–10
The First Passover   12:1–36
Israel's Exodus   12:37–13:16

Setting Up the Section

The slaughter of the firstborn of the Egyptians raises tremendous moral issues. God uses the tenth plague as the means to release His people from slavery. This text insists that we examine and accept the meaning and application of God's judgment at work in His creation and in the lives of His people.

📖 **11:1–10**

THE TENTH PLAGUE FORETOLD

Throughout this account, Moses' purpose is not merely a chronological review of historical events, but to explain theologically the significance of what happens to Egypt and Israel as a result of the plague of the firstborn and the first Passover. Thus, he sacrifices chronological smoothness in deference to theological explanation. Verses 4–8 are Moses' final retort to Pharaoh, made immediately after his demand that Moses leave. Verses 1–3 are cited before the announcement of Moses to Pharaoh that the firstborn of Egypt will be slain. This explains how Moses knew that this was the final plague, and why Pharaoh will nonetheless reject the warning. Verses 9–10 are also a parenthetical explanation of why Pharaoh stubbornly refuses to heed the warning of the plagues. This plague is the final blow, which will compel Pharaoh to release the Israelites.

📖 **12:1–36**

THE FIRST PASSOVER

Like the Feast of Unleavened Bread and the redemption of the firstborn, the Passover was to become a permanent part of Israel's religious liturgy (12:24–25). There were several purposes for the Passover celebration, some of which were to be understood at a later time. The Passover is a memorial of the deliverance of Israel, accomplished by the mighty power of God (3:20; 13:9, 14, 16). The Passover and its related celebrations, the Feast of Unleavened Bread and the redemption of the firstborn, were intended to serve as occasions for instruction for the future generations of Israel (12:26–27; 13:8, 14–16).

The Passover celebration is a means of incorporating or excluding the Gentiles in the covenant of God to Abraham (12:38, 43–49). No uncircumcised person could partake of the Passover. The Passover lamb is a model of the Messiah, the Lamb of God, through whom God would bring redemption to both Israel and the Gentiles (12:5–7, 46–47).

Critical Observation

The similarities between the Passover lamb and the Lamb of God are perhaps not immediately perceived, but consider what we know about the Passover lamb and the Lamb of God today: The lamb was to be without defect (12:5), just as Jesus was without blemish (1 Peter 1:19); the shed blood of the lamb saved Israel's firstborn (Exodus 12:12–13, 22–23), just as the blood of Christ saves mankind from God's judgment (1 Peter 1:18–19; Revelation 5:9); and just as no bone of the Passover lamb was broken (Exodus 12:46), so no bone of Jesus was broken (John 19:32–36). Thus, the Old Testament prophet, Isaiah, spoke of Israel's Savior as a Lamb (Isaiah 53:6–7).

For the Israelites, the Passover and the tenth plague serve as a judgment on the gods of Egypt, whom the Israelites had worshiped (Joshua 24:14), and as evidence of the grace of God in the lives of His people. The plagues point out the sin of the Egyptians and their need to repent and believe in the God of Israel.

The firstborn of Israel are not spared because they are more worthy or more righteous than the Egyptians, but because of the grace of God alone. God made provision for non-Israelites to partake of the Passover if they were circumcised (acknowledging their faith in the Abrahamic Covenant; see Genesis 17:9–14; Exodus 12:48–49). Since there were many non-Israelites who left Egypt with Israel (Exodus 12:38), it is likely that a number were converted and physically spared from death through the process of the plagues and the provision of the Passover.

📖 12:37–13:16

ISRAEL'S EXODUS

Verses 31–42 give a historical overview of the Exodus, from the command to leave issued by Pharaoh to an account of the departure, showing that God's promises have been carried out in accord with His schedule—to the very day. Verses 43–51 conclude with further instructions for the Israelites regarding the celebration of the Passover in the future, especially focusing on the participation of foreigners. God would have Israelites (and the readers of New Testament times as well) know that the institution of the Passover was done in accordance with direct divine revelation—designed and pre-scribed by God.

The Passover is proof of God's possession of Israel. The firstborn of Israel belonged to God as a result of the Passover, and all of Israel was God's possession as a result of the Exodus. All of the commandments and requirements which God placed upon the Israelites were predicated upon the fact that they were a people who belonged to Him.

EXODUS 13:17–14:31

THE RED SEA: ISRAEL'S DELIVERANCE AND EGYPT'S DEFEAT

Charting Israel's Course	13:17–22
Changing Israel's Course	14:1–9
Calming Israel's Fears	14:10–14
Divine Instruction and Intervention	14:15–20
Israel's Deliverance and the Egyptians' Destruction	14:21–31

Setting Up the Section

This text portrays the hardness of humanity's heart, which leads ultimately to destruction. The sea, which destroyed the Egyptians, is the instrument of God's wrath, but it is also the instrument of Israel's deliverance.

📖 13:17–22

CHARTING ISRAEL'S COURSE

Israel's passing through the Red Sea is one of the most dramatic events recorded in the Old Testament. It rid the Israelites, once for all, of Pharaoh's dominion and released them from their obligation to return to Egypt, after traveling a three-day journey into the wilderness to worship God (as had been described by Moses to Pharaoh). This was, in fact, the birth of the nation of Israel.

There were three possible land routes for Israel to take to reach Canaan. The shortest route would have been to cross the land belonging to the Philistines, but they would have encountered war and lost heart (13:17). It may seem strange that God wants to avoid a military confrontation, when in verse 18 (see also 6:26; 12:41) it reads that the Israelites are armed for battle. The expression used here has been understood to refer only to the orderly way in which the Israelites (nearly two million people, counting women and children; see 12:37) departed Egypt. Others understand that the Israelites did come out of Egypt at least partially armed, but all seem to agree that Israel was not at all prepared to fight a full-scale battle at this point in time. Instead, the nation moved in a southeasterly direction, avoiding the Philistines.

Verses 21–22 describe a cloud and fire in which God is present (14:24; 40:38; Numbers 9:15–23; 14:14; Deuteronomy 1:33; Nehemiah 9:12, 19; Psalms 78:14; 105:39; 1 Corinthians 10:1). This provides the Israelites with a visible manifestation of His presence, protection, and guidance.

📖 14:1–9

CHANGING ISRAEL'S COURSE

Moses' leadership (beyond the guiding pillar and cloud) was to bring about a change of course for the Israelites, one that would perplex the people. The Israelites are instructed to turn back and camp near Pi Hahiroth, between Migdol and the sea. God's instructions explain that this change of course, while it puts the people in a seemingly vulnerable position, is intended to encourage Pharaoh's pursuit. God knew Pharaoh would think the Israelites were miserably lost or misguided and that recovering them would be easy. Pharaoh's attack would result in his defeat, to the glory of God (14:4).

📖 14:10–14

CALMING ISRAEL'S FEARS

The Israelites are terrified by the sight of the rapidly approaching Egyptians (14:10). They begin to reason that God has failed them. Moses, confident that God will deliver them from the Egyptians, tries to reassure the people. Even Moses begins crying out to God, not unlike the Israelites before him (14:10, 15), anxious for deliverance.

📖 14:15–20

DIVINE INSTRUCTION AND INTERVENTION

Why does God rebuke Moses (14:15)? Because Moses knows that God has guided the Israelites to this place—between the Red Sea and the Egyptians. The pillar has led them there (13:21–22; 14:19), and God has explained His plan to Moses—so that He could gain glory through Pharaoh and his army (14:1–4). Moses knew that God had promised to bring the Israelites into the land of Canaan, which was across and beyond the Red Sea (Genesis 15:13–21; Exodus 3:7–8, 16–17; 6:4; 12:25; 13:5). Moses also knew that God had given him power through the use of his staff. God's gentle rebuke of Moses implies that Moses should have understood these things.

In spite of Moses' lack of faith, God graciously responds to his cry for help. He instructs Moses to raise his staff and stretch out his hand over the sea, making it possible for the Israelites to pass through on dry ground (14:16). The Egyptians, God informs Moses, will enter the sea behind them, resulting in their destruction and God's ultimate glory (14:17–18). God does more than just speak; the angel of the Lord, manifested in the pillar of cloud and fire, moves from the front of the Israelites to the rear, giving light to them and paralyzing the Egyptians in darkness (14:20).

📖 14:21–31

ISRAEL'S DELIVERANCE AND THE EGYPTIANS' DESTRUCTION

Stretching forth his hand over the sea, Moses brings about a strong wind, turning the seabed to dry ground (14:21). Even more amazing than the courage of the Israelites to enter the seabed is the fact that the Egyptians follow them there. The Egyptians are blind to the incredible dangers of doing so by the hardness of their hearts.

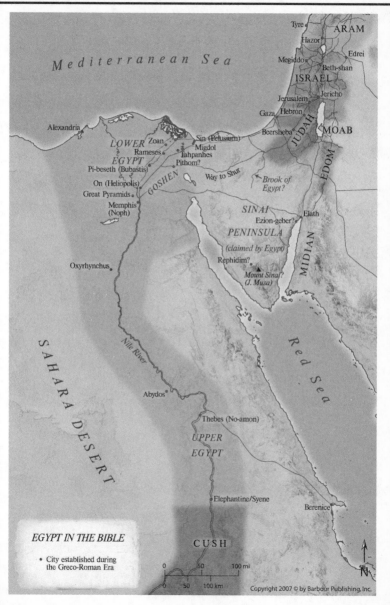

EGYPT IN THE BIBLE

- City established during the Greco-Roman Era

Copyright 2007 © by Barbour Publishing, Inc.

109

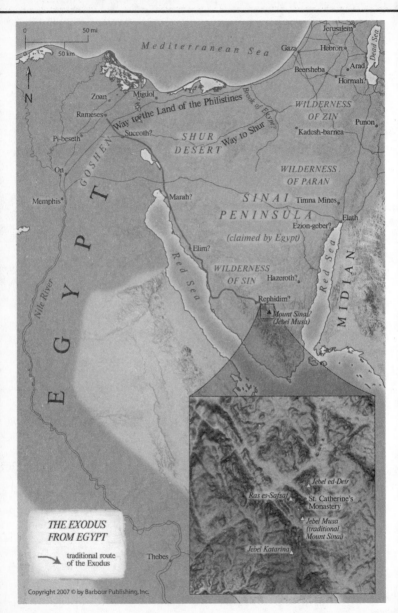

THE EXODUS
FROM EGYPT

→ traditional route
of the Exodus

Copyright 2007 © by Barbour Publishing, Inc.

In the morning watch, which is from 2:00 a.m. until dawn, God brings confusion to the Egyptian troops (14:24). The poetic description of Psalm 77:16–19 makes it seem that a thunderstorm causes the confusion. The Egyptians try to retreat, but instead plunge headlong into the waters (14:27–28).

Critical Observation

The destruction of the Egyptians in the Red Sea is the culminating act of divine judgment that began with the hardening of the Egyptians' hearts. God began to judge the Egyptians at the time that Moses returned to Egypt and appeared before Pharaoh. Each plague was a judgment of the gods of the Egyptians (12:12). The Bible references the hardening of Pharaoh's heart (and sometimes his officials' or his army's hearts) fourteen times in Exodus. Of these fourteen instances, six refer to God hardening Pharaoh's heart (9:12; 10:1, 20, 27; 11:10; 14:8), three refer to Pharaoh hardening his own heart (8:15, 32; 9:34), and five are indefinite (7:13, 22; 8:19; 9:7, 35).

EXODUS 15:1–27

THE SONG OF THE SEA

Setting Up the Section

Israel's first great affirmation of faith is expressed in a song. Some have titled this song the "Song of the Sea." The mood of the song is triumphant. The structure has two parts: what God has done for Israel at the Red Sea and what God will surely do for Israel in the future (15:11–21).

📖 15:1–12

GOD'S VICTORY OVER THE EGYPTIANS

Moses apparently wrote the song and led Israel as they sang it. In psalmlike fashion, the acts of God are viewed as evidence of His nature and character. With dramatic poetic strokes, God's sovereignty is evidenced by His control over the forces of nature (wind) and His ability as the Creator to cause nature to act unnaturally (the piling up of the water). In spite of the Egyptians' power and confidence, God simply blew them away, causing them to sink in the sea (15:10). The greatest army on the face of the earth is no match for the God of Israel. The greatness and the goodness of God are recognized by the Israelites as they reflect on God's victory over their enemies.

Demystifying Exodus

This song reveals the fulfillment of God's plan for the deliverance of Israel. God told Moses that Pharaoh would not release the Israelites until God's mighty hand compelled him to by performing miracles (3:19–20; 6:1). Now, after their passing through the Red Sea, Israel praises God for what He has done (15:6, 9, 12). God revealed through Moses that He was going to judge the gods of Egypt (12:12). Now, after the Exodus, Israel proclaims God as the one unique God (15:11). By the Exodus, God said that Israel would know He was the God who delivered them (6:7). Here, the Israelites sing their praises to Him for deliverance (15:2). This praise song reveals that God accomplished what He had sought to accomplish in the events of the Exodus.

15:13–21

GOD'S FUTURE VICTORY OVER ISRAEL'S ENEMIES

The second half of the song focuses on Israel's deliverance that is yet to come, and the defeat of the enemies who will resist Israel in Canaan. The NIV underscores the shift from the past defeat of the Egyptians to the future defeat of Israel's enemies by rendering the verbs of verses 13 and following in the future tense. The plagues and passing through the Red Sea are the beginning of Israel's journey home.

The "Song of the Sea" provides the Israelites a mechanism for recalling God's great act of deliverance at the Red Sea, and it directs their attention to the character of God, producing hope and confidence in His future protection and blessing.

15:22–27

ISRAEL'S PROTESTS AT THE WATERS OF MARAH

The Israelites travel into the Desert of Shur, and for three days they find no water. When they realize the water at Marah is bitter, they quickly turn to anger at Moses for leading them to such a place. This reveals their lack of faith and hardness of heart. The transformation of the waters of Marah, which means "bitter" (Ruth 1:20), is a miracle. No one knows of any wood which could produce the result described here. The casting of the wood into the water must have been a symbolic act, like Moses raising his staff over the waters of the Red Sea.

Take It Home

The Israelites failed to see the relationship between the affirmation of their faith in their worship (15:1–21) and the application of their faith in their daily walk (15:22–26). Israel had just proclaimed her faith in God as her warrior (15:3), but she was unable to trust in God as her provider (15:22–26). If God could deal with the waters of the Red Sea, surely He could be trusted to deal with the waters of Marah.

When we gather to worship God, we sing many hymns and choruses which express our faith in God, and yet too often we forget the truths that these hymns affirm. We must learn to apply in our daily walk those truths which we affirm in our public worship.

EXODUS 16:1–36

OBEDIENCE BOOT CAMP

Growling Stomachs and Grumbling Saints 16:1–3
The Bread of Heaven 16:4–36

Setting Up the Section

In the passage, Israel is guilty of two sins: greed and grumbling. Both of these sins are symptomatic of an even more serious underlying sin. Exodus 15:26 provides the background for God's provision of manna for His people. God's instructions regulating the gathering and use of the manna serve as a test of Israel's faith and obedience.

📖 16:1–3

GROWLING STOMACHS AND GRUMBLING SAINTS

In this passage, there is a definite relationship between the Israelites' growling stomachs and their grumbling lips. In verse 3, Israel greatly exaggerates the benefits of Egypt and the direness of their current predicament, and they fail to perceive the hand of a sovereign God in their sufferings. They are struggling with submitting to the wisdom of their leaders, and they are complaining because they feel like they have no control over their situation.

📖 16:4–36

THE BREAD OF HEAVEN

God reveals His glory to the Israelites by manifesting Himself in the cloud (16:10) and satisfies their physical needs by providing quail and manna (16:11–14). God's daily provision of manna in the wilderness teaches the Israelites to look daily to God for their sustenance. The regulations for collecting the manna—gathering only the needs of the day—taught them self control that kept their hope for deliverance in God and not in the manna. The greatest danger Israel faced was not starvation in the midst of a wilderness, but the wrath of God.

Take It Home

The tension here is a part of the broader tension between divine sovereignty and human responsibility. God provided the manna that Israel needed, but He commanded them to collect, cook, and keep it in accordance with His instructions. This illustrates the fact that divine sovereignty and human responsibility are related. God provides, but we must obey. In this relationship, God asks us to have self-control, but also provides the catalyst to produce it.

EXODUS 17:1–16

GOD'S GRACE TO ISRAEL

| Massah and Meribah: Water from the Rock | 17:1–7 |
| The Lord Is My Banner | 17:8–16 |

Setting Up the Section

Leaving the Desert of Sin, where the provision of manna had commenced (Exodus 16), the Israelites went from place to place as the Lord directed them. While Israel's later wandering in the wilderness is the result of their sin at Kadesh-barnea (Numbers 13–14), the wanderings in this chapter are designed to serve as Israel's "boot camp" experiences.

17:1–7

MASSAH AND MERIBAH: WATER FROM THE ROCK

Moses names the place where he draws water from the rock *Massah* (test) and *Meribah* (quarrel). This incident is typical of Israel's stubbornness and rebellion against God (Deuteronomy 9:6–8, 24; Hebrews 3:10). The grumbling of the Israelites in the wilderness is a persistent problem. Furthermore, the sin of this first generation of Israelites is almost identically reproduced by the second generation of Israelites some years later (Numbers 20:1–13). The problem of grumbling is common to every generation, in every age. Thus, we find the events of Massah and Meribah frequently referred to throughout scripture (Numbers 20:1–13; Deuteronomy 6:16–17; 8:15, Psalm 95:7–9; 1 Corinthians 10:1–13; Hebrews 3, 4).

Israel's lack of water is by divine design, for God is testing them by their response to adversity (Deuteronomy 8:2, 16; Psalm 81:7). It reveals the sinful condition of their hearts and is a reminder that God is always blessing them on the basis of His grace, not their works.

THE LORD IS MY BANNER

Scripture often reveals one dramatic event immediately after another. The attack of the Amalekites right after the Israelites' testing of God is an opportunity for them to demonstrate their confidence in God's desire for their good. The image of Moses holding up his staff to call on the power of God to defeat the Amalekites is a powerful one. What a simple but powerful picture of the interplay between our limited strength and God's all-powerful might. The image of the Lord as His people's Banner is used elsewhere in the Bible.

Take It Home

Is it possible that you are in a kind of wilderness? God may have purposed this season so that you could come to know Him in a much more intimate way than you have previously. Just as God meant Massah and Meribah for Israel's good, He means your wilderness experience to be for your good as well.

EXODUS 18:1–27

THE TYRANNY OF THE URGENT

Jethro's Arrival   18:1–12
Jethro's Advice   18:13–27

Setting Up the Section

Moses' father-in-law, Jethro, having heard of God's protection and deliverance of the Israelites, comes to visit in order to reunite Moses with his wife and children. The first half of the chapter reveals several symptoms of a serious problem in Moses' life, which prompts not only Jethro's arrival, but also his advice about achieving balance.

JETHRO'S ARRIVAL

The arrival of Jethro, accompanied by Zipporah, Gershom, and Eliezer, is apparently a pleasant surprise for Moses. We are not told precisely when or why Moses and his family are separated, but the last mention of them is in chapter 4. One might conjecture that Moses sent his family back to Jethro at a time when he feared for their safety. Perhaps, too, he felt that the pressures of confronting Pharaoh and of leading Israel were too great to have the additional responsibilities of a husband and father.

Jethro acts out of wisdom, compassion, and concern for Moses' best interest. This is a magnanimous act, especially after the deceptive explanation Moses gave for his return to Egypt (Exodus 4:18). Jethro rejoices with Moses, praising God for His grace manifested toward Israel, as evidenced by Moses' report (18:9–10). Also, Jethro seems to acknowledge, for the first time, the superiority of God over all other gods—unique in that Midianites were generally idolaters (Numbers 25:17–18; 31:16). Jethro demonstrates his newfound faith by offering sacrifices to God and sharing the sacrificial meal (Exodus 18:12).

Critical Observation

There is a tendency among Christians to minimize the failings of a man like Moses in this situation. The assumption is that the saints who are described in the Bible always do the right thing for the right reasons. Instead, we should interpret Moses' actions in light of the fact that, while we know he is God's chosen leader, he is also an imperfect human being. The text here is not extolling Moses' virtues, but his vices. Here is a person who we can identify with, an individual with flaws just like us. Yet he is used by God nonetheless and blessed by the keen advice of those who care about him.

📖 18:13–27

JETHRO'S ADVICE

Jethro is baffled by the inefficiency he has witnessed. It is apparent from his questioning that he does not agree with the way Moses is handling things. Moses' response reveals his distorted perception and several misconceptions regarding his role as a leader.

While Moses deals with the Israelites individually, Jethro advocates dealing with them collectively (18:19–20). Moses is unable to manage because he fails to see that he needs a strong team to support him. He is dealing with nearly two million people, and he is trying to do so by himself. He is, according to Jethro, wearing himself out (18:18). Moses has allowed his sense of public duty to overshadow his sense of personal responsibility.

Jethro's advice is that Moses rearrange his time so that priority is given to teaching the people God's principles and precepts, and prescribe guidelines for solving problems when they arise.

Take It Home

Jethro's advice is good for all. How can you facilitate the ministry of others by encouraging and equipping them to do what they do best? Faith is required to trust God to enable you to do what He has called you to do. Faith is also required to enable you to leave what you should not do to others.

EXODUS 19:1-25

THE PREAMBLE TO ISRAEL'S CONSTITUTION

God's Purpose for the Decalogue	19:1–6
Preparing for the Appearance of God	19:7–15
The Manifestation of God on the Mountain	19:16–25

Setting Up the Section

Chapter 19 serves as a preamble to the commandments given by God to Israel. It reveals the purpose of the commandments, as well as the perspective we should have toward them.

📖 **19:1–6**

GOD'S PURPOSE FOR THE DECALOGUE

Apparently, it is not necessary for God to summon Moses (19:3). This may be due to the fact that it is on Mount Horeb (synonymous with Mount Sinai) where Moses first encounters God (chapters 3 and 4). At the burning bush, God promises Moses that the nation will come to worship Him "at this mountain" (3:12). Thus, Moses seems to know that he is to ascend the mountain to speak with God. From the mountain, God speaks some of the most significant words found in the Old Testament (19:4-6). God's statement declares to the Israelites His faithfulness to His covenant, their distinction from the Egyptians, and His promise to keep Israel the special object of His care.

God uses an image of the eagle's care for its offspring. In the book of Deuteronomy, Moses explains the image more fully (Deuteronomy 32:11). While there are times when God seems (to the Israelites) to have abandoned His people, in reality God is simply stirring up the nest, forcing the Israelites to try their wings.

This declaration also describes how Israel's deliverance is for the purpose of being brought to God so that the nation could be His prized possession. In the Abrahamic Covenant, God promises Abraham that Israel will become a great nation and the special object of His blessing. The blessing of Israel is also meant to be a source of blessing to all nations (Genesis 12:2). While this would ultimately be fulfilled by the coming of the Messiah, there is also a more immediate application. God purposed to bless the nations by establishing Israel, His servant, as a mediatory people, sharing with the nations the way of entering into fellowship with God.

Israel must keep God's covenant (as defined by the law) to maintain their status as God's people. Israel's calling is to a position of both privilege and responsibility. To whom much is given, much is required. Israel is given the commandments as a distinction from other nations so that they can fulfill their priestly calling.

19:7–15

PREPARING FOR THE APPEARANCE OF GOD

To this point, God has only indicated that the people must keep their covenant by obeying the laws which He is about to set down. The Israelites anticipated the law with eagerness, demonstrating their implicit trust in the character of God. Verses 10–15 outline the steps which the Israelites must take in order to purify and prepare themselves for the appearance of God on the third day.

Why are these boundaries so serious to God? To press past the barriers which were constructed to satisfy one's curiosity would be to demonstrate an attitude of irreverence. It is this irreverence which God finds as such a serious sin. Remember, it is irreverence which results in Uzzah being struck dead, even though his intentions (to keep the ark from falling from the ox cart) are well meaning (2 Samuel 6:6–7). It is also Moses' irreverence (in the striking of the rock) that keeps him from entering into the promised land (Numbers 20:12).

Irreverence is the by-product of an inadequate sense of the holiness of God. The Israelites do not yet have an adequate grasp of the holiness of God. The manifestation of God on Mount Sinai is a spectacular demonstration of God's power and majesty. His coming necessitates preparatory consecration, and it also motivates continual consecration, as people could see themselves in the light of His glory and grace (Exodus 19:23).

19:16–25

THE MANIFESTATION OF GOD ON THE MOUNTAIN

This text describes the splendor and the majesty of God as He manifests Himself to Israel on the mountain. Exodus 19 prepares us for the glorious giving of the law by God to His people—an occasion marked by God's purity, power, and holiness.

The law contained not only the regulations of God, but also the account of God's mercy and grace in saving and keeping His people. Each generation is to teach the next generation the goodness of God, and each new generation is to ratify the covenant for itself (Psalm 78:5–7).

Critical Observation

The Mosaic Covenant was never given as a means of earning righteousness by law keeping. The new covenant is promised because the Mosaic Covenant could not be kept by Israel (Jeremiah 31:31–34). Whenever Israel failed with regard to the law, it was not just a matter of violating the law in some minute particular, but it was a result of unbelief (Psalm 78:21–22, 32–33, 37).

The proper interpretation and application of the law is best determined by a study of the Old Testament prophets, who focus on the essence of the law rather than the particulars of its expression (Hosea 6:6–7; Micah 6:6–8). The law (in its broadest form—the Pentateuch, the first five books of the Bible) is intended to serve as a record of God's faithfulness to His promises and to His people. The Ten Commandments, along with the rest of the laws of God, are given to serve as the covenant between God and His people, and as their national constitution, by which the nation would be guided and governed.

Critical Observation

When Paul or the other apostles speak disparagingly of the law, it is not the law as given by God and properly interpreted and applied, but the law as interpreted and applied by the Judaizers, who sought to pervert it into a system of works oriented righteousness. In order to refute their false teaching, Paul finds it necessary to teach the proper perspective of the law. The law, writes Paul, is provisional and preparatory, and is superseded by the new covenant. The law was good—but the new covenant is far better.

Take It Home

The law is a gracious provision for the nation of Israel, albeit a temporary one. The new covenant would be far better, but the old covenant is a necessary prerequisite and preparation. In the first covenant, God's majesty and might are manifested to all, but only a select few could draw near. In the new covenant, all who wish to can draw near, but only a few behold His majesty. The first manifestation of God on Mount Sinai portrays the marvelous truth of the holiness of God, and the separation which that demands. The second manifestation of the Lord (on Mount Calvary) reveals the marvelous grace of God, by which He draws near to us and by which we may draw near to Him. How careful we must be to keep both the holiness and the grace of God in perspective.

EXODUS 20:1–26

THE TEN COMMANDMENTS

The Characteristics of the Commandments   20:1–17
Pure Worship   20:18–26

Setting Up the Section

The Decalogue, also called the Ten Commandments, is one of the keys to understanding the Old Testament. It is the central core of the lengthy Mosaic Law.

📖 20:1–17

THE CHARACTERISTICS OF THE COMMANDMENTS

In Exodus 20, God expresses the essence of the Old Testament law in ten principle statements. In chapter 19, we learn that the giving of the law is directly related to Israel's calling to be a kingdom of priests and a holy nation (19:6). If Israel is to represent God, they must be like God. The law defines how God's holiness is to be manifested in the lives of men and women.

The Ten Commandments are both a corporate constitution for Israel and an intensely personal revelation from God to His children. The *you* in the commandments is not plural, but singular. Each individual is therefore urged to enter into the joy of service by adopting this covenant and by obeying the laws which are contained therein. The Decalogue is not only a constitution, it is God's standard for Israel's culture.

📖 20:18–26

PURE WORSHIP

Verses 18–21 contain the account of the Israelites' reaction to the giving of the law. It also offers God's reason for giving it as He did—to keep the people from sinning (20:20).

While God evidently spoke the Ten Commandments in the hearing of all the Israelites (19:9; 20:19, 22) the people were so struck by the revelation that they asked Moses to act as a go-between for them from then on, which he did (20:21).

Verse 20 mentions two kinds of fear. First, the people are told not to fear, but then they are told the fear of God will be with them. The first fear is a tormenting fear (which enslaves). The second is a respectful fear (which demonstrates trust with acknowledgement of power). The latter is the fear that will keep the people from sinning.

Verses 22–26 include specific instruction regarding worship. Idolatry is clearly prohibited, but also there seems to be a prohibition against making images to represent God (20:22). An altar, on the other hand, was an acceptable form of worship. The Israelites built altars both at a central location once they settled and along the way when God revealed Himself (Genesis 35:7; Joshua 8:30). The specific instruction regarding uncut stones was probably to distinguish the Israelite altars from the Canaanite altars.

Another distinction between the two was the prohibition of stairs leading up to the altar. This seems to be simply to keep the priest from exposing himself as he went to the altar to make a sacrifice.

The simple description of the altar—made of earth or stone—could serve to keep the emphasis of the worship on God rather than man's efforts.

EXODUS 21:1–23:33

BEYOND THE TEN COMMANDMENTS

Setting Up the Section

The Ten Commandments set out in broad strokes God's law for His people, outlining how we are to relate to Him and honor His image in others. The Mosaic Law continues for two more chapters in Exodus, outlining God's design for protecting servants, persons, and property, and further explaining the role of social responsibility, mercy, and justice in the nation of Israel.

📄 21:1–22:15

PROTECTION FOR SERVANTS, PERSONS, AND PROPERTY

The laws in this chapter relate to the commandments in which God prohibits killing and stealing. Though they differ from contemporary times and customs, they do explain the moral law and the rules of natural justice. God's people are to have a unique approach to everything, including their servants and other property. God commands the Israelites to respect their servants as human beings—even preserving their family bonds and allowing their families to go free with them in the Year of Jubilee. In being made free, servants become a picture of God's mercy and a living example of the eventual freedom that is possible in Christ, through His own sacrifice and grace.

Demystifying Exodus

Who were servants in ancient Israel? Foreign slaves were often war prisoners. However, impoverished Israelites sometimes sold themselves or their children so that they could work and be cared for. In other cases, judges sold some persons for their crimes, and creditors were, in some cases, allowed to sell debtors who could not pay. Forced Hebrew slavery for any reason was not practiced and is ranked in the New Testament with the greatest of crimes.

God gives and maintains life. In these laws dealing with murder, we see how fiercely He protects and values it. God's harsh punishment for ungrateful and disobedient children is designed in part to encourage parents to be very careful in training their children and setting a good example in learning self-control and respect.

22:16–31

SOCIAL RESPONSIBILITY

The people of God answer to God, not only for what they do maliciously, but for what they do without intent. In this portion of the law, God calls His people to always be ready to show mildness and mercy, according to the spirit of these laws. When one does harm to a neighbor, he or she should make it right, even when not compelled by law. God calls upon the Israelites to honor those around them and God Himself by being generous and living justly.

23:1–9

LAWS OF MERCY AND JUSTICE

The Law of Moses includes many straightforward, practical requirements. Every element of the law enables the Israelites to act as God's people and to worship Him with their conduct, thus separating themselves from the pagan world. The Israelites are called to remain fair and honest, allowing nothing to compromise God's justice by lessening faults, aggravating small ones, excusing offenders, accusing the innocent, or misrepresenting the truth in any way.

23:10–19

SABBATH LAWS AND FESTIVALS

The Sabbath laws require that both the seventh day of each week and each seventh year are treated as sacred opportunities for rest and rejoicing in God's provision and power. It teaches not only the importance of mercy, but the need for dependence on God by forcing people to trust that God will bless their faithfulness with plenty.

The Israelites have a weakness for idolatry, and therefore God requires them to be rigorous in honoring Him during three annual festivals. They are required to come together before the Lord, rejoicing in and honoring His faithfulness. They are not to arrive empty-handed but with sacrifices that demonstrate their loyalty and love for God.

23:20–33

GOD'S ANGEL TO PREPARE THE WAY

In the closing verses of Exodus 23, God promises to prepare the way for the nation of Israel, drive out their enemies, and bring them into the promised land. He commands the Israelites to be sensitive and attentive to the angel He is sending ahead of them and to worship Him alone. He promises to provide for them and make them prosper in their new home.

Take It Home

Have you allowed your life to crowd out time for worshiping and celebrating God's goodness? This is the blessing intended for all of God's children—to come together in gratitude and to enjoy and honor Him on a regular basis. Indeed, periodic rest from the duties of the world helps us anticipate the heavenly rest which we all crave—when all earthly labors and cares shall cease. How can you seize upon the blessing of a day of rest and worship more practically amidst a hectic life?

EXODUS 24:1–18

THE MAGNIFICENT MEAL ON MOUNT SINAI

The Call and the Confirmation   24:1–11
The Tablets of Stone   24:12–18

Setting Up the Section

Centuries before the scenes described in this text, God promised Abraham a seed (a son, which would become a great nation), a land (the land of Canaan), and the promise that this nation would be blessed and be a blessing to all nations (Genesis 12:1–3). The promises God made were ratified as a covenant between Himself and Abraham in Genesis 15. Now the Mosaic Covenant, which has been spelled out in the Ten Commandments, is formally imposed upon Israel by the God who has delivered her out of Egypt.

📄 **24:1–11**

THE CALL AND THE CONFIRMATION

The ratification of the Mosaic Covenant is the key to the remainder of the book of Exodus. God is the initiator of this covenant with His people Israel. A distinction is drawn between the Israelites and God, but there is also a distinction made between Israelites. These same distinctions are paralleled in the tabernacle, where the priests have greater access to God than the people, and the high priest alone can enter the Holy of Holies, once a year. Such distinctions are abolished in the new covenant.

Demystifying Exodus

Covenants had several common elements. Usually they involved promises or commitments to which the parties bound themselves. There was often a sacrifice made, followed by a meal, which included some of the sacrifice. There was also a memorial, some kind of physical token of the oath, which served to remind the parties of their commitments. There was a curse attached to the one who broke the covenant which he had made. There was always a sense of solemnity in the making of a covenant, for it was a serious step of commitment.

Moses understood that the covenant God was making with Israel needed to be ratified by the nation. Once the Israelites have verbally ratified this covenant, Moses carries out the ratification process by the use of symbols and representatives. Moses offers covenant sacrifices (these are not sin offerings), making an altar with twelve pillars for the twelve tribes of Israel. The blood sprinkled upon the altar and upon the people links the people with the covenant sacrifices.

The covenant meal, eaten by the seventy-five leaders of Israel in the presence of God, is the final act of ratification. The leaders (seventy elders, plus Nadab and Abihu, Aaron, Moses, and his servant, Joshua) are representatives who act on behalf of the entire nation, teaching and interpreting the law.

On the mountain, the elders of Israel see God enthroned, but from a distance. This perhaps explains why there's no account of fear on the part of the elders. This also helps to explain why Moses could later ask to see God, as though he had not seen Him earlier (33:17–23).

The ratification of the Mosaic Covenant had great meaning for the Israelites of that day. It clearly defined Israel's relationship with God, and what was expected of each Israelite. The covenant also spelled out the consequences, both of obedience and of disobedience. Israel could always know where she stood with God.

24:12–18

THE TABLETS OF STONE

The second call of Moses to the top of Mount Sinai is for the purpose of giving him the commandments written on stone by the finger of God (24:12). It is also for the purpose of revealing the blueprints for the tabernacle. From chapter 25 to the end of Exodus, the tabernacle is the principle subject. The tabernacle was designed to institutionalize God's presence among His people on an ongoing basis, as the mountain had served on a one-time basis.

While Moses puts Aaron and Hur in charge as he prepares for his trip, note that it is not until later (Numbers 11; Deuteronomy 1) that Jethro's advice of a team of leaders helping him (Exodus 18) is actually put into practice. Once again, the seventh day is set apart from the other six, this time by God's personal arrival in a cloud. Unfortunately, the forty days of Moses' absence provide a test which Israel fails (see Exodus 32).

The wonder of the revelation of God to the elders of Israel is that God does not strike them dead. The wonder of the revelation of God to Moses is that it is described from the perspective of the Israelites, at the base camp, rather than from Moses himself. Why didn't Moses give a firsthand account? We know Moses was a very humble man (Numbers 12:3), who was not intent upon glamorizing his own experiences. Perhaps Moses simply had too much awe and reverence for the things he experienced to try to recreate or capture it.

Take It Home

As we consider the Mosaic Covenant, we are reminded of the gospel. The gospel is the news that God has provided as a means of relating to people, through the new covenant, which was achieved through the sprinkling of the blood of Christ. The gospel is the message of an everlasting covenant, which men and women can enter into with God.

EXODUS 25:1–31:18

A PLACE TO WORSHIP

Setting Up the Section

Now that Israel has been delivered from Egypt, they need a place where they can worship their God, a place where He can be present among them. Once God gives Moses the law, He follows with specific instructions for such a place—the tabernacle.

📖 25:1–9

OFFERINGS FOR THE TABERNACLE

The gifts for the tabernacle are given voluntarily, as an act of gratitude. God also required compulsory giving and sacrificing by the Israelites, however in this instance, there is no need to compel the people to get excited about building God's dwelling place among them. And as we see later, their giving actually exceeds what could be used.

In verses 8–9, Exodus refers to the structure that was to be built as a *sanctuary* ("place of holiness") and a *tabernacle* ("dwelling place"). These words stress the fact that God is worthy of worship and that He is choosing to live with His people.

📖 25:10–26:37

THE FURNISHINGS OF THE TABERNACLE

The tables on which God describes His will for the Israelites are called *the Testimony.* In the New Testament, Christians associate this same word with the good news of Christ's work that the disciples and apostles testify to in the Gospels. Here the law, God's testimony to His people, is placed in an ark overlaid with gold that is kept in the Holy of Holies. Above the ark, God's visible glory hovers.

The *ark of the covenant* (25:10–22) functioned as God's throne. The solid gold lid of the box was called the mercy seat (25:17). This is where the high priest made his yearly offering on the Day of Atonement (Leviticus 16).

The table for the bread of the presence was replenished weekly (25:23–30). This was a constant thank offering placed before God. Some think it was also a reminder of the testimony that Israel was to be to the world around them.

The lampstand (25:31–40), the *menorah*, is often seen today as a symbol of Israel. Some see the place of the lampstand in the original tabernacle as a symbol of God's Word which lights the darkness. Others see it as a symbol of Jesus, light of the world.

The curtains and the veil were similarly constructed (26:1–35). The curtains outlined the tabernacle while the veil provided a boundary for the innermost holy chamber. The screen served as a front door (26:35–37).

Take It Home

While many elements of the tabernacle are attributed with symbolic properties, the mercy seat is seen by some as the most rich. As the lid of the ark of the covenant (seen as God's throne), it provided temporarily what Jesus' sacrifice permanently offered to believers. It was the place of a blood sacrifice that atoned for sin. In fact, the same word that is translated *mercy seat* in verse 17 is the word used to describe Jesus in 1 John 2:2—atoning sacrifice.

📖 27:1–20

OTHER CRUCIAL INSTRUCTIONS

God is very specific in His description of the other elements of the tabernacle; nearly everything is not only functional but also symbolic and instructive in its form.

The altar of burnt offerings stood just inside the entrance to the court (27:1–8). Some see this as an apt picture of this sacrifice being the first step to fellowship with God.

The curtain around the courtyard was an added boundary, though a shorter one, to protect the innermost holy place of the tabernacle (27:9–19). It was in the courtyard that the priests did their work and the people offered their sacrifices.

These instructions regarding the oil that was in the lamps form a transition from this information about the tabernacle furnishings to the following information about the priests' ministry (27:20–21).

THE PRIEST'S CLOTHING

Chapter 28 describes the clothing of the priest: "a breastpiece, an ephod, a robe, a fitted tunic, a turban, and a sash" (28:4 NET). The *ephod* was an apron-like piece of clothing that fit over the robe. Verses 6–14 describe the ephod in detail.

Verses 15–30 describe the breastplate. While we often think of military metal breastplates, this one was made from the same material as the ephod.

Demystifying Exodus

Verse 29–30 outline the decision-making function of the breastplate. There is much we do not know about the Urim and Thummim. We know they helped with decisions, probably yes or no kinds of decisions, and were kept in the pockets of this breastplate. They are usually compared to casting lots or throwing dice, but we don't have enough details to understand the exact process the priest used for them.

CONSECRATION OF THE PRIESTS

In the consecration of the priests—Aaron and his sons—God demands solemnity and ceremony. Ultimately, the model for the priesthood is Jesus, called by God to intercede for His people and anointed by His Spirit clothed with glory and beauty (Hebrews 3:1–2). Hebrews 2:10 instructs that in the new covenant all believers are priests, offering spiritual sacrifices and relating directly to God. For the Israelites, the priesthood established here would be their intercessors and their representatives before God for generations to come.

INCENSE, ATONEMENT, WASHING, AND ANOINTING

The priests are instructed to burn incense every morning and evening, the same time that the daily burnt offerings are made. The incense is to be left burning continually throughout the day and night as a pleasing aroma to the Lord. It is made of an equal part of four precious spices (stacte, onycha, galbanum, and frankincense) and is considered holy. The offering of incense foreshadows the gifts brought to the infant Jesus ("God with us") by the wise men.

THE PRIESTS AND THE SABBATH

This passage reveals how God gifts His servants. God chose Bezalel and Oholiab and anointed them with His Spirit "with skill, ability, and knowledge in all kinds of crafts" (31:3 NIV). Indeed, God has made these two skilled artists so that they can construct the temple exactly according to His commandments. The example of these two artists commissioned and gifted by God Himself reminds us that whatever our life's work or calling, we can use it to honor God.

Critical Observation

The importance of keeping the Sabbath has already been described in detail, yet God returns to it. He goes one step further saying that the Sabbath signals the special relationship that exists between God and Israel—it is a sign of the Mosaic Covenant, just as circumcision is a sign of the Abrahamic Covenant. Immediately after God issues this reminder, Moses encounters the Israelites in the full swing of their rebellion—too impatient to wait to rest in God's true presence. God's emphasis on His people's need for ritualistic rest and worship has obviously not been honored by the impatient Israelites.

EXODUS 32:1–35

THE REJECTION OF GOD AND THE REVELATION OF MAN

Israel's Idolatry	32:1–6
Divine Indignation and Human Intervention	32:7–14
Moses and God Respond	32:15–35

Setting Up the Section

In the story of the golden calf, Israel is guilty of impatience for God's manifestation in the tabernacle, but it is her idolatry that condemns her.

📖 32:1–6

ISRAEL'S IDOLATRY

There is a cause and effect relationship between the absence of leadership and the practice of idolatry. While Moses is gone for forty days and nights (24:18), receiving instructions about building the tabernacle, the Israelites use his absence as a pretext for taking immoral action, seizing the opportunity for creating an image of God.

📖 32:7–14

DIVINE INDIGNATION AND HUMAN INTERVENTION

The Mosaic Covenant, ratified approximately one month before Israel's idolatry, defines the relationship Israel has with God. In Moses' appeal for his people on Mount Sinai, he does not refer to the Mosaic Covenant, because the law can only condemn; it cannot save.

When Moses appeals to God, he appeals to the Abrahamic Covenant, made centuries before. The law is God's provisional covenant, given to humanity because of its depravity, but it is not the cure. If the promises of the Abrahamic Covenant are to be fulfilled, it would have to be by some other covenant than the Mosaic Covenant.

The Mosaic Covenant could not change human hearts—the root problem of sin. Striving to keep the law in order to be saved or sanctified is true folly, because we all suffer from the same ailment—sin. Idolatry seeks to replace what cannot be seen with something that can be seen—it is physically oriented. Thus, the underlying issue of idolatry is faith, since faith focuses on what is not seen (Hebrews 11:1).

📖 32:15–35

MOSES AND GOD RESPOND

The irony of the dialogue between Moses and God (Exodus 3–4), in which God provides Aaron as Moses' spokesman, is shown here. Moses is empowered by his fear of God, whereas Aaron is fumbling because of his failure. God reveals His righteousness in response to the sins of the Israelites; Aaron reveals his unrighteousness. It is not enough for us to recognize merely the depravity of humanity; we must resist it.

🏠

Take It Home

This is Israel's first great act of rebellion and sin since the ratification of the covenant. The Mosaic Covenant was based on the righteousness of men, and thus served only to condemn. The new covenant is based on the righteousness of the Messiah, Jesus Christ, and thus can be counted on to forgive humanity and save them from their sin. The old covenant gave no assurance of the forgiveness of sins; the new gives us absolute confidence and boldness.

EXODUS 33:1–34:9

THE PRESENCE OF GOD WITH HIS PEOPLE

Outside the Camp	33:1–11
Meeting God	33:12–34:9

📖 33:1–11

OUTSIDE THE CAMP

Because of Israel's sin, God deals with His people from a distance as they travel through the wilderness. Although this is a fulfillment of Israel's first inclination and request (20:18–21), when it actually happens the nation mourns.

Israel's removal of ornaments and jewelry is an appropriate act of repentance, because these ornaments are similar to those which had been contributed to make the golden calf (32:2–4) and were associated in the ancient Near East with pagan gods. To put off these ornaments demonstrates Israel's sincere repentance over their idolatry in the preceding chapter.

The grace of God is seen even in God's threat to remove Himself from Israel's midst. God states that the purpose for keeping a distance between Himself and the Israelites as they travel on toward the promised land is that their sinfulness would require Him to destroy them. The threatened consequence for Israel's idolatry is losing God's intimate presence among them. God's grace is evident as well in the provision of Moses as the mediator for the people.

In the midst of Israel's sin, and the threat of God withholding His presence, God provides a tent where not only Moses, but all the people, can go to seek God. This provides the people a means of worshiping God and offers them a hope for a future fellowship with God.

Take It Home

The Israelites mourn because they have only the promise of prosperity, but not God's intimate presence among them. In our day and time, prosperity is touted as the proof of God's presence. It's simply not true. Learn from the Israelites to desire the presence of God more than mere prosperity.

33:12–34:9

MEETING GOD

The remainder of this text is divided into Moses' three petitions to God. Each request is followed by God's response, which then becomes the basis for a further petition of Moses. Once he is assured of the presence of God in the midst of His people, Moses makes a personal request to see the glory of God.

Moses has already faced war with the Amalekites, a war only won by prevailing prayer (Exodus 17). Now more than ever, he is aware of the rebelliousness and waywardness of the Israelites. And Aaron has so far proven to be a liability. Also, the Mosaic Covenant, which gave such hope initially, is now known to pronounce only a curse and not to promise blessing, due to the sinfulness of the people. No wonder Moses is concerned about setting out for Canaan. Moses wants to know not only the person God is sending with him, but also the plan God has for the people. He is also seeking to know God more intimately, to know God's character in order to better understand how to please Him.

God promises Moses He will be with him and provide the means to get the Israelites to Canaan. Furthermore, He promises Moses that the Israelites will ultimately live safely in Canaan. This is indicated by the term *rest*, used here and elsewhere in the Old Testament. This word conveys the end of an evil, an enemy, hostility, or adversity. When God promises Moses rest, He assures him that the things Moses fears most will be overcome, and that the task which God has given him will be completed.

Moses is not willing to enjoy God's favor alone while Israel's destiny hangs in the balance. So in his second request, he petitions God's presence not only be with him, but with everyone. Notice how Moses twice links himself with Israel in order to associate God's favor for them with His favor for Moses. God assures Moses that He will be present with Israel, as well as with him.

Later, after Moses' request to see the glory of God (33:18), the glory of God will fill the

EXODUS 36:8–39:43

THE TABERNACLE, THE DWELLING PLACE OF GOD

Characteristics of the Tabernacle   36:8–39:43

Setting Up the Section

The description of the tabernacle provides the first biblical revelation as to how God dwells among His people, and what this suggests for the church today.

📄 **36:8–39:43**

CHARACTERISTICS OF THE TABERNACLE

When the people left Sinai for Canaan, they would need some portable place for God's presence to be manifested. The tabernacle serves as a meeting place between God and humans, and is known as the "tent of meeting" (35:21). Since the tabernacle is a tent, the problem of portability is solved.

The tabernacle also solves the problem of having a holy God dwell in the midst of sinful people. The tent curtains, and especially the thick veil, serve as a dividing barrier between God and the people. Beyond this, the tabernacle is sanctified and set apart as a holy place. Also, the tabernacle is a place of sacrifice so that the sins of the Israelites could be atoned for. While the solution is not permanent, it does facilitate communion between God and His people.

The tabernacle displays wealth and beauty in a reflection of God's glory within. According to this calculation, there would be some 1,900 pounds of gold, 6,437 pounds of silver, and 4,522 pounds of bronze. The excellence of the tabernacle, both in its materials and its workmanship, is a reflection of the excellence of God. The tabernacle is also a holy place, because abiding in it is a holy God (30:37–38).

While the tabernacle is composed of varied elements, it is its unity—in design, function, and purpose—that is celebrated and emphasized in the text. It is God's masterwork amidst His people, proclaiming His presence and hinting at His glory.

Take It Home

The tabernacle and, eventually, the temple of God are the forerunners for the modern church. The New Testament Epistles teach us that the dwelling place of God's Holy Spirit is now the church—not the church building, but each Christian who is part of the body of Christ (Ephesians 2:19–22). In the new covenant, believers are called to consider their body a temple of the Lord, and treat it with appropriate reverence, just as the Israelites were called to approach the tabernacle and the temple with great reverence for God's holiness (1 Corinthians 6:18–20).

newly constructed tabernacle (40:34–35). On various occasions during Israel's sojourn in the wilderness, God's glory is manifested to the people. On a number of these occasions, the glory of the Lord appears to stop the people from sinning.

The glory of God is almost always some visible manifestation of God's presence and of His splendor. For Moses, and ultimately with the entire nation, the sight of God's glory would serve as an assurance of God's presence,.

The Bible consistently teaches that no person is able to see God face-to-face and live. God speaks of Moses as being able to see His back, but not His face. In the context of the passage, this means that Moses will be able to see all of God's goodness, but not some of His other attributes. Let us not fail to appreciate the wonder and the honor of this revelation of God to Moses. While it is only the back of God, it is all Moses can survive—and it is more than any man had yet been privileged to see.

Critical Observation

While Moses met with God at the tent of meeting (33:7), the renewal of the Mosaic Covenant took place at the top of Mount Sinai. The revelation of God's glory to Moses took the place of the manifestation of God to the seventy elders of Israel. The dimension of God's character that encourages Moses is the goodness of God. It is this side of God that gives Moses (and Israel) hope of forgiveness and God's renewed presence among them. God grants Moses this vision of His glory along with Israel's forgiveness, reclaiming them as His own people once again.

EXODUS 34:10–35

A NEW BEGINNING

The "New" Old Covenant   34:10–28
The Transfiguration of Moses   34:29–35

Setting Up the Section

Moses returns from the mountain with a radiantly beaming face, a reflection of the glory of God. Every time he speaks to God face-to-face, the radiance will be renewed. Every time he speaks to Israel with his beaming face, the people know that God is speaking to them through Moses, giving him credentials that they dare not ignore.

📄 **34:10–28**

THE "NEW" OLD COVENANT

The covenant made here is virtually a renewal of the former covenant; however, there are some differences. The first covenant was based on the miracles God had done in delivering the Israelites from Egyptian bondage, while this covenant looks forward to the miracles that are instrumental in Israel's possession of the land of Canaan (34:10–11).

Ironically, the miracles God formerly accomplished in Egypt resulted in the Egyptians driving the Israelites out of their land; now, the miracles God promises to accomplish will drive the Canaanites out of Israel's land.

There are a number of differences between the way this new covenant is given and the way in which the former was given. Moses goes alone to the mountain, apparently not even accompanied by Joshua. No promises are made this (second) time by the Israelites, although the blessings of this covenant are still conditional.

The "code of the covenant" given here is significantly shorter than that found in chapters 20–23. The first code emphasizes social matters, such as the treatment of slaves and just compensation for losses caused by negligence or theft. In this abbreviated code of the covenant, the emphasis falls on Israel's walk with God, which had quickly been interrupted by Israel's idolatry and apostasy.

📄 34:29–35

THE TRANSFIGURATION OF MOSES

Predictably, the people are at first frightened by the brightness of Moses' countenance, but then they are eventually able to draw near enough to hear Moses speak and to accept his words as from God Himself. Moses begins to employ a veil that he will remove when he speaks with God and will leave it off until he has conveyed God's words to the people. Then, the veil will be put on until the next time he speaks with God. The text indicates that Moses does this on a number of occasions, with some degree of regularity.

The greater intimacy of Moses with God is apparent by the people's actions here. In the past, the manifestations of the glory and majesty of God were more distant, so that the people wanted to keep their distance from God and have Moses to be their intermediary (20:18–20).

Take It Home

Moses' authority is evident in his radiant face, a sign that he had been speaking with God. Christians today have the ministry of the Holy Spirit, who dwells within and bears witness internally to those to whom the new covenant is proclaimed (John 16:8–16). Whenever we speak the Word of God in truth, the Holy Spirit bears testimony within the listener, validating the truth of what has been said, just as Moses' radiant face gives the Israelites confidence that his testimony and leadership are from God.

EXODUS 35:1–36:7

ISRAEL'S OFFERINGS

Setting Up the Section

Chapters 35–40 conclude by describing the construction of the tabernacle, and climax at God's descent into the midst of the camp. The theme of this section is the presence of God in the midst of His people.

📄 35:1–36:7

ISRAEL'S OFFERINGS

The excitement and enthusiasm of the Israelites is evident by the abundance of their gifts. In fact, the text informs us that the gifts exceed the need, so much that Moses is asked to command the people to stop giving. The Israelites' giving includes both material goods and technical services—both of the highest quality.

Because giving is done willingly, joyfully, and unanimously, it is not mandatory—the motivation of the Israelites is extremely high. The tabernacle is the means of God personally dwelling among His people (25:8), and the people are eager to have this promise fulfilled. This is a onetime need, for which the people have been amply enabled to contribute. With such motivation, God could easily allow the nation to provide the skills and materials for the tabernacle voluntarily.

There were other ongoing needs in Israel, however, which were not so glamorous, and of a much longer duration. To insure these needs are met, God makes giving a compulsory matter. There is an ongoing need for the support of the priests and Levites, who devote themselves to the service of God in the tabernacle.

THE CONSECRATION OF THE TABERNACLE AND THE PRESENCE OF GOD

Setting Up the Section

This is the climax of the story of Exodus: The tabernacle is completed, and the glory of God descends upon it. It is also an introduction to Leviticus. God commands the anointing of the priesthood, who will dominate the next story in the history of the Israelites and receive God's instructions regarding the use of the carefully constructed tabernacle.

📖 40:1–16

DIVINE INSTRUCTIONS: ARRANGING AND ANOINTING

There is a distinct change in the personal pronoun employed in chapter 40 from *they* (39:43) to *you* (40:2). The shift is from the construction of the tabernacle, in which all the people were involved, to the setting up of the tabernacle and the anointing of it, which was the responsibility of Moses (40:1, 16).

There is a descending order of holiness of the items referred to in the chapter. We begin in the Holy of Holies, the most holy place in the tabernacle, and end in the courtyard, the least holy place.

📖 40:17–33

THE TABERNACLE IS ASSEMBLED AND RAISED

There is a mood of excitement and anticipation among the Israelites who have spent months carefully following God's specific instructions. Amazingly, the tabernacle is constructed on Israel's first anniversary as a free nation (12:2), and just about nine months from the time of her arrival at Mount Sinai. It also appears that the tent is erected on this one day, since the materials are all made and ready before this time (39:32–43). God's precise timing emphasizes how far the Israelites have come since they escaped Egypt.

Moses' role finally seems to have evolved into something more provisional (almost priestly), which continues until Aaron and his sons are anointed and installed as the official priesthood of Israel. Moses offers incense (40:27), burnt and grain offerings (40:29), and washes himself (40:31), like Aaron and his sons.

THE GLORY OF GOD DESCENDS UPON THE TABERNACLE

Since the cloud has been present with the Israelites from the time they left Egypt and never departed from them, there is a sense in which nothing new occurs here. What was once distant (either before or behind the nation, or far away, atop Mount Sinai) is now in the very midst of the camp. The second fact is even more significant. The appearance of the glory of God in the tabernacle takes place after Israel's great sin (the golden calf), which is reported in chapter 32. Finally, the glory of God settles on the tabernacle to abide there, not just as a momentary manifestation of God.

Imagine the Israelites' delight in seeing the tabernacle set up for the first time and intensified by the splendor of God's glory descending upon it. The cloud, the visible manifestation of the glory of God, descends upon the tabernacle to dwell in the midst of the people and to guide them into the promised land. The joy of God's presence is all the more glorious in the light of Israel's "fall" in chapter 32.

The glory of God descending upon the tabernacle is the realization of Israel's highest hopes, of Moses' most noble and impassioned petition. The glory of God in the tabernacle is so awesome that even Moses could not enter it. Remember that Moses had seen more of God's glory than any other human being alive—in the burning bush (chapter 3), in the plagues and exodus of Israel, and from inside the cloud atop Mount Sinai (chapters 19, 24). At his request, he had seen even more of God's glory when he was privileged to view the back of God (33:17–34:9). But the glory of God in the tabernacle is greater than that which Moses (or any other Israelite for that matter) could behold.

Take It Home

The presence of God is indeed dear to the Israelites, who had never had the presence of God closer to them. Nevertheless, God is still separated from the people. Even Moses could not enter into the presence of God in the tabernacle, and only the high priest could enter into the Holy of Holies once a year. Christ has torn the veil away—He dwells within each individual believer, not just in the midst of the nation.

LEVITICUS

INTRODUCTION TO LEVITICUS

Though many see Leviticus as a book addressing the priests of Israel, the information here was actually written for the people, yet includes specific instructions for the priests. The laws relate to the entire nation of Israel, but it was the priests who were to teach others how to live as God's holy people and to regulate worship in the tabernacle (also called *sanctuary*, or *tent of meeting*), where God's holy presence dwelled.

AUTHOR

Moses is generally ascribed as the author of the first five books of the Old Testament, or the Pentateuch (which means "five books" or "five scrolls"). These books are also known as the Law of Moses, or Mosaic Law. It is most likely that Moses wrote during the time when Israel was wandering and intermittently camping in the desert for forty years during the second half of the fifteenth century BC.

PURPOSE

In the Hebrew text, the first word of the book of Leviticus, translated "and He called," serves as the title of the book, though its English title means "of the Levites." The book served as a handbook for the priests God put in place after the institution of the Mosaic Covenant at Mount Sinai. The specific details are many, and this preciseness was to ensure the Israelites that the continuing presence of God was with them. The laws on both ceremonial holiness and personal holiness were supposed to teach the Israelites about their holy God and how to live set apart as His people. Not only does God tell the Israelites how to worship, but He gives them practical ways to live out holiness in everyday life.

THEMES

The book of Leviticus is comprised of twenty-seven chapters including many regulations and guidelines. The rules are not arbitrary, though. Each of the seemingly minute details in Leviticus deals with the main theme of holiness.

The phrase that is repeated most often in Leviticus is a variation of God's command, "Be holy as I am holy." During this time, Israel was a new nation. God's laws were designed to teach them how to become set apart—holy people who imitated God's character.

The tent of meeting was built by the Israelites as a holy place to house the presence of a holy God. Sinful people could not approach their God, though, because He was the essence of holiness. The rituals and offerings detailed in Leviticus are God's compassionate design to allow His people to find atonement so that they could approach Him in worship and experience a covenant relationship with Him.

Leviticus can be divided into two major sections, separated by chapter 16, which deals with the annual Day of Atonement. Chapters 1–15 deal with what we might call priestly holiness, by giving instructions about sacrifices and rituals that relate to one's holiness. Chapters 17–27 deal more with what we could call practical holiness—that which is worked out in daily life.

HISTORICAL CONTEXT

During the writing of Leviticus, the Israelites were camped at the base of Mount Sinai in the desert after their deliverance from Egypt and before their entrance into the land of Canaan. It was at Mount Sinai that God entered into a covenant relationship with the Israelites. He would be their God, and they would be His people. God communicated to His people through their leader, Moses, how they should live out their covenant responsibilities.

Leviticus is the third book in the Pentateuch. It is closely connected with the book of Exodus and often repeats or expands on instructions God gave through Moses there. Exodus records God's detailed instructions to the Israelites for how to build His holy tabernacle. Leviticus follows up with regulations God communicated from that tabernacle. The laws of Leviticus did not initiate sacrificial offerings, but they did serve to regulate them.

CONTRIBUTION TO THE BIBLE

The book of Leviticus is quoted or referred to in the New Testament at least forty times (more than any other book in the Bible). Many of Jesus' teachings, particularly those on the Great Commandment, come from Leviticus (19:18). New Testament teachings on holiness tie directly to Levitical teachings (1 Peter 2).

The greatest theological contribution of Leviticus is an introduction to atonement. The sacrificial system detailed in Leviticus reveals human sinfulness and introduces atonement through a substitutionary blood sacrifice. To fully understand the reason for and importance of Jesus' ultimate sacrifice, a student of the Bible would need to understand the Old Testament system's purpose and flaws.

OUTLINE

LEVITICUS 1:1–17

THE BURNT OFFERING

Setting Up the Section

In Exodus, God gives Moses instruction for how to build the tabernacle (2:1–8; 38:1–7). In Leviticus, He gives Moses instruction for how to offer sacrifices at the tabernacle. The burnt offering illustrates God's principle of atonement, where humanity's sin is answered through a sacrificial shedding of blood.

📖 1:1–2

THE COMMAND

The Israelites were camped at the base of Mount Sinai when Moses received their instructions. The burnt offering is a voluntary and personal offering, and instructions are given for individuals (1:2). The sacrifice is not for specific sins, but rather for the general state of sinfulness. The purpose of the burnt offering is to make atonement for the sin of the offerer and to gain God's acceptance.

📖 1:3–9

BULLS

The sacrificial animal had to be the best quality (without defect) and male (1:3). Bulls were valuable livestock, and the male would be able to produce additional offspring. It would be a true sacrifice for an Israelite to offer a young, productive animal.

Both offerer and priest participate in the sacrifice (1:4–9). The offerer is responsible for the slaughter, and the priest handles the sprinkling of blood and burning of the offering on the altar of sacrifice. By laying his hands on the animal, the offerer identifies his sins with the offering. The animal becomes a substitute for the individual. While many sacrifices benefit both the offerer and the priest, because both are allowed to eat from the sacrificed animal, the burnt offering is completely consumed by fire.

When an Israelite wanted to find acceptance with God in order to worship, he had to come with a burnt offering. This is to acknowledge and make provision for his sinfulness. The sacrifice allowed the Israelites to come into the presence of a holy God in the tent of meeting.

SHEEP AND GOATS

Sheep and goats were livestock of considerable value, and the best male of the flock was required as the offering. One of the unique contributions of the burnt offering is that it illustrates sacrifice in its purest form. A valuable animal is given up wholly to God without expectation of anything in return, other than the benefit of finding acceptance with God.

Demystifying Leviticus

The Israelites of Moses' day understood the burnt offering in terms of what they already knew about it, not its future fulfillment. The key to understanding the meaning was what had already been revealed (see Genesis 8, 22; Exodus 10, 18, 20). Through Noah's example, the Israelites saw that God's blessing came after an offering, not after good deeds. In Abraham's story, they saw the sacrifice as substitution. So when the Israelites placed their hands on the head of a sacrificial animal, they would have known it was dying in their place.

BIRDS

God gives three options for animal sacrifices (herd, flock, or bird). This is because the poor could not afford a bull, sheep, or goat. God did not keep people from coming into His presence because they could not afford to sacrifice (14:21–22, 30–32). A dove or young pigeon was a true sacrifice for those who were poor, just as a bull or goat was a sacrifice for those who owned livestock, making it pleasing to God (1:17).

Take It Home

Real sacrifice is seldom practiced today in the church. We tend to give away our leftovers, while we keep what is new and best for ourselves. The kind of costly sacrifice seen in the burnt offering is what God expects from true disciples who give up all to follow Christ. When we give ourselves to God, as living sacrifices (Romans 12:1–2), it is completely as a pleasing offering. May God enable us to practice this kind of sacrifice in our own lives.

LEVITICUS 2:1–16

THE GRAIN OFFERING

Setting Up the Section

The second offering explained in Leviticus is the grain offering. This name *grain offering* refers to the material most often used, but the Hebrew name for this offering indicates its primary function, which is "gift." At this time, the Israelites were camped in the desert, where they could not grow grain, so this offering (most likely wheat or barley) was a great sacrifice. To sacrifice this seed to God was an act of faith because they would have to depend on God to provide more.

2:1–3

UNCOOKED GRAIN

Like the burnt offering, the grain offering required the highest quality sacrifice (2:1–3). The grain had to be fine, meaning finely ground flour. To make fine flour entailed a great deal of extra effort. The grain offering was also sacrificed by fire and produced a pleasing aroma to the Lord (2:2).

The Israelites are instructed to make the grain offering after the burnt offering (Numbers 28; Joshua 22:23, 29; Judges 13:19, 23). Since there is no blood shed in this offering, it does not atone for sin. Contribution to the grain offering is allowed because a person's sinfulness has already been atoned for in the burnt offering.

2:4–10

COOKED GRAIN

The oil used in this offering (2:4) would probably have been olive oil, also a sacrifice since it was not readily available in the desert. All the sacrificial materials were difficult to obtain in the days of Moses, though of course, these laws would continue on into the settlement of the land.

Critical Observation

The Israelites had to depend on God for even basic needs while camped at Mount Sinai, but when they were in Canaan, it would be easy to enjoy their blessings and forget to depend on God. The grain offering was one way for the Israelites to remember that God is both Creator and Sustainer.

Only a handful of the grain offering was burned on the altar; the rest was given to the priests, Aaron and his sons (2:2–3, 9–10). The greater portion of the offering served as the livelihood of the priests, just as the tithe was God's means for supporting the Levites (Numbers 18:21–24). The sacrificed portion was called the "memorial portion" (Leviticus 2:2, 9, 16 NET), and the other portion was called "a thing most holy" (2:3, 10; 5:17 NASB).

Demystifying Leviticus

The grain offerings in the King James Version of the Bible are referred to as "meat offerings." The word *meat*, as it was used by the translators of the King James Version, did not have the same meaning as the term today. This was a term that simply referred to food, and in a general way could refer to grain (either in its raw or cooked form).

📖 2:11–13

YEAST AND SALT

Through the grain offering the Israelites acknowledge God's provision for their needs. Since the purpose of the grain offering is worship, not atonement, the offerer could contribute. However, only certain additions were allowed. Salt was allowed, but leaven and honey were forbidden. The Hebrew word translated *honey* indicates fruit (not bee) honey. When this kind of honey is burned, it ferments—a form of decay which is associated with death and thus is to be avoided (the same is true of yeast).

The grain offering was associated with the burnt offering, and the blood sacrifice could not be associated with leaven, which was known to corrupt.

Known to preserve and purify, salt was added to the grain offering. Salt may have reminded Israel of the enduring covenant with God, since salt does not burn or turn into a gas but basically stays the same through fire (2:13).

Demystifying Leviticus

The salt added to the grain offering has significance as "the salt of the covenant of your God" (2:13 NIV). A "covenant of salt" is also found in Numbers 18:19 and 2 Chronicles 13:5. Salt was used symbolically in covenants in the ancient Near East. The salt used in the grain offering represents purity and longevity, reminding Israel of their long-lasting covenant with God.

2:14–16

FIRSTFRUITS

The grain offering of firstfruits (Leviticus 2:14–16) was that which was first harvested from a crop (Exodus 23:19). The offering was accompanied by incense as a sensory symbol of the pleasure the offering would bring God. Again, the expense was a reminder that sacrifice is costly, but pleasing God is the highest good.

Here's a review of the offerings and the laws that governed them:

First Regulations:	Additional Regulations:
(More "laity" directed)	(More priestly in orientation)
Burnt Offering, ch. 1	Law of Burnt Offering, 6:8–13
Grain Offering, ch. 2	Law of Grain Offering, 6:14–23; 7:9–10
Peace Offering, ch. 3	Law of Peace Offering, 7:11–34
Sin Offering, ch. 4	Law of Sin Offering, 6:24–30
Guilt Offering, ch. 5, 6:1–7	Law of Guilt Offering, 7:1–10
Ordination Offering, 6:19–23	Ordination Offerings, 8:1–9:24 Priests and offerings, 10:1–20

Take It Home

How do we develop real trust in God? Leviticus suggests it is by giving sacrificially. This is the kind of giving we see when the Israelites offer their firstfruits, trusting God to provide an additional harvest. Sacrificial giving requires faith in God as the One who faithfully supplies our needs and who gives us our daily bread.

LEVITICUS 3:1–17

THE PEACE OFFERING

Setting Up the Section

The burnt offering focuses on God's righteousness and an individual's atonement through an animal sacrifice. The grain offering focuses on the Israelites' dependence on God. The peace offering is made on top of the burnt offering (3:5) and focuses on the Israelites' peace with God—the peace of mind and wholeness that comes with knowing God is at peace with us. There is also a strong element of fellowship signified by the sharing of the meal together. This is why some translations translate it "fellowship offering."

Three principle passages in Leviticus deal with the peace offering: 3:1–17 (the mechanics of the sacrifice); 7:11–34 (the meaning of the sacrifice); and 19:5–8 (the law of leftovers).

📖 3:1–5

FROM THE HERD

In the day of Moses, an Israelite would begin to make a peace offering by selecting an animal without any defect (male or female) from his herd or flock (3:1, 6). He would then take this animal to the doorway of the tabernacle, where he would lay his hand on its head, identifying his sin with the animal and himself with its death, and slaughter it. Inside the tabernacle, the priests would collect the shed blood and sprinkle it around the altar (3:2, 8, 13). After skinning the animal and cutting it into pieces, the priests would then burn the fat, kidneys, and part of the liver on the altar (3:3–5, 9–11, 14–16).

The process is much like that of the burnt offering, except in the peace offering the entire animal is not consumed. The blood, fat, and organs are burned (3:3–5, 9–11, 14–16), but the rest is given to the priests and the offerer (7:30–34; 10:14–15).

Critical Observation

Some Bible versions have translated *peace offering* as *fellowship offering*. Both *peace* and *fellowship* are appropriate. The word *peace* has the connotation of "wholeness" or "completeness." The Israelites became whole when they were accepted by God in worship (19:5). The meal that the offerer enjoyed, along with fellow Israelites, signified the peace that the sacrifice brought about. Today, through Christ's death, we can have peace and fellowship with God and peace and fellowship with others.

FROM THE FLOCK

The process for a sacrifice from the flock is the same as one from the herd. At the end of the chapter, though, Israelites are instructed never to eat the fat or blood of an animal (3:16–17; 17:10–13).

Critical Observation

Each sacrifice by an Israelite was a certain type for a specific purpose. Every offering had exact rules. Because of the consequences for failing to observe the rules, individuals had to be certain about the specifics of each offering. In part, this was a safeguard against mindless ritual. People could not go through the motions of sacrifice without thinking about the purpose.

LEVITICUS 4:1–35

THE SIN OFFERING

Unintentional Sins	4:1–2
The Priest's Sins	4:3–12
The Community's Sins	4:13–21
A Leader's Sins	4:22–26
An Individual's Sins	4:27–35

Setting Up the Section

Offerings in Leviticus 1–3 are organized by sacrificial animal. The sin offering in chapter 4 is organized by categories of people: high priest (4:3–12); congregation of Israel (4:13–21); leader (4:22–26); and individual Israelite (4:27–35). The sin offering is for a specific sin, as opposed to a state of sinfulness addressed by the burnt offering. Also, while chapters 1–3 are concerned with the process of sacrifice, chapters 4–6 emphasize the result of the process: forgiveness. (The sin offering is further explained in 5:1–13 and 6:24–30.)

UNINTENTIONAL SINS

The sins addressed through the sin offering are those that, for some reason, are not immediately apparent but are eventually known. The text notes that the sin offering is to be made immediately after the knowledge of sin is present (4:14, 23, 28).

4:3-12

THE PRIEST'S SINS

If the high priest sinned, he would bring guilt on the entire congregation of Israelites (4:3), so the offering was necessary to atone for the sin for everyone. The priest himself would bring a bull to the tabernacle, lay his hand on it, and slaughter it (4:3-4). He would then sprinkle some of the blood on the tabernacle veil and some on the altar of incense (4:5-6). The remaining blood was poured at the base of the altar of burnt offering (4:7). The fat of the offered bull was burned as with the peace offering, but its body was burned completely outside the camp (4:11-12, 21). The offerer received none of the meat.

4:13-21

THE COMMUNITY'S SINS

When the entire community sins, there is a sin offering to atone for the collective sin (4:14). The process is the same as the sin offering of the priest.

4:22-26

A LEADER'S SINS

Even unintentional sin makes a person guilty (4:22). When a leader is aware of his sin, he is to sacrifice a male goat as a sin offering. The process is similar to that of the priest's offering, with two exceptions: Blood is not sprinkled at the veil, and the animal's body is not burned. (The meat of these sacrificial animals could be eaten in a holy place by the male priests [6:24-30].)

With each category, the person or people involved are found guilty due to sin. In each case, a blood sacrifice is needed for atonement.

Demystifying Leviticus

The Old Testament prophecy of Isaiah spoke of the Messiah, whose shed blood would atone for our sins (Isaiah 53:4-6). When John the Baptist saw Jesus, he proclaimed, "Look, the Lamb of God, who takes away the sin of the world!" (John 1:29 NIV). Hebrews demonstrates that Jesus is the sinless Lamb of God (Hebrews 9:11-14; 1 Peter 1:13-21). Jesus is the sin bearer, who died once for all, so sin could be cleansed and we could approach a holy God.

4:27-35

AN INDIVIDUAL'S SINS

An individual Israelite could offer a male goat or a female lamb as a sin offering. The process would have been the same as that of the leader's sin offering.

In chapter 4 we see a repeated sequence: There is sin, resulting in guilt; there is a blood sacrifice, resulting in atonement and forgiveness. This explains why only the blood and fat of the sin offering are used and the rest is thrown away. God is demonstrating in a dramatic way that only blood can atone for Israel's sin.

Take It Home

The ancient sin offering has something to say to Christians today. Whenever we sin, we need to remember that God used Christ's shed blood to provide forgiveness. Confession and repentance is the means for experiencing that forgiveness. Every sin, no matter how insignificant it seems, requires the blood of Christ to be shed. Let us not forget that while forgiveness is free, it is not cheap.

LEVITICUS 5:1–19

SIN AND GUILT OFFERINGS

Setting Up the Section

Leviticus 5:1–13 continues to explain the sin offering (see chapter 4) and begins to address sins specifically. In verses 14–19, the sin offering and the guilt offering are combined.

Critical Observation

Leviticus 4–7 presents both sin and guilt offerings. The two themes intermingle throughout. The Bible closely ties sin and guilt together. Take, for example, 5:5–6 and 5:15. If a person is *guilty* he may need to bring a *sin offering*, but if a person *sins* he may need to bring a *guilt offering*. The two concepts are seemingly inseparable.

📖 **5:1–13**

MORE ON THE SIN OFFERING

Chapter 5 addresses specific sins such as ignoring a call to testify, touching something or someone ceremonially unclean, or speaking without thinking (5:1–5). The guilty person would confess his or her sin and give a female lamb or goat as a sin offering (5:6).

Verses 7 and 11 show God's grace in providing an exception for those who are poor. They could offer a less expensive blood sacrifice (doves or pigeons), or even fine flour. So while not everyone could afford a peace offering, everyone was afforded the opportunity to experience forgiveness. (In fact, Psalm 69:30–33 seems to imply that all the poor really need to bring is a "song.")

THE GUILT OFFERING

The guilt offering is similar to the sin offering. The guilt offering seems to have been used for a breach of God's commandments, even if unintentional or for a sin where restitution could be made. Just as with the sin offering, atonement could be found through a guilt offering. Unlike the sin offering, restitution was also necessary to make up for what a person did or did not do by giving part of the value of the sacrificial ram to the priest.

Take It Home

One of the reasons we sometimes continue to carry our guilt is that we refuse to recognize that the debt has been paid. For the believer, our guilt offering is Jesus Christ. But God doesn't ask us to pay for our guilt; He only asks for confession and repentance. We can confess sin and leave the guilt behind.

LEVITICUS 6:1–30

MORE OFFERING RULES

Setting Up the Section

Chapter 6 flows directly out of chapter 5, including additional details related to the guilt offering, burnt offering, grain offering, and sin offering.

MORE ON THE GUILT OFFERING

A guilt offering was necessary in the case of disobedience against God's laws, specifically those relating to other people. If, for example, an Israelite cheated his neighbor, he would need to make a guilt offering. The same goes for a number of sins that affected others (6:4–5). A sin against one person was seen as a sin against the entire community, and ultimately God. The penalties teach that restitution is necessary before forgiveness (6:6).

6:8–13

MORE ON THE BURNT OFFERING

Priests would sacrifice burnt offerings every morning and evening for the congregation of Israel. These verses focus heavily on how to make sure sacrifices are completely consumed by not allowing the fire to go out (6:9), and how to handle disposing of ashes (6:11).

6:14–23

MORE ON THE GRAIN OFFERING

These details show priests how to burn the memorial portion of the grain offering and what to do with the leftovers (6:15–16). The priests could eat what remained, but only in a consecrated area since it was still a holy offering (6:16). The seemingly tedious details ensure that priests are obedient to God rather than following their own way.

Critical Observation

The Israelites brought their offerings to the Lord, but the priests served as His representatives. With the coming of Christ and His death and resurrection, we no longer need an earthly intermediary; we have direct access to God through Jesus (Hebrews 4:14–5:10).

6:24–30

MORE ON THE SIN OFFERING

These additional rules relate to holiness. The tabernacle is a holy place because the presence of God dwells there, and the sin offering is a serious, sacred ritual that the priests are not to take lightly.

Demystifying Leviticus

The passages in Leviticus 6:8–7:38 address Aaron and his sons, the priesthood, directly. They form a kind of handbook of priestly procedures. The priests were keepers and protectors of the law, so these specific and serious words would have been written, not handed down through oral tradition.

EVEN MORE RULES

Setting Up the Section

After a few more rules about the guilt offering, the majority of chapter 7 gives additional regulations for the peace offering, including the grain offerings that should accompany it and how to handle the leftovers.

📄 **7:1–10**

THE GUILT OFFERING AGAIN

The first verses give additional regulations concerning the guilt offering. The focus is on keeping it holy; it is not something to be taken lightly. Because of the offering's holy nature, only the priests (or males in their family) could partake in eating the meat of a sacrificed animal after the kidneys and the fat around them were burned on the altar to God (7:3–6). Likewise, the cooked grain offering belonged to the priests (7:9–10). Even then, they could be eaten only in a holy place (7:6).

📄 **7:11–38**

THE PEACE OFFERING AGAIN

Verse 11 begins the additional rules to help the priests administer the peace offering. Along with the fat of a sacrificial animal that is offered to God, an appropriate grain offering is also necessary. If the peace offering is out of thanksgiving, both leavened and unleavened cakes are to be offered. Part is burned on the altar, and the rest goes to the priests (7:12–13).

Since the fat and blood of the animal are offered to God, and the breast and the right thigh go to the priest, the rest of the sacrificial animal is left for the offerer. So after the ceremonial sacrifice, the Israelite would eat a festive meal with what remained. This is perhaps the most striking feature of the peace offering.

Critical Observation

Throughout scripture, the meal has a deeply religious significance. The festive meal that was part of the peace offering added to this significance. Here, the meal is a symbol of the peace the Israelite has with God and with others through the sacrifice.

Considerable emphasis is placed on what happens to the leftovers from the peace offering (7:15–18; 19:5–8). They had to be eaten on the day of the sacrifice in the case of thanksgiving (7:15), or by the next day in the case of a vow or freewill offering (7:16–18; 19:5–8). Anyone who was unclean or had touched something unclean could not eat of the meal; disobedience meant being cut off from the rest of the Israelites (7:20), a severe consequence.

Demystifying Leviticus

For an Israelite to be cut off from his people (7:20, 25) was the ultimate punishment. The Israelites were a communal people, so to be cut off signified loss of identity and covenant relationship. The phrase "cut off" indicates the offender was taken outside the camp and put to death or possibly banished forever.

Verses 22–26 offer another reminder that the Israelites are absolutely not to eat any of the fat or blood of sacrificed animals (or any other animals, for that matter). Eating fat means the possibility of an Israelite being cut off from his people (7:25), and eating blood means he will certainly be cut off (7:27).

The fat of the sacrificial animal, along with its breast meat and thigh, are offered to the Lord, but the priests keep the meat after burning the fat. This is one of the ways that God provides for the physical care of the priests (7:28–35).

LEVITICUS 8:1–36

PRINCIPLES OF PRIESTHOOD: ORDINATION

Setting Up the Section

Leviticus 8 describes the origin and ordination of the Aaronic priesthood. This chapter portrays the fulfillment of God's commands pertaining to the ordination of Aaron and his sons, as detailed in Exodus 29.

📖 8:1–4

THE CHOICE

God announces Aaron's ordination through Moses. Aaron was made high priest and his sons were made priests because God had chosen them, not because of any merit they possessed on their own.

Demystifying Leviticus

The Aaronic priesthood is just being formally established in chapter 8, but the concept of priesthood is not new to the Pentateuch, the first five books of the Bible. In a curious incident in the life of Abraham, a priest king by the name of Melchizedek is introduced (Genesis 14:18–20). Also, Joseph's wife is the daughter of an Egyptian priest (Genesis 41:45, 50; 46:20), and Jethro, Moses' father in law, is known as "the priest of Midian" (Exodus 2:16; 3:1; 18:1). At Mount Sinai, God proclaimed that He had delivered Israel from bondage and set her apart to be a "kingdom of priests" (Exodus 19:6). Instead of creating the concept of priests, Leviticus 8 is the first mention of Israelite priests.

📖 8:5–13

THE CLOTHES AND THE OIL

Worship of God is a serious matter, shown in part through the detailed preparation in verses 5–13. While other Israelites are often purified through washing their hands, the priests are symbolically purified through full-body baths (8:6). The elaborate ceremonial garments would have set apart the priests in appearance and in service to God. The oil represents a divine anointing (8:10–13).

Critical Observation

God took the sin of His priests very seriously. Being in close proximity to God brought with it correspondingly high standards of conduct. This is indicated in several ways in Leviticus. God frequently indicates that disobedience to His commands could bring death (8:35; 10:6–7, 9; Exodus 28:35, 43; 30:20–21). Chapter 10 shows this played out with two priests, plus the implications it has for the entire priesthood.

📖 8:14–36

THE SACRIFICE

Before the priests could be accepted into God's holy presence, they would have to make sacrificial offerings (8:34). Moses had been serving in the high priest function before Aaron's ordination, so he performs the sacrificial rites of the sin offering and burnt offering (8:14–21; see chapters 1, 4). In a special ordination ritual, a second ram is used to symbolize how the priest should hear God's voice, do righteous deeds with his hands, and walk in the ways of God (8:24). Additional offerings are made, and the portions that are not burned are given to Aaron and his sons for a ceremonial meal (8:31). The ordination is complete seven days later, only after the priests show their obedience to God (8:35–36).

Take It Home

Aaron and his sons were obedient to the things God asked of them, and God sanctified them. First Peter 1:2 reminds us that obedience is still a mark of personal holiness.

LEVITICUS 9:1–24

PRINCIPLES OF PRIESTHOOD: MINISTRY

Preparation	9:1–14
Service	9:15–24

Setting Up the Section

Leviticus 9 turns the focus from Moses to Aaron. Aaron and his sons are now commanded to offer sacrifices, first for their own sins and then for the sins of the nation.

📄 9:1–14

PREPARATION

After the ordination of Aaron and his sons is complete, Moses calls them and the leaders of Israel. He tells Aaron to make a sin offering and burnt offering for his own atonement, and then he tells him to educate the Israelites about their responsibilities (9:3–4). The Israelites obeyed and drew near to God (9:5).

Aaron and his priestly sons perform their first ritual duties. Aaron makes a sin offering and burnt offering for himself and his family (9:8–14). They would have to be pure before God before they could offer sacrifices on behalf of the people.

📄 9:15–24

SERVICE

As God's representative of the nation of Israel, Aaron makes a sin offering, burnt offering, grain offering, and peace offering for the people (9:15–18; see chapters 1–4).

The purpose of these offerings is to make preparations for the revelation of God's glory to the people (9:23–24). The Israelites' response to God's presence is joyful worship (9:24).

Demystifying Leviticus

At the sight of God's glory, the people fell facedown (9:24). This was a typical symbol of submission in the Near Eastern cultures.

Take It Home

The Old Testament priests had to be washed in order to carry out their priestly duties. This terminology is now applied to all who are in Christ as a royal priesthood (1 Peter 2). Priests are those whose sins have been atoned for, so that they are free to minister to other sinners. This atonement for the New Testament priest is that which Christ, our great High Priest, has made through the shedding of His blood on the cross (Hebrews 4:14–5:10).

LEVITICUS 10:1–20

PRINCIPLES OF PRIESTHOOD: A DANGEROUS JOB

Playing with Fire	10:1–5
Following the Rules	10:6–11
Understanding Holiness	10:12–20

Setting Up the Section

At the end of chapter 9, fire consumes what is left of the people's sacrifice, and at the beginning of chapter 10, fire comes from God's presence, consuming two of Israel's priests. Nadab and Abihu are sons of Aaron who die because they exercise their priestly duties in a way that dishonors God. The priesthood was an exceedingly dangerous job, for those who drew near to God in service dared not do so casually or irreverently.

📄 10:1–5

PLAYING WITH FIRE

The exact sin committed by Nadab and Abihu, the two oldest sons of Aaron, is not clear; the text says they were offering unauthorized fire before God (10:1). What is clear is that their actions were in direct disobedience to God's commands.

The death of Nadab and Abihu dramatically conveys that priests were allowed to approach God, but that privilege demanded corresponding honor toward Him and His laws (10:3).

📄 10:6–11

FOLLOWING THE RULES

After taking Aaron's oldest sons outside the camp, Moses gives additional rules (10:6–7), so Aaron and his other sons do not become unclean as a result of improper mourning.

In verses 8–11, God speaks directly to Aaron. His words indicate that Nadab and Abihu may have sinned as a result of drinking while on duty (10:9), and He makes a clear distinction between what is holy and what is common (10:10). He also emphasizes the priests' role of teaching the Israelites God's law (10:11).

📖 10:12–20

UNDERSTANDING HOLINESS

Verses 12–15 are instructions to the Aaronic priests conveyed through Moses. They provide a backdrop for understanding Moses' anger when he suspects the sin offering is not properly carried out (10:16–18). Typically, when a goat is given for a sin offering, the breast meat is eaten by the priests. When Moses does not see the meat, he thinks Aaron's other sons have disobeyed God's instructions, but the situation is answered successfully by Aaron. Because of the recent tragedy, Aaron thinks eating of the offering is inappropriate, so it is burned.

Demystifying Leviticus

At the beginning of chapter 8, Moses is the prominent leader, as he has been throughout the account of the Exodus. In chapter 10, however, Aaron is installed as high priest, and he very much comes into his own. Moses' provisional priestly role seems to come to an end here. He is the great prophet, but Aaron is the great priest.

LEVITICUS 11:1–47

CLEAN AND UNCLEAN: FOOD RULES

Land Creatures	11:1–8
Water Creatures	11:9–12
Flying Creatures	11:13–23
The Solution	11:24–47

Setting Up the Section

The third major section of Leviticus (chapters 11–15) defines what is clean and unclean. The label *clean* and its counterpoint *unclean* comprise a prominent theme in Leviticus. The importance of distinctions between the holy and the profane is introduced in 10:10. To get a good grasp on Leviticus, it is important to understand what clean and unclean mean and how they relate to holiness.

📖 11:1–8

LAND CREATURES

Chapter 11 explains clean/unclean food regulations in particular. (There is no clear reason for why certain creatures were considered clean and others were not.) Three animal categories are listed: land, water, and flying creatures. These same distinctions are found in Genesis 1, where God creates all life that is in the heavens, on earth, and under the waters.

Demystifying Leviticus

Various Bible translations name different animals as clean or unclean in chapter 11, and the names of the animals listed may not point to the exact creature we think of today. When a translator deals with Hebrew terms and attempts to isolate and identify a specific creature, it is not always easy, or even possible, to do so with exact accuracy. However, that should not affect the understanding of the principles of cleanness and uncleanness.

Two basic stipulations must be met before a land animal can be considered clean and, therefore, something an Israelite could eat: The creature must have a divided split hoof and chew its cud (11:3). Of course, some animals fit one category but not the other, but the rules are clear that both are necessary (11:4–8).

11:9–12

WATER CREATURES

To be considered clean, animals that live in the sea have to meet two qualifications as well: They must have fins and scales (11:9). The Israelites are not only to avoid unclean creatures, but they are to detest them (11:10–12).

11:13–23

FLYING CREATURES

Instead of qualifications for birds, God provides a list of unclean birds to avoid. The list includes birds that eat other animals or feed off dead carcasses (11:13–19). Flying insects are also mentioned. Essentially, all flying insects are unclean, unless they have jointed jumper legs (11:20–23).

11:24–47

THE SOLUTION

An additional category of unclean animals includes ones that creep or swarm, such as mice and lizards (11:29–31, 41–43).

Touching an unclean creature that is dead would make an Israelite categorically unclean. Even eating a clean animal without going through the proper sacrificial procedure would do the same thing (11:39). The last half of the chapter provides solutions for the problem of uncleanness.

Critical Observation

Essentially, the death of even a clean creature made it unclean, which would, of course, make it difficult to eat since generally all animals are killed before they can be eaten. So all meals that include meat would become an act of worship, since the only way an animal could be killed and stay clean is if it were offered as a sacrifice to God in front of the door of the tent of meeting (see Leviticus 17).

The offenses in chapter 11 are relatively minor, so a person or object could be made clean with water, and the state of uncleanness lasted only until evening (11:32). The exception is a clay pot or oven; it had to be destroyed (11:33, 35).

"Clean" and "unclean" are categories more than conditions. There is a direct relationship between what is clean and what is holy in scripture. Only what is clean can become holy. God emphasizes the Israelites' identification as His people by reminding them, "I am the LORD who brought you up from the land of Egypt to be your God; thus you shall be holy, for I am holy" (11:45 NASB).

Take It Home

In the Levitical system, those declared unclean by priests suffered both humiliation and isolation. The practical result meant a person could not approach God in worship until made clean again. Being unclean restricted fellowship with both God and other people. In the new system, we have been made clean and acceptable through Christ. We can draw near to God (James 4:8), and we can be holy as God is holy (1 Peter 1:15–16).

LEVITICUS 12:1–8

CLEAN AND UNCLEAN: MOTHERS ONLY

Unclean Mothers	12:1–5
Purification	12:6–8

Setting Up the Section

Chapters 12–15 continue to define what is unclean, along with the process of purification. Chapters 12 and 15 address uncleanness related to sexual reproduction, and chapters 13 and 14 address skin ailments.

📖 12:1–5

UNCLEAN MOTHERS

These verses describe the categorical uncleanness a woman experiences after childbirth. The act of having a child itself is not considered sinful, but the flow of blood and other discharges associated with birth cause uncleanness. It may be that reproductive blood and semen are seen as holy fluids. When one comes into contact with something holy it renders one temporarily unclean (note, for instance, that handling the scrolls of scripture make one's hands unclean). (See chapters 15 and 17.)

After the birth of a boy, a woman is isolated at home for seven days. After the child's circumcision on the eighth day, she is required to wait another thirty-three days before worshiping at the sanctuary (12:2–4). After the birth of a girl, a mother's period of uncleanness doubles, with fourteen days at home and sixty-six days before she is allowed to go to the sanctuary (12:5). The reason for this discrepancy is unclear, though some think that "life" is the issue here and the longer one is unclean it means the longer one is in contact with principles of life—so, since a baby girl has a womb, the period of uncleanness is twice as long.

📄 **12:6–8**

PURIFICATION

An unclean mother has to sacrifice both a burnt offering (lamb) and a sin offering (pigeon or dove) to be considered clean again. Provisions are made for mothers without much money by allowing them to substitute two birds for a lamb (12:6–8).

LEVITICUS 13:1–59

CLEAN AND UNCLEAN: PROBLEM SKIN, MILDEW

Rashes and Infections	13:1–23
Spots and Balding	13:24–46
Mildew	13:47–59

Setting Up the Section

The laws in chapters 13 and 14 declare that serious skin disease (physical evidence of decay) made an individual unacceptable before a holy God and unacceptable within the Israelite community. Chapter 13 in particular helps the priests identify these skin disorders.

📄 **13:1–23**

RASHES AND INFECTIONS

If an Israelite had any kind of symptom of a skin disease, he was taken to a priest to be examined through clinical-type instructions (13:1). A deep sore or raw skin would indicate decay and, therefore, cause a person to be unclean (13:3, 15).

Infection also indicated decay and made a person unclean (13:6–8, 18–23). If a priest was unsure, the affected Israelite was quarantined (13:5), followed by additional examination (13:5–7, 21). A condition that did not spread was purified through water, but a spreading rash or other disorder pointed to infection (13:6–8). A chronic disease was also considered infection and made a person unclean for the duration of the disease (13:9–11). If a disease was cured or shown not to be infectious, the person was considered clean (13:12–13, 23).

While the practices described in this section certainly have potential for health benefits, it appears that, at the most fundamental level, the issue is "wholeness." Notice in verse 12 that if a person is covered from head to toe, he is considered clean.

Demystifying Leviticus

The term *leprosy*, used in many Bible translations, is most likely not used to describe the disease we know as leprosy. It is more likely a generic term referring to a number of skin disorders rather than a specific disease. The NIV better translates the original term as "infectious skin disease."

📖 **13:24–46**

SPOTS AND BALDING

The same rules apply for suspicious spots or burns (13:24–40). A man who experiences normal balding is clean (13:40–41), but a disorder on the skin of his head is examined the same way other disorders are examined by a priest (13:42–44).

Any person found to have an infectious skin disease is to be put outside the camp to live. He was also forced to announce his unclean state to anyone he encountered and to take on the posture of a mourner (13:45–46). He would also be cut off from fellowship with other Israelites and could not approach God in worship.

📖 **13:47–59**

MILDEW

The Israelites are instructed to deal with mildewed clothing in a similar way to diseased skin. Just as infectious diseases could spread, so could mildew. Priests examined and isolated contaminated clothing (13:49–51). Clothes with spreading mildew, or mildew that would not wash out, were burned (13:52, 55, 57).

LEVITICUS 14:1–57

CLEAN AND UNCLEAN: CLEANING INFECTIONS AND MILDEW

Outside Camp	14:1–8
Inside Camp	14:9–32
Mildew Matters	14:33–57

Setting Up the Section

The laws in chapters 13 and 14 declare that serious skin ailments make an individual unacceptable before a holy God and even within the Israelite community. Chapter 14 in particular outlines the purification process.

OUTSIDE CAMP

Those with symptoms of skin disease were sent outside the camp in a kind of quarantine, presumably so others would not catch the disease (14:3). This would have been significant, as it separated an individual from both his community and the sanctuary of God.

Critical Observation

The Old Testament law says the unclean could never come into the presence of the holy God, yet God's Son took on human flesh and lived among humanity. In His ministry, He avoided the self righteous, who considered themselves clean by their own merits, and He sought out those who were regarded unclean. The new covenant, in the person of Christ, broke down the barrier that the Old Testament law and its sacrificial system could not. Jesus Himself went "outside the camp," seeking to save the unclean. As Christians, we are called to do likewise (Hebrews 13:12–13).

If the priest finds the condition to be healed after a week, there is then a cleansing ceremony including hyssop, known for healing properties (Psalm 51:7; Matthew 27:48), and two clean birds (Leviticus 14:4–7). Additional bathing and washing then took place, along with shaving all hair to allow the person back into the camp (14:8).

Demystifying Leviticus

The killing of a bird in the ceremony was not so much a sacrifice as a symbol. The life of one bird is exchanged for the life of the other, who is given freedom from death and decay and "new" life.

INSIDE CAMP

After the ceremonial cleansing, the affected person has seven days of additional examination that includes additional shaving (14:9). That is followed by the sacrifice of three lambs for guilt, sin, and burnt offerings (14:10–13), along with a grain offering. The ceremonial smearing of blood (14:14) is similar to the priestly consecration ritual (see 8:24). The oil ritual (14:14–18) accompanied the atonement that made the unclean person clean.

Three sacrificial lambs would have been expensive, so special exceptions were made for the poor, as with other offerings (14:21–22).

MILDEW MATTERS

Rules relating to mildew (a general term for anything from mold to dry rot), which was something that would cause decay in the home, are similar to those relating to human skin disease (14:33–57). These instructions deal with the homes the Israelites would build once in Canaan (14:34). Verse 34 likely indicates that God is the Creator of all living things, not that He is sending mildew as some kind of test or punishment.

The examination periods (14:37–42) are similar to those for skin disease in chapter 13. In the same way an unclean person is sent out of the camp, contaminated building stones are put outside the city (14:40). The cleansing ritual for a home (14:49–53) is the same as for the person who is unclean (14:4–7).

Take It Home

While the priests could pronounce a person unclean or clean, he could not heal a person with a disease. We see the same thing as the focus in the New Testament turns from external symptoms to what is going on in a person's mind and heart. The scribes and Pharisees of Jesus' day did not have this grasp of the meaning of "clean" and "unclean." They could not understand why He spent time with people considered unclean. They failed to see Him as the One who could make humans clean, the One who could bring wholeness. Let us focus more on what's going on inside ourselves and others, and let us point others toward the restoration found in Christ.

LEVITICUS 15:1–32

CLEAN AND UNCLEAN DISCHARGES

The Male Kind	15:1–18
The Female Kind	15:19–32

Setting Up the Section

Chapter 15 picks up where chapter 12 leaves off, declaring certain discharges as unclean. Both men and women have what might be called normal (15:16–18, 19–24) and abnormal (15:2–15, 25–30) discharges. Aside from practical hygienic concerns, the laws once again address the subject of holiness.

📖 15:1–18

THE MALE KIND

Verses 1–12 refer to a man with a discharge from his body as unclean. The word translated *body* could mean a person's body, but it is also used as a euphemism for a man's sexual organ. The nature of this particular discharge is not clear, but it is likely some kind of infection. Because infections often contain dead matter, the man would be considered unclean. And since some infections can spread, anything or anyone the man touched would also be unclean.

Verses 13–15 address his purification. Those who touch the unclean man could become clean simply by washing their clothes and bathing (15:5–12). The man himself has a period of isolation (15:13) and then can renew relationships with God and fellow Israelites after sacrificing birds as a sin offering and burnt offering (15:14–15).

Verses 16–18 address semen discharge, a normal male function. The answer to the day-long unclean condition is to bathe and wash any affected clothing. Even intercourse between a married couple resulted in both the man and woman being unclean until evening and having to bathe (15:18).

📄 15:19–32

THE FEMALE KIND

A woman's regular menstruation would make her unclean for seven days (until the period is completely over). Anything she sat on was considered unclean, and anyone who touched her or anything she had touched would be unclean for a day (15:19), requiring bathing and washing (15:20–23). If the woman's husband had sex with her, then he would also be unclean for seven days (15:24). Purification came through water.

Verses 25–30 address an unusually long period or other associated discharge, which are considered to make a woman unclean. The same rules apply as with normal menstruation (15:25–27), but the woman has to go through the same sacrificial ceremony as the man with the abnormal discharge (15:14–15, 29–30).

Critical Observation

The laws concerning the unclean state during abnormal discharges (15:25–30) shed light on the story of the hemorrhaging woman who sought healing from Jesus in Luke 8:43–45. Not only was she seeking physical wholeness, but the healing would bring her relational wholeness as well.

Take It Home

Verse 31 of this chapter emphasizes the reason for the clean/unclean laws. Since the tabernacle housed the presence of a holy God, those who were declared categorically unclean could not enter into that presence. In addition, the laws reminded the Israelites that they were a people who had been set apart by God. As Christians today, our holiness is not judged by these kinds of laws, but it is good to remember that when we approach God through prayer or worship, we are approaching a holy God.

LEVITICUS 16:1-34

THE DAY OF ATONEMENT

Preparation	16:1–5
Sacrifice	16:6–19
Cleansing	16:20–34

Setting Up the Section

Chapter 16 serves in part as a kind of addendum to chapters 8–10, as it addresses the expectations of the Aaronic priesthood. It opens with instructions God gives Moses to give to Aaron after the death of Aaron's two sons in chapter 10. The focus of these regulations is to make the people of Israel clean (a topic explained in detail in chapters 11–15). The chapter ends with a command for the high priest to make atonement for all the sins of Israel once a year. This is the introduction of the annual Day of Atonement.

📄 16:1–5

PREPARATION

Even the high priest could not enter into the Holy of Holies whenever he wanted (16:3), so the opening instructions are to prepare Aaron to enter into that sacred place (Exodus 28, 39; Leviticus 16:4). Before he could enter into the Lord's presence, Aaron would have to make a sin offering for himself and his family, as well as a burnt offering. He would also go through an elaborate bathing and dressing process (Leviticus 16:4) to illustrate the contrast between God's purity and human sinfulness.

Critical Observation

In the course of his daily sacrifices, Aaron, the high priest, represented God, so his clothing was beautiful and extravagant. But when he entered the Holy of Holies to perform the annual atoning ritual, he went before God in simplicity and humility.

📄 16:6–19

SACRIFICE

The two goats Aaron brings on behalf of the people serve a special purpose. One will become the sacrificial sin offering for the people; the other will provide atonement by symbolically taking on the people's sin and then being sent away (16:7–10, 15). The bull sacrifice is a sin offering for Aaron and his family (16:11), and the subsequent goat sacrifice is a sin offering for the people (16:15).

God's dwelling place (the tabernacle) is emphasized with the cloud of incense (16:12–13) to veil the glory of God so that Aaron can enter into His presence. Atonement is made for the holy place, including the altar, since the sin of the people defiles the tabernacle (16:16–19).

CLEANSING

After taking care of the holy place, Aaron symbolically lays the sins of the entire nation on the head of the second goat and sends it away in the desert so it can not return (16:20–22). Atonement is made complete with burnt offerings for Aaron and the people (16:24) and with completing the sin offerings (16:25–27).

The people participate in the day through solemn rest and intentional humility (16:31).

Take It Home

Unlike the other Jewish holidays, the Day of Atonement was not a festive event. It was a day of national mourning and repentance. The Israelites were told to humble themselves (16:31), which most likely included fasting. No work was done since it was on the Sabbath. This would thus be the only appointed holy day characterized by mourning, fasting, and repentance. The Day of Atonement was a time for dealing with unknown sins that had gone unaddressed in the past year. Even unknown sins hinder our fellowship with God and others. This kind of reflection and repentance should be a regular part of the Christian life.

LEVITICUS 17:1–16

PRECIOUS IS THE BLOOD

Sacrificial Blood   17:1–9
Lifeblood   17:10–16

Setting Up the Section

Leviticus 17 is a transitional chapter. It concludes the previous sixteen chapters, which focus on the sacrificial process, by applying the value of blood to the daily practices of the Israelites. It also introduces the following chapters that deal with the practice of holiness in the everyday life of the Israelites. If the first sixteen chapters of Leviticus were addressed primarily to the priests of Israel, this chapter is addressed mainly to the people of Israel. If the previous chapters dealt with the sacred—the tabernacle, the sacrifices, and the priests—this chapter deals with the secular, the normal course of life for the Israelite.

SACRIFICIAL BLOOD

The regulation of verses 3–7 presupposes that an Israelite will be tempted to slaughter one of his animals for its meat. Slaughtering any animal had to take place as an offering at the tabernacle (17:4, 8–9; see chapters 1–7, 16); otherwise it is considered bloodshed. An Israelite has to make a peace offering in order to voluntarily slaughter and eat an animal.

Demystifying Leviticus

The people of Moses' day had learned a killing ritual from surrounding pagan cultures. There was no purely secular slaughter, but only a sacred ritual. An Israelite who slaughtered an animal was performing some type of worship, either of God or of a goat idol (17:7). God commands the Israelites to exchange past practices for those that worshiped Him.

LIFEBLOOD

The regulation of verses 10–13 prohibits anyone living in Israel to eat the blood of any animal (17:10–11, 13). Blood is equated with life and God's atonement of the Israelites (17:11), so anyone who ate it would be "cut off" from his people, an expression that, at best, means expulsion from the nation and, at worst, execution.

Hunters are instructed to cover the blood of game they kill (17:13). An animal killed by another animal could be eaten, but the one who does so will become unclean (11:39–40; 17:15).

Critical Observation

Any animal that was slaughtered had to be offered to God as a sacrifice. Any blood that was shed was shed as a part of a sacrifice. Thus, any meat an Israelite ate (even from his own herd or flock) had to be first offered to God as a part of a sacrifice at the tent of meeting. And since the peace offering is the only sacrifice that the Israelite could eat, every time the Israelite wanted to eat meat, he had to make a peace offering.

RELATIONSHIP RULES

Setting Up the Section

The Israelites had been the slaves of Pharaoh. The Exodus freed the Israelites from bondage to Egypt, but it also brought them under the yoke of their God, who had delivered them. These people were to live under a new order, spelled out in the covenant that God made with them. God spells out clearly what kind of behavior He expects from His people. This chapter begins a new section of Leviticus that offers practical guidelines for how the Israelites are to live as a holy people.

📄 18:1–5

A COVENANT RELATIONSHIP

Verses 1–5 address the Israelites' motivation for obeying the laws that God is going to lay down in the following chapters. God reminds the Israelites of their relationship to Him. Knowing they had a tendency to mimic the cultures around them, He also gives specifics for how they should live as the people of God by following His ways and statutes (18:3–4).

📄 18:6–23

RELATIONAL BOUNDARIES

These verses define for the Israelites the boundaries of God-honoring relationships (see chart). The progression is from inner boundaries that prohibit sexual relationships with close relatives (18:6–18) to middle boundaries that limit sex within and outside of marriage (18:19–20) to outer boundaries of unnatural relationships (18:21–23).

Demystifying Leviticus

The regulations concerning sex related uncleanness serve in part to clearly separate sex from religious worship. The separation is particularly important to the Israelites because of the pagan worship rituals of the Canaanites, whose fertility cult engaged in sexual union as an act of worship (Numbers 25:1–9). Since the Israelites had been known to imitate other people (Exodus 32:6), these laws set apart the Israelites' worship from that of their pagan neighbors.

Verses 6–18 begin with the closest relationship (mother and child) and progress from there to a man and his sister-in-law. In ancient Israel, familial relationships were the social cornerstone of the community, so keeping them pure would have been extremely important.

Verse 19 reiterates the law found in chapter 15, and verse 20 is a reminder of the seventh commandment. Verses 21–23 remind the Israelites not to imitate the pagan people around them.

📖 18:24–30

CONSEQUENCES

For the Israelites, the land of Canaan represents God's blessings. The last part of this chapter stresses the fact that the sins of the Canaanites defiled the land and would lead to their expulsion (18:24–25). It also warns the Israelites that if they fail to live according to God's laws when in Canaan, then they will lose the blessing of the land (18:28). At the conclusion of Leviticus, God spells out in greater detail the blessings of obeying Him (chapter 26).

Critical Observation

After God led the Israelites out of captivity in Egypt, He made a covenant with His people, known as the Mosaic Covenant because it was communicated through Moses. God introduced the Ten Commandments, part of the covenant, with the words "I am the LORD your God" (Exodus 20:2). When the covenant was reiterated to the next generation, the same phrase was used (Deuteronomy 5:6). In Leviticus 18, it shows up again. The words, used forty-seven times in chapters 18–26, are a reminder to the Israelites of their identity as people of God.

Take It Home

Sexual boundaries matter to God, and they should matter to us as Christians. Still, God offers renewed purity and forgiveness. Look at the love Jesus shows the Samaritan woman at the well (John 4), the woman caught in adultery (John 8), and the prostitute who honored Him (Luke 7). We can let our pasts be in the past. We can receive Christ's words, "Go and sin no more" (John 8:11), and also receive His love and grace.

HOLY, HOLY, HOLY

Being Holy	19:1–8
Loving Others	19:9–18
Living Holy	19:19–37

Setting Up the Section

The Mosaic Covenant was established so Israel would be a holy nation (Exodus 19:6), set apart as God's people. Leviticus hammers home the importance of holiness for the Israelites. The book provides instructions for holiness involved with special ceremonies, holy days, and how to approach the tabernacle. Chapter 19 provides detailed, specific ways to practice everyday holiness that include respect for God and for others.

📖 19:1–8

BEING HOLY

God had Moses assemble all the Israelites to offer this command: "You shall be holy, for I the LORD your God am holy" (Leviticus 19:2 NASB). The law is God's standard of holiness, instructions on how to imitate His character. What follows is a refresher course on the Ten Commandments (19:3-4) and a repeat of ceremonial law surrounding the peace offering (19:5-8).

📖 19:9–18

LOVING OTHERS

After the reminders, God inserts new instructions that lead to God's second overarching command: "You shall love your neighbor as yourself; I am the LORD" (19:18 NASB). Holiness would be practiced as the Israelites loved their neighbors. This includes the vulnerable (19:9-11, 14-15), fellow Israelites (19:11-13, 15-16), foreigners (19:10, 33-34), and even enemies (19:17-18).

Critical Observation

Leviticus 19 is important because of the prominence of its teaching in the New Testament. Both our Lord (Matthew 5:43; 19:19; 22:39; Mark 12:31, 33; Luke 10:27) and the apostles (Romans 13:9; Galatians 5:14; James 2:8; 1 Peter 1:16) make a great deal of the two great commandments that are given here: "You shall be holy, for I the LORD your God am holy" (Leviticus 19:2), and "You shall love your neighbor as yourself" (19:18). In the context of this chapter, it becomes clear that the Israelites' enemies are included in the broad category of "neighbor," something Jesus also taught (Matthew 5:44–48).

🕮 19:19-37

LIVING HOLY

The rest of the chapter lists miscellaneous laws. They are reminders to be a set-apart people who do not mix with other cultures (19:26-29). The people are reminded to create God-honoring relationships (19:20-22), to maintain fairness (19:36), and to practice compassion rather than oppression (19:33-34).

Demystifying Leviticus

The holy behavior that God required was seen in acts He had already performed on behalf of His people. God's holiness was manifested by His compassion on the Israelites when they were oppressed in Egypt. So, too, holiness is to be manifested by the people of God by the way they treat others.

LEVITICUS 20:1-27

CAPITAL CRIMES

Molech and Mediums	20:1-6
Family Business	20:7-21
Follow the Rules	20:22-27

Setting Up the Section

Chapter 20 falls into the broader context of chapters 18-20, which stress practical holiness in the everyday life of the Israelite. Chapter 18 has focused primarily on the family, chapter 19 instructs Israel to love their neighbor, and chapter 20 follows up by detailing the capital punishment for serious sins forbidden in the previous chapters. The actions highlighted become crimes as well as sins.

🕮 20:1-6

MOLECH AND MEDIUMS

Verses 1-6 show a co-participation between God and His people in condemning those who are guilty of capital crimes. In fact, those who close their eyes to sin also become guilty (20:4-5). The child sacrificed here is a reflection of the surrounding pagan cultures.

Critical Observation

These capital crimes are violations of God's covenant with Israel. The crimes in Leviticus that call for a death penalty are all crimes against God's covenant, which emphasizes that God set Israel apart from the surrounding nations to distinguish them by means of holiness as His people (Exodus 19:5-6). The Mosaic Covenant is the definition of the holiness that God requires in order for Him to dwell among His people and for them to be His holy nation.

FAMILY BUSINESS

The relational sins listed in chapter 18 are repeated here, this time with the penalty. (See chart.)

Verse	Relationship	Penalty
18:7	Mother and son	Death, 20:11
18:8	Stepmother and son	Death, 20:11
18:9	Brother and sister/Brother and maternal half-sister	Cut off, 20:17
18:10	Father and granddaughter	Burned, 20:14
18:11	Brother and paternal half-sister	Cut off, 20:17
18:12	Nephew and aunt (father's sister)	Barrenness, 20:20
18:13	Nephew and aunt (mother's sister)	Barrenness, 20:20
18:14	Nephew and aunt (wife of father's brother)	Barrenness, 20:20
18:15	Father and daughter-in-law	Death, 20:12
18:16	Brother and sister-in-law	Barrenness, 20:21
18:17	Father and stepdaughter/Father and step-granddaughter/Husband and mother-in-law	Burned, 20:14
18:18	Husband and sister-in-law	None

FOLLOW THE RULES

When God made certain sins crimes as well, the Israelites were strongly motivated to obey God's laws and to avoid sin. In these verses, God gives a general exhortation to follow His laws (20:22). The result of disobedience will be loss of their promised land in Canaan. God had promised the Israelites a land flowing with milk and honey, a symbol for blessing (20:24), but He requires obedience and sanctified (set apart) lives that imitate His own character (20:26). As an example, He lists another crime that is influenced by pagan culture and deserving of the death penalty.

Take It Home

There is a difference between crimes and sin. Chapter 20 highlights capital crimes, but in God's eyes all sin brings death (Romans 6:23). There is no room for self-righteousness if God views all sins as capital offenses. If we are not guilty of one form of sin, we are surely guilty of another; and seen from God's point of view, the kind of sin we commit matters little. As James explains, to be found guilty of offense at one point is to fall short in all points (James 2:1–13).

LEVITICUS 21:1–24

HOLINESS: TRUE/FALSE, PART 1

Setting Up the Section

Chapters 17–20 are addressed to the Israelites in general, defining how holiness is to be practiced in the everyday activities of life. Chapters 21 and 22 return to addressing the Aaronic priesthood. Of particular importance is how they are to avoid being defiled and to remain holy. Each section is marked by the statement, in slightly modified forms, "I am the Lord, who sanctifies you" (21:8, 15, 23; 22:9, 16, 32).

📖 **21:1–9**

MOURNING AND MARRIAGE (PRIEST)

Priests had to remain ceremonially clean so that they could approach God and make offerings on behalf of the people. This meant they could not bury the dead, except in the case of close blood relatives (21:1–3). All Israelites (especially priests) were forbidden to shave their heads or the edges of their beards or to cut their skin as a sign of mourning (19:27; 21:1–5, 10–12; Deuteronomy 14:1). An ordinary Israelite had greater freedom in choosing a wife; priests could marry a widow but not a divorcee (21:7). Even a priest's daughter was held to higher standards (21:9).

📖 **21:10–15**

MOURNING AND MARRIAGE (HIGH PRIEST)

If there is a high standard for the priests (21:1–9), there is an even higher standard for the high priest (21:10–15). The high priest could not participate in standard mourning traditions (21:10), or even leave the tabernacle to take part in burying near relatives (21:10–12). And the high priest could marry only a virgin of his own people (21:13–15).

📖 **21:16–24**

STAY BACK

The Aaronic priesthood began with Aaron and his sons and would continue through his line of descendants. Those who had physical defects would not be able to participate in sacrificial offerings (21:16–21). The sacrificial animal had to be without defects, and so did the priest doing the offering. The priest with the defect could eat the food the priests were allowed, but he could not approach the altar (21:23).

Critical Observation

Aaron's position as high priest did not make him holier than others, though it did hold him to a higher standard. God chose Aaron and his descendants, just as God chose the Israelites. A look at Aaron's life reveals that neither he (Exodus 32) nor his sons (Leviticus 10) were holy by their own merit. Even though a priest was ceremonially pure, he still could approach God only by means of sacrifice and atoning blood.

LEVITICUS 22:1–33

HOLINESS: TRUE/FALSE, PART 2

Setting Up the Section

As with chapter 21, chapter 22 addresses the Aaronic priesthood with a continued emphasis on how to avoid being defiled and how to remain holy. Each section is marked by the same statement, in one form or another, "I am the LORD, who sanctifies you" (21:8, 15, 23; 22:9, 16, 32).

📖 22:1–9

KEEP IT CLEAN

Priests were tasked with approaching God's holy presence in the tabernacle and offering blood sacrifices that would atone for sin. This means they had to remain clean. Attempting priestly duties while unclean would cause defilement, and that person would be cut off from God (22:3). The priests were to respect the rules for cleanness and uncleanness in chapters 11–15 (22:4–9).

Demystifying Leviticus

The nature of defilement is not that of specific sin, but of external ceremonial defilement. Leviticus begins by defining defilement in very concrete terms, but as the Old Testament revelation unfolds, the prophets emphatically teach that God is not nearly as interested in the external ceremonial acts of people as He is in the attitudes of their hearts and the resulting righteousness.

📖 22:10–16

THE PRIEST'S FOOD

These verses add a few details regarding how priests are to handle the food left over after sacrificial offerings (see chapters 2–7).

📖 22:17–33

WHAT TO GIVE/NOT GIVE

Verses 17–33 are additional regulations for sacrificial offerings (see chapters 1–7). Because the blood is atoning or purifying in nature, a sacrificial animal has to be without defect (22:19–22, 24–25). Those who had defects, some simply in their appearance, were not to be offered. The priests followed laws related to holiness in order to teach the Israelites that God is holy (22:31–33).

Critical Observation

Since chapters 21–22 were addressed to Israel's priests, the priests of Jesus' day would have seen the teachings directed at them. It was their misunderstanding of the text, and their misapplication of it, that resulted in their immediate and intense opposition to Jesus' teachings and practices.

Take It Home

In chapters 21–22, God says six times, "I am the LORD, who sanctifies you." He set Israel apart from the nations, and He set the priests apart from the people. God commands the priests to avoid outward defilement because they are already holy, by God's sanctification. They are to avoid the prohibited things, not because avoidance would make them clean, but because these things would make them unclean. There is a world of difference between avoiding something to keep yourself from sin and avoiding something to make yourself holy. May God grant us to understand and to apply the principles of Leviticus and the law as our Lord taught us to do, for His sake.

LEVITICUS 23:1-44

ALL IN GOOD TIME

The Weekly Sabbath	23:1–3
Spring Holy Days	23:4–22
Fall Holy Days	23:23–44

Setting Up the Section

The Lord's appointed times are festivals and holy days that commemorate significant times and events in Israel's history. The commemorative holidays show truths of God's salvation, love, and plans. The appointed times create a sacred rhythm in the lives of the Israelites.

🔖 23:1–3

THE WEEKLY SABBATH

Sabbath means "rest." The Sabbath celebration has its roots in the creation of the world (Genesis 2:1–3). God blessed the seventh day and sanctified it, separating it from the others in kind and character. The Sabbath becomes a day of rest in a week otherwise filled with toil and work.

🔖 23:4–22

SPRING HOLY DAYS

The Israelites celebrate Passover (Leviticus 23:4–5) and the Feast of Unleavened Bread (23:6–8) together. The first month in the sacred Jewish calendar is marked by Passover, a day celebrating Israel's deliverance from captivity and birth as a nation. It is the most important festival. The Feast of Unleavened Bread is an extension of Passover. This is a time for the Israelites to remember their identity as God's people.

The Festival of Firstfruits (23:9–14) is a time for the Israelites who were camped in the desert to be reminded of the hope of future blessings in Canaan (23:10). On this day, the first sheaf of barley is harvested, but nothing can be eaten until the sheaf is waved before God as an act of thanksgiving for His provision. The priest would also make a burnt offering together with a grain offering and a drink offering of wine (23:12–13).

The Festival of Pentecost, or the Feast of Weeks (23:15–22), gets its name from the counting of fifty days from the Sabbath following Passover. It coincides with and celebrates God's giving of His law at Mount Sinai. The feast also includes several offerings to God, and the Israelites are instructed to leave the edges of their crops unharvested for the poor and the foreigner as well (23:22).

Demystifying Leviticus

The Jewish calendar is based on the relative motion of both the moon and the sun. Each month is defined by phases of the moon. The first of every month coincides with a new moon, and the fifteenth of every month coincides with a full moon. The calendar keeps the months and their respective seasons together by inserting a leap month, meaning most years have twelve months, but some have thirteen. The primary markers in the calendar are the sacred holidays.

📖 23:23–44

FALL HOLY DAYS

The Festival of Trumpets (23:23–25) is known today as Rosh Hashanah. It is a day marked by assembling together, doing no regular work, and commemorated by blowing trumpets with fanfare. It is a reminder that the Day of Atonement is approaching and a time for the Israelites to reflect on the year and their relationship to God.

Following the somber reflection of the Day of Atonement, the Feast of Tabernacles (23:33–43) is the joyous holiday of the manifest presence of God. As a reminder to younger generations of God's deliverance of the Israelites in Egypt, they are all to live in booths (temporary shelters made of tree branches and palm leaves) for seven days.

Take It Home

The story of God's deliverance and salvation is told without words through the tastes of Passover, waving of the sheaf during Firstfruits, waving of loaves on Pentecost, the sound of trumpets, and temporary tabernacles. These days speak of past and future deliverance, and they provide markers each year in the life of a Jew. Do you have any kind of sacred rhythm in your own life? Are there any visual markers that help you remember God's presence?

Religious Month	Canaanite Name	Babylonian Name	Gregorian Placement	Holy Day
First	Abib	Nisan	March or April	Passover; Feast of Unleavened Bread; Wave Offering of Firstfruits
Second	Ziv	Iyyar	April or May	
Third		Sivan	May or June	Pentecost
Fourth		Tammuz	June or July	
Fifth		Ab	July or August	
Sixth		Elul	August or September	
Seventh	Ethanim	Tishri	September or October	Trumpets; Day of Atonement; Feast of Tabernacles
Eighth	Bul	Cheshvan	October or November	
Ninth		Chislev	November or December	
Tenth		Tebeth	December or January	
Eleventh		Shebat	January or February	
Twelfth		Adar	February or March	
Thirteenth		Adar II	March	This is the leap month

LEVITICUS 24:1–23

LAMP, LOAVES, AND LOUDMOUTH

Setting Up the Section

Leviticus 24 addresses how the Israelites should care for the dwelling place of God and how they should deal with someone who blasphemes God's name. The first nine verses concern the ritual of maintaining the lamp and the loaves. Justice is also to become a matter of consistency (24:10–33). In all three sections, the element of continuity in ritual is present.

📄 24:1–4

KEEP THE FIRES BURNING

The golden lampstand has already appeared in the Pentateuch several times (Exodus 25:31–40; 27:20–21; 37:17–24; 40:25–26). It is housed in the holy place to provide light in the darkness of the tabernacle. Even in the daytime, the many layered coverings of the tent would keep out sunlight, so the light of this lamp is required. The emphasis of these verses is that the light must be kept burning at all times. The key word is *continually* (Leviticus 24:2–4). Virtually the entire nation plays a role in this task of keeping the golden lamp burning.

📄 24:5–9

GIVE US OUR WEEKLY BREAD

There are two reasons the continual changing of the loaves is important. First, they are a part of the sacrificial offerings (24:7). To fail to provide fresh loaves each week would hinder the sacrificial process, which is symbolic of an everlasting covenant (24:8). Second, these loaves (or, more accurately, what remained of them) are a part of the food that sustains and nourishes the priests (24:9). To fail to provide for the priesthood would be to hinder the priestly process, so the loaves are always to be on hand.

📄 24:10–23

THE PERIL OF PROFANITY

The next group of verses addresses the case of a man who had blasphemed God's name. The Israelites were not sure how to interpret God's law, so they asked for a ruling (24:10–12). In clarifying the law as it applies to this man's offense, Israel is taught how the law applies to them personally. In addition, God's people are taught some important principles that apply to a much wider range of offenses.

The one who defames God's character is to be taken outside the camp. All the witnesses lay their hands on his head as an act of recognizing their part in the crime, and then the entire congregation of Israelites would stone the offender as a way to identify with God and His holiness (24:14–15).

Critical Observation

God's instructions to the Israelites relating to blasphemy are such that justice would be carried out consistently, without variation, without deviation, and without cessation. The principle of equality in punishment is consistently taught in the Old Testament. In Deuteronomy 17:2 and 17:7, the principle of equality in punishment is applied to men and women. It is most clearly taught in the book of Numbers (Numbers 15:13–16; Deuteronomy 29:10–13; 31:11–12).

God then gives general rules for how to deal with blasphemy. God's holiness is emphasized by the severe punishment prescribed for someone who blasphemes. The other rules in verses 17–22 show that the punishment provided should match the crime committed.

LEVITICUS 25:1–55

SUPER SABBATH

Sabbath Year	25:1–7
Jubilee Year	25:8–34
Neighborly Ways	25:35–46
Strange Company	25:47–55

Setting Up the Section

Leviticus 25 reveals God's compassion for the poor and oppressed. The Sabbath Year and the Year of Jubilee are part of God's gracious provisions for all His people. The two events are interrelated, so they are dealt with at the same time. Verses 1–34 lay down God's law pertaining to the land, while verses 35–55 apply to people.

25:1–7

SABBATH YEAR

During the Sabbath Year, the land is given its rest (25:2–3, 5). Following these commands would require great faith since letting fields lie fallow for a year would mean trusting God to provide as He promises (25:18–22). The land regulations are also a provision for the poor, since anyone is allowed to eat from the crops but no one could harvest them for sale (25:6–7). This provided them with food in times of need and the possibility of a new beginning.

Demystifying Leviticus

The "laws of the land" were designed to hinder greed by keeping in check those who would try to accumulate vast land holdings at the expense of others.

📄 **25:8–34**

JUBILEE YEAR

The Year of Jubilee was like a super Sabbath. Every fifty years, God proclaimed a year of freedom and liberation from bondage following the Day of Atonement (25:9–10). On the Sabbath Year, all debts are canceled (Deuteronomy 15:1–2), but in the Year of Jubilee, the Israelite who has sold himself to another is released, and the land that has been leased to another is restored to its original owner. The Year of Jubilee is a reminder that God owns the land (25:23).

Loans were to be made without any consideration of how many years were left to repay the loan (Deuteronomy 15:7–11), but leases were made by calculating the number of years remaining until the Jubilee (Leviticus 25:14–16, 26–28). One is an act of generosity, considered more a gift than a loan, and the other is a business arrangement that is regulated to ensure a fair deal.

📄 **25:35–46**

NEIGHBORLY WAYS

The first type of poverty addressed (25:35–38) is temporary. God's solution is a no-interest loan. In verses 39–46, God instructs the Israelites how to help a fellow Israelite who is so poor he has to sell himself. That person is to be treated not as a slave, but with dignity as a hired worker who could leave his employment if treated unfairly (see Deuteronomy 15:16–17; 24:15). At the Year of Jubilee, the servant has to be released so he can return to the property of his forefathers (Leviticus 25:41).

While an Israelite could not be a slave because he was ultimately God's servant, not another person's (25:42), non-Israelites could be bought as slaves. However, they were also to be treated well.

Critical Observation

One of the most significant prophecies of Israel's restoration, couched in Jubilee terminology, is found in the book of Isaiah: "The Spirit of the sovereign LORD is upon me, because the LORD has chosen me. He has commissioned me to encourage the poor, to help the brokenhearted, to decree the release of captives, and the freeing of prisoners, to announce the year when the LORD will show his favor" (Isaiah 61:1–2 NET). It is this text that our Lord read in His hometown synagogue (Luke 4).

STRANGE COMPANY

A poor Israelite could sell himself to a wealthy foreigner, but he kept the right to redemption (25:47–48) at any time by a relative or himself (because he ultimately belonged to God). If that did not happen, though, the nation of Israel was responsible to make sure he was not mistreated (25:53) and that he was released in the Year of Jubilee (25:54).

Take It Home

Israel was to show compassion to the poor and the oppressed in order to imitate God. The instructions given to the Israelites concerning the poor among them was to ensure that God's people imitated Him, both in attitude and action. While this is an Old Testament text, the principles here are relevant today. Loving our neighbor as ourselves is part of living out God's character.

Verses:	35–38	39–46	47–55
Problem:	Cash flow shortage	Poverty	Dire Poverty
Solution:	Loan	Slave of Israelite	Slave of Stranger
Conditions/ Obligations:	No interest to be charged	No harsh treatment A day laborer Released (Jubilee)	Right of Redemption Not deal harshly Released (Jubilee)
Goal/Purpose:	So he can dwell in the land	So he can dwell in the land	So he can dwell in the land (implied)
Motivation:	God's deliverance from Egypt	They are God's servants	They are God's servants

LEVITICUS 26:1-46

A WELCOME WARNING

Setting Up the Section

Leviticus 26 is one of the clearest warnings in the Pentateuch (and is reiterated more emphatically in Deuteronomy 28). God's standards for Israel's conduct and the results of obedience or disobedience are given well in advance of punishment or blessing. This chapter does not contain just words of warning, though. It also reveals some of the greatest words of hope found in the Bible.

📖 26:1-13

BLESSINGS

God reminds the Israelites that they are His people (26:1-2) and then promises blessings if they will act as His people (26:3-13). In its broadest definition, God's blessings are conditioned by Israel's keeping of the Mosaic Covenant (26:3-4). At the heart of that covenant is worshiping God alone and observing the Sabbath (26:1-2).

The blessings God promises Israel are directly related to her possession of the land of Canaan: peace (26:6), prosperity (26:4-5, 9-10), and the presence of God (26:11-12). Those promises end with a reminder of past blessings and of God's faithfulness (26:13).

📖 26:14-39

CURSES

The curses are virtually a reversal of the promised blessings. Instead of prosperity, disobedience will bring poverty (26:16, 26). Instead of peace and security, disobedience will bring insecurity, peril, and fear (26:16, 17, 21-22, 25, 31-32, 36-39). Instead of God's presence, disobedience will bring separation (26:17, 21, 23-24, 28, 34-35).

Demystifying Leviticus

There are a number of passages that are parallel to Leviticus 26. Exodus 23:22-33 is the first recording of the promise of blessings and curses, based upon Israel's obedience to the Mosaic Covenant. In Deuteronomy 28, the blessings and curses are repeated in greater detail for the second generation of Israelites who are about to possess the land of Canaan. Joshua 24:20 is a brief summation of the warnings of this chapter, and the writings of the prophets reveal some direct dependence on it (Isaiah 49:1; Ezekiel 34:25-30; 37:21-28). Leviticus 26 is key to understanding the history of Israel.

ASSURANCE

God deals with Israel's sin and with repentance at its roots, at the level of motivation. Israel's disobedience is the result of her hatred of God's laws (26:15). But God's motivation in discipline is to have Israel turn back to Him (26:41). God assures Israel of an ultimate hope by reaffirming His love for them. In the end, God assures Israel that He will restore her not based on obedience to the Mosaic Covenant, but because of His own faithfulness (26:40–45).

Take It Home

The benevolence of God is underscored in this chapter, even with its gruesome warnings. God's desire is for restoration; to have Israel turn back to Him (26:18, 21, 23, 27). And in the end, despite their unfaithfulness, God assures Israel that He will restore them based on His faithfulness, not their deeds (26:40–45). Israel is always assured of God's love and of His good purposes for His people. May we find hope in the faithfulness and mercy of God in our own situations.

BLESSINGS (26:1–13)	CURSES (26:14–39)
God Confirms Covenant (9)	God's Vengeance for Covenant (25)
God's Presence	**God's "Absence"**
God turns toward His people (9)	God sets His face against them (17)
God will dwell among them (11)	God sends them into captivity (38–39)
God walks among them (12)	God becomes their adversary (33)
Peace	**Peril**
Security (5)	Soul pines away/sudden terror (16)
Peace of mind (6)	Terror, fear, panic (36–37)
Beasts won't harm them (6)	Beasts destroy and decimate (22)
Prevail over their enemies (7–8)	Attacked by enemies—raids (16) Struck down by enemies (17) Ruled by enemies (17) Flee, but none pursue (17) Delivered into enemy hands (25) Scattered among nations (33) Destroy themselves—cannibalism (29)
Prosperity	**Poverty**
God gives rains in season (4)	God withholds the rains (19)
Crops will grow abundantly (4–5) Old grain cleared out for new (10)	Crops don't grow (20) Enemies raid and steal crops (16) Famine—lack of bread (26) Land is desolate (32)
Israelites fruitful and increase (9)	Consumption, fever, waste away (16) Wild animals decimate (22) Pestilence in cities kills (25) Israelites kill and eat their own (29)

LEVITICUS 27:1–34

THE VALUE OF A VOW

Setting Up the Section

The key to the structure of chapter 27 is found by the categories of things that are vowed as offerings to God. In a systematic way, this chapter deals with the various kinds of things that men and women may promise to dedicate to God. Regulations appropriate to each are then specified. The vows of Leviticus 27 are voluntary promises to offer a particular gift to God. But God, knowing human nature, makes provisions for vows that are made irresponsibly.

📖 27:1–8

PEOPLE

People could be devoted to God (Judges 11:30–31; 1 Samuel 1:11) to serve in ministry or to serve the priests in non-ceremonial roles. The monetary values set for these different categories of people (based on age and gender) serve to discourage vows that are not well thought out, as the money would have to be presented if the offered person was not presented to fulfill what had been promised.

📖 27:9–13

ANIMALS

In these verses, regulations are given regarding the gift of clean and unclean animals that could be offered to God (27:9–13) and used or sold. The vowed animals had to meet sacrificial standards and could not be replaced with a less valuable offering. If a man wanted to renege on a vow, he had to buy back the animal and pay a penalty.

📖 27:14–25

PROPERTY

The house in verses 14–15 is not attached to family land but is a piece of property that would not revert to the owner in the Year of Jubilee. The value of the house would be established by the priest, and if the offerer wanted to redeem the house, he had to pay that value plus a penalty.

A portion of inherited family land could be dedicated to God (27:16–21), but it would revert to the owner or his heirs in the Year of Jubilee. To redeem the field, the donor would be required to pay fifty shekels of silver for every certain amount of seed required for planting. The number of years remaining until Jubilee would determine the value of the gift. If the man who dedicated this field attempted to negate his vow by selling this property to another, then it would become property of the priests in the Jubilee year.

Someone could purchase another person's fields and devote them to God (27:22–25). In that case, the priest determines the property value and expects payment the same day, but the land would revert to the original owner at Jubilee.

📄 27:26–34

PROHIBITIONS AND TITHES

Unacceptable gifts include things that already belong to God (27:26), including tithes (27:30–33).

Demystifying Leviticus

Simply viewed, offering a vow is practicing a kind of credit card act of worship. It is a promise to worship God with a certain offering in the future, motivated by gratitude for God's grace in the life of the offerer. There is a delay in making the offering if the offerer is not able, at that moment, to follow through. The vow is made, promising to offer something to God if God will intervene on behalf of the individual, making the offering possible. Often the vow was made in a time of great need (see Genesis 28:20–22; Numbers 21:10–3; Judges 11:29–40; 13; 1 Samuel 1:10–11; Jonah 2:9).

While earlier chapters of Leviticus deal largely with compulsory offerings and obedience, the last chapter concludes by focusing the Israelites' attention on voluntary worship. The voluntary act of worshiping God by means of vows is the highest form of Old Testament worship. The legislation of this chapter assumes that people will make offerings in response to love, not to law.

Take It Home

These regulations taught the Israelites that it is a costly matter to break a vow. How many promises or commitments have been made to you—by a parent, friend, or business associate—that have been forgotten or ignored? How many times can you recall making a commitment you later regretted? This chapter highlights the importance of following through on promises and thinking them through before committing.

NUMBERS

INTRODUCTION TO NUMBERS

The book of Numbers derives its name from the two censuses taken of the nation of Israel at the beginning and the end of this book. Before being referred to as *Numbers*, this writing had also been known as *In the Desert* (or *Wilderness*), referring to the fact that the Israelites spent forty years in the desert.

AUTHOR

Many evangelical scholars consider Moses the author of Numbers. Additional support for Moses as the author is found in the fact that Jesus calls the first five books of the Bible "the book of Moses" (Luke 24:27, 44).

PURPOSE

The instructions included in the book of Numbers are intended to prepare the people to travel to Canaan. The families are counted and they are organized. Numbers accounts for the forty years the Israelites wandered in the wilderness and moves from the judgment that fell on the first generation that left Egypt to the hope of the second generation who would see God's promise come true.

OCCASION

This book covers a history of thirty-nine years in the travels of the Israelites from Mount Sinai to the border of the promised land. Throughout this book, Israel is sometimes seen as a complaining and rebellious nation, often needing God to intervene with discipline. In the midst of His discipline, however, this book also clearly establishes the reality that God will still keep His covenant and will continue to provide for the needs of His people. Thus, Numbers does not end with failure but with a generation ready to enter the promised land because of God's mercy and grace.

THEMES

Numbers highlights certain critical theological themes, including God's covenant with Abraham and His power to deliver. Along with that is the essential theme of the obedience (or disobedience) of the people. In addition, many of the laws that are described in Exodus are either restated or expanded upon in Numbers.

CONTRIBUTION TO THE BIBLE

Numbers is an important part of the first five books of the Old Testament. It links the book of Exodus to the book of Deuteronomy. Exodus shows the movement of Israel from Egypt to the early years of Sinai. Numbers picks up the next forty years, taking the Israelites from Sinai to the plains of Moab. Then Deuteronomy picks the story up in the plains of Moab and the final preparations to enter Canaan.

ISRAEL AT SINAI AND THE JOURNEY TO KADESH

NUMBERS 1:1–12:16

ISRAEL AT SINAI AND THE JOURNEY TO KADESH

Setting Up the Section

The book of Numbers opens with a census, a counting of the people. The nation of Israel is organized by tribes. This census prepares the tribes for their march, identifying those who will be fit for battle once the people enter the land. As a number of scholars have pointed out, this number is really more of a military registration than a simple census.

Verse 1 gives us a telling reference point. This census takes place in the second month of the second year after the Israelites have left Egypt. The Passover described in Numbers 9:1 was to have happened in the *first* month of the second year. So, while the facts and figures are included at the beginning of the book of Numbers, the census actually happens after the first Passover feast is commemorated.

📖 1:1–54

THE CENSUS PREPARATION AND RESULTS

The Lord commands Moses to take a census of all the Israelites, with an exclusive emphasis on those who will be able to function as soldiers (1:1–4). This census is taken by tribe, with a tribal leader listed (1:5–16). Each tribe is identified by the son of Jacob from whom they descended. Jacob was the grandson of Abraham. His name is later changed to Israel, thus the people as a whole are referred to as *Israelites*.

In verses 17–46, Moses provides the results of the census, with the numbers rounded off to the nearest hundred. The total is 603,550 men.

Following is the summary of each tribe:	
Reuben: 46,500	Ephraim (son of Joseph): 40,500
Simeon: 59,300	Manasseh (son of Joseph): 32,200
Gad: 45,650	Benjamin: 35,400
Judah: 74,600	Dan: 62,700
Issachar: 54,400	Asher: 41,500
Zebulun: 57,400	Naphtali: 53,400

Notice that Ephraim and Manasseh are both sons of Joseph. This means actually only eleven of Jacob's sons are represented. The missing son (and tribe) is Levi. God has a special purpose for the descendants of Levi (1:47–54). The Levites are not to be included as soldiers, but are to care for the tabernacle and all that belongs to it. They are to camp around it, protect it, and be responsible for dismantling it and setting it back up as the camp moves. This assignment elevates the role of the Levites and puts a priority on the role of worship among the people.

Take It Home

God orders the Levites to be set apart for the worship of God, which surely indicates a priority on worship. How important is worship to you? How much of your life do you set aside for it? Do you prepare for the role worship will play in your life, or do you leave it to the "professionals?"

📖 2:1–34

THE ARRANGEMENT OF THE CAMP

In order for the Israelites to live their nomadic lifestyle without falling into complete chaos, there would have to be some structure. In this case, the tabernacle becomes the hub around which the tribes are organized. The campsites are described in relation to the tabernacle—north, east, south, or west (2:1–31). Each tribe has a banner, or standard, that displays the tribe's symbol (2:1–2).

Campsites

	^ NORTH ^			
	Naphtali	Asher	Dan	
Ephraim				Judah
Manasseh		**TABERNACLE** (surrounded by Levites)		Issachar
Benjamin				Zebulun
	Gad	Simeon	Reuben	
		SOUTH		

This order held significance not only for camping and breaking camp, but also for traveling. The ark of the covenant always leads the way, carried by the priests, and the tribes to the east and south march ahead of the tabernacle, while those to the west and north march behind it.

Marching Diagram

Rear of the Column>>>>>   Front of the Column>>>>>>

Dan Asher Naphtali	Ephraim Manasseh Benjamin	Kohathites Carry the Tabernacle Furnishings	Reuben Simeon Gad	Gershonites and Merarites Carry the Tabernacle	Judah Issachar Zebulun	Levites Carry the Ark

📖 3:1–4:49

THE RESPONSIBILITIES OF THE LEVITES

Setting Up the Section

The Levites are given the care of the tabernacle. Once the people enter Canaan, the Levites will have no specific piece of land. Instead, they will be scattered throughout the land and will live off a portion of the offerings brought by the people.

The opening verses of chapter 3 include the names of the sons of Aaron: the first high priest, Nadab (the firstborn), and Abihu, Eleazar, and Ithamar. We don't know the exact nature of the error that causes Nadab and Abihu to be killed in the line of duty, but we know it was an improper worship connected to the censors (3:1–4).

The remainder of chapters 3 and 4 offers a double census of the descendants of Levi and a description of their responsibilities. The organization of the Levites through the rest of Numbers is according to the three sons of Levi. The priests, however, are a subset of the descendants of Kohath, those who would descend specifically from Aaron's family line.

- Descendants of Gershon: the curtains and coverings (3:21–26)
- Descendants of Kohath: the furniture and utensils (3:27–32)
- Descendants of Merari: the boards and bars (3:33–37)

Demystifying Numbers

Verses 40–51 discuss the substitution of the Levites for the firstborn sons and cattle of each of the other tribes. Traditionally, the firstborn belonged to the Lord, so they could be expected to be offered to the tabernacle for service (the sons) and sacrifice (the livestock). In this case, though, the Levites stand in the place of these firstborn, offering their service to the tabernacle instead.

When a family came to offer their firstborn to the tabernacle, or later, the temple, they had the opportunity to give money to redeem their son back into family life. The same thing happens here with the 273 firstborn who outnumber the Levites. A price is paid for their redemption—1,365 shekels, which is given to Aaron and his sons.

This practice of redeeming provides a kind of foreshadowing picture of the ransom that Christ paid in being the only begotten Son of God, who took our place and became the sacrifice.

While chapter 3 lists the duties of each family of Levi's descendants, chapter 4 delves deeper into their ministries.

The Kohathites between thirty and fifty years of age numbered those who could care for the holy objects of the Tent of Meeting after the priests had prepared them for removal (4:1–20). Rather than loading these objects onto wagons or animals, the Kohathites carry them. The items had to be covered before the Kohathites dealt with them, so they wouldn't be killed by touching them or looking at them. This is not an affirmation of the worth of these items as much as the purity of God.

The census of the Gershonites between thirty and fifty years of age numbered those who would carry the curtains of the tabernacle under direction of Aaron and his sons, especially Ithamar (4:21–28).

The census of the Merarites between thirty and fifty years of age numbered those who could carry the poles and tent pegs of the tabernacle, also under direction of Ithamar (4:29–33). These items would have been quite burdensome.

Verses 34–39 summarize the census, which numbers the Levites for service at 8,580.

Demystifying Numbers

Why put so much effort into the breakdown of the tabernacle? Partly because it highlights the seriousness with which God's holiness should be taken. In this scenario, this meticulous amount of care is an expression of respect.

CLEANSING THE CAMP

Setting Up the Section

As the Israelites prepare to go on the move, they must purify themselves. This pursuit of purity is meant to impact all their social interactions. In this chapter, God focuses the attention of the nation on dealing with three specific issues: physical impurities, moral impurities, and marital impurities.

In verses 1–4, Moses is to identify the ceremonially unclean people: any man or woman who has a skin disease (often wrongly interpreted as leprosy), a discharge (whether natural or related to infection), or is unclean because of contact with a dead body—human or animal. While the purpose here is associated with purity rather than health, the actions probably benefited the whole community.

Next are moral impurities (5:5–10). The Lord orders anyone who has wronged another to make full restitution to the one who was wronged. This restitution involves more than simply returning the offended person to the point before the loss, but also adding 20 percent. If the restitution can't be made directly to the person, then it is made to the family. If not the family, then to the priest. Under these guidelines, there is no excuse for not making wrongs right again. This is more than a matter of community; it is a matter of cleansing oneself before God who sees all.

Finally there is the issue of marital impurity. Verses 11–31 outline a test by which a man can ferret out suspected infidelity on the part of his wife. The test requires an offering and a drink of holy water with tabernacle dust (some consider this to imply a bitter herb) mixed in. The result of the test depends on how the woman's body responds to the liquid.

While this test seems foreign to contemporary minds, the first purpose it serves is to put the man and his wife in the midst of spiritual leadership—the tabernacle priest. An important point of this procedure is that it places the woman before God for Him to determine if she is guilty or innocent. The husband isn't free to act on his suspicions any way that he chooses.

Critical Observation

The test for infidelity described in verses 11–31 seems like a double standard to the contemporary mind. Where was the man with whom the woman was unfaithful? What if the woman suspected her husband of infidelity? The hard truth is that in this tribal culture, women were not given the same rights as men. There seems to be no demands made, for instance, on the husband who falsely accuses his wife. There are elements of this practice, however foreign it sounds to us, that did serve to protect women to a certain point.

In reality, the point of this test is to protect paternity rights so that a child by another man does not inherit the estate of the husband. That is why the negative consequences involve the shriveling of the "thigh" (a euphemism for the womb), which would result in a miscarriage.

📖 6:1–27

THE NAZIRITE VOW AND AARON'S BLESSING

Verses 1–20 outline the vow of the Nazirite. This is typically a temporary vow of spiritual dedication.

There are three marks of this vow, called a separation to God: abstaining from wine and grape products (6:3–4), not touching dead bodies (6:6–8), and not cutting one's hair (6:5).

The first two conditions are similar to the rules for priests during their terms of service. Wine would hinder the priests' vigilance (Leviticus 10:6–11), and the high priest could not even enter the place where a relative's corpse lay, although the ordinary priests could attend to a close relative (Leviticus 21:1–4, 11). Uncut hair, however, is peculiar to the Nazirite and symbolizes his commitment (Numbers 6:7). The word translated *Nazirite* is related to the Hebrew term which carries the idea of both a vow and a crown. This may contain a deliberate suggestion that the long hair functions as a crown—evidence of the vow.

If the vow is broken, for instance if someone can't escape touching a dead body, the Nazirite must pay a penalty and start fresh (6:9–12). When the period of dedication ends, he has to shave his head and burn the hair in the flames of the fellowship offering (6:13–21).

Critical Observation

Jesus is referred to as a Nazarene because he was from a town called Nazareth. This is an entirely different matter than the Nazirite vow discussed here.

There are examples of Nazirites in the Bible though. Samson was a Nazirite from birth (Judges 13; 16:17–20), and many think Paul made such a vow as well (Acts 18:18; 21:20–26). Apart from the priesthood, the Nazirite expressed the highest form of separation to the Lord. He was a token of Israel's dedication to God. Unlike some contemporary vows, the law was clear that vows had to be fulfilled (Deuteronomy 23:21–23), so the Nazirite vow, though temporary, was binding.

Numbers 6:22–27 contains the blessing God gives the Israelites. It is a frequently quoted spiritual blessing. God's face, described in this blessing as shining on His people, is a symbol of His presence. His favor is implied by the picture of Him turning His face toward the Israelites. Thus, this blessing is a prayer for God's presence and favor.

📖 7:1–89

THE DEDICATION OF THE TABERNACLE

Setting Up the Section

Chapters 7–9 describe the dedication of the tabernacle. The events of chapters 7–9 actually precede the events described in chapters 1–6.

Numbers 7 is the second longest chapter in the Bible. It describes the twelve-day festival in which the people bring gifts to be used in the tabernacle. Each day different tribes send a representative to offer the gifts. There is much repetition, but to the original readers of Numbers, this repetition is understood as an emphasis.

Moses completes the tabernacle setup as he has been instructed (7:1). In verses 2–11, the leaders of the tribes offer six covered carts (one for every two leaders) and twelve oxen (one for every leader). Moses daily accepts the carts and oxen for twelve days. He gives two carts and four oxen to the sons of Gershon, to carry the curtains and coverings of the tabernacle (3:21–26). He gives four carts and eight oxen to the sons of Merari, to carry the heavy boards and bars of the tabernacle (3:33–37). None are offered to the sons of Kohath, though. They are required to carry the holy objects on their shoulders (3:27–32). Even though the tribes offer the same gifts, Moses lists them separately, honoring each one (7:12–83).

Verses 84–89 serve as a summary of the gifts, and then God speaks to Moses. His message begins with chapter 8.

GOD DIRECTS MOSES

In verses 1–4, God gives instructions regarding the lampstands. They are to be mounted so their light falls forward, resembling a tree. This symbolizes the fact that God is the giver of life to mankind. It also may symbolize the fact that Israel is to be a light to the world. The light from this lamp also shines brightly upon the showbread, which symbolizes the daily provision of God.

Verses 5–26 prescribe how the whole Levite workforce (in place of the firstborn Israelites; 3:40–51) is dedicated and purified for their work, and how those who retire at age fifty may continue to help the younger Levites as guards in the tabernacle. The male members of the Levites are to be set apart by

- being cleansed by water and shaving their hair;
- washing their clothes;
- offering burnt, sin, wave, and grain offerings.

Without being made clean through an offering and a spiritual washing, the Levites could not serve God.

Take It Home

In this passage of Numbers, God is establishing what it means to be set apart for His service. Though we worship differently today, this issue of seeing ourselves as God's servants is still important. First Peter 2:9 tells us that all believers are a holy priesthood. We are set apart unto God for His purposes and glory. When Jesus Christ came, He did not do away with the priesthood; instead, He widened it so that all those who come to God through faith in Him become a holy priesthood, set apart for the work of God.

OBSERVANCE OF THE PASSOVER

Setting Up the Section

In Numbers 9:1–10:10 there are three very important aspects of life in Israel established—the Passover celebration, the presence of God in the cloud covering the tabernacle, and the silver trumpets that function as a kind of public address system.

On the first month of the second year after the people had come out of Egypt, God commands them to commemorate the Passover (9:1–14). Comparing Numbers 9:1 with Numbers 1:1 makes it obvious that this celebration must have preceded the census described at the opening of Numbers.

There are provisions made for those who are unable to celebrate the Passover at the appointed time, but the death penalty awaits those who do not celebrate at the appointed time if they are able (9:13). This underscores the priority on worship that runs throughout Numbers.

Critical Observation

The Passover is the celebration that remembers God's faithfulness in protecting the Israelites from the angel of death. The Passover also shows the grace of God. God not only spared the firstborn, but He also rescued the people and brought them out of slavery to the promised land.

The Israelites are to celebrate the Passover annually, as a way of remembering the grace and the mercy of God. These two great themes come to their fullest expression on the cross of Jesus, where Jesus stood as the Passover Lamb for mankind.

The means of guidance for the sons of Israel is the movement of the cloud over the tabernacle (9:15–23) and the sounding of two silver trumpets (10:1–10). Despite the failings of the nation, the cloud is always present. In fact, the presence of the Lord is seen all day: a cloud by day and fire by night. The Israelite people are not only reminded of the past, they also have the daily reminder of the present: God is with them. He is their God and they are His people.

Take It Home

When the cloud moves, the Israelites are to move. God directs the people to go where He wants them to go, when He wants them to go. The people, then, had to respond by obeying His direction. This passage contains eight references to God's orders and the Israelites' obedience (9:18, 20, 23). This underscores a subtheme of Numbers: It is a dangerous thing to know what God demands and not do it.

10:1–36

THE DEPARTURE

God commands Moses to make two hammered trumpets of silver (10:1–10). They are to be blown for several reasons: to gather the people, to sound an alarm for the camps to begin to move, and to mark celebrations (like the monthly festival mentioned in verse 10).

According to verse 9, these trumpets also act as a kind of prayer that God will hear His children and rescue them from their enemies.

On the twentieth day of the second month of the second year, Israel sets out in military array for the first time. The cloud leads them from the wilderness of Sinai to the wilderness of Paran (10:11–36). Because of the organization described in the previous chapters (instructions about which families would care for what parts of the tabernacle, and in what order they would travel), all the people have to do is follow the directions they have been given (10:13–17).

Verses 11–12 give a quick summary of the journey, then verse 13 begins a more detailed account.

Moses talks his brother-in-law, Hobab, into continuing on in the journey. Hobab understands the places to camp and how to function in the desert, so his presence has some advantages. Moses even promises Hobab that if he comes along, he will share in the blessings promised to the Israelites. (Though Hobab initially resists, he apparently changes his mind because his descendants are listed with the Israelites in Judges 1:16 and 4:11.)

Though Hobab's expertise is certainly useful to the Israelites, God does the leading. Verses 35 and 36 include two short hymns that celebrate God's direction. The first is a prayer for protection as the group moves. The other is a prayer for fellowship as the group settles.

📖 11:1–35

DISSENSION IN THE RANKS

Setting Up the Section

The people have now become frustrated with their circumstances. The inconveniences and sacrifices required of them are great, and they begin to complain. They have lost sight of God's promises and have become focused on their immediate suffering.

In verses 1–3, only three days into their journey from Sinai, the people begin to complain about their difficulties—and God responds. Fire from the Lord may imply lightning, but the text is not that specific. When the people cry for help, Moses intercedes for them. The place is called *Taberah*, which means "burning." Yet, in the following verses, the complaining continues.

In verses 4–9, the Israelites still don't return their attention to God, and instead keep their focus on the next problem in their lives. In this case they complain about the food God has provided: manna. It seems that they forget the sweat, labor, pain, and enslavement that had been a part of their lives in Egypt and remember only the food.

Critical Observation

The manna God provides is like a seed of grain, and looks like small, clear drops. The name is commonly thought to be derived from an expression of surprise, "What is it?" More probable is it derives from a word that means "to allot," denoting an allotment or a gift. Generally, manna has been associated with a byproduct of the tamarisk tree found in northern Arabia.

The mixed multitude of verse 4, sometimes interpreted *rabble*, or *riffraff*, that seems to instigate this round of grumbling is not clearly defined here, though it likely refers to the non-Israelites who traveled with the group out of Egypt (Exodus 12:38).

Upon hearing the cries of widespread dissatisfaction from the people, God is considerably angered, and Moses is distressed (Numbers 11:10–15). The dissension is so great that Moses becomes exasperated at the people for making his role as a leader unbearable, and resentful toward God for assigning him this overwhelming burden of leadership. Prior to this, Moses worked hard to intercede for the people. Now, temporarily, his focus is on finding an end to his own misery.

The conversation between God and Moses in verses 16–35 deals with the situation on two levels—the immediate problem of feeding the people and the long-term problem of leading the people.

The first strategy is for Moses to appoint seventy elders among the Israelites (11:16–17). Seventy of these men, a number suggestive of a full complement of persons, are to be endowed with the Spirit of God for assisting Moses in bearing the burdens of the people as spiritual leaders. This spiritual dimension differentiates this group from those appointed for administrative and judicial tasks in Exodus 18:25–26.

The next strategy is a double-edged sword. God provides directions for the larger populace to consecrate themselves prior to receiving the blessing from the Lord (Numbers 11:18–23). In this case, though, the so-called blessing described in verses 19–20 is one that will wear out its welcome. Notice the emphatic nature of the description in verse 19—not one, two, five, ten, or even twenty days, but for an entire month (more than twenty-nine days) they will receive meat.

Demystifying Numbers

Consecration is a term used here to describe the process of purification through bathing. The purpose, which is what makes it a spiritual process, is to be prepared to receive the presence of the Lord. Ritual purity was necessary before offering sacrifices and as preparation for celebrating festivals such as Passover. Here, it is to prepare for God's blessing.

In verses 21–23, Moses reminds God of the numbers of the people. The promised meat would need to be in astronomical quantities. In his disbelief, Moses challenges God's ability to meet the needs of the people in the wilderness. Still, in verses 24–25, he follows through with the first stage of the instructions (11:16).

The promise God gives in verse 17 is fulfilled in verse 25, but according to the text, it seems to be a one-time event that proved God's presence.

Two of the men—Eldad and Medad—who had been registered among the seventy elders remained in the camp and prophesied there. An unknown young man (perhaps Joshua, who voices the complaint of 11:28) gives witness of this phenomenon back to Moses, who is still gathered at the Tent with the other sixty-eight. The generosity that Moses exhibits here seems to imply that he has gathered his spiritual and personal resources after his lack of faith evidenced in verses 16–35. While there aren't many specifics about why these two men didn't join the others, the fact that they face no judgment from God makes it appear benign, though it doesn't seem so to Joshua.

Critical Observation

Joshua, the son of Nun, is introduced in the account of the Israelites as a leading warrior in the first battle against the Amalekites (Exodus 17:8–14). When Moses meets with the Lord at the Tent of Meeting, which is at first outside the camp of Israel (Exodus 33:7–11), the young Joshua remains at the Tent even after Moses departs. Here, Joshua acts as an assistant to Moses, calling for Moses to force Eldad and Medad to cease their prophesying. Joshua perhaps sees these two men as a threat to Moses' leadership.

Moses' response to Joshua contrasts considerably with that of his earlier expressions of complaint and despair (11:28–31). Instead of feeling threatened, Moses commends the event. An undercurrent in Moses' response may be his own desire for further relief from the heavy responsibility of leadership, but it also reveals a heart open to God's leadership.

Verses 31–32 describe the wind that brought the quail to the camp. The magnitude of the quail is measured in three ways:

- The breadth of distribution: a day's journey in each direction, or twelve to fifteen miles
- The depth of the piles: about 3 feet high (though some interpret this as the level at which the quail flew)
- The amount individually collected: at least ten homers over a two-day period, a volume estimated at between thirty-eight and sixty-five bushels. The homer is the largest dry volume measure in the Hebrew vocabulary.

Some of the birds are eaten right away, while most of them are spread out around the camp, presumably for drying the meat after cleaning and salting it. While the people are processing and eating the quail, the Lord's anger burns against many of those who had gathered too much, and they are struck down and die, possibly from food poisoning.

In verse 35, the journey continues toward Hazeroth. This precise location is conjecture.

Take It Home

Grumbling is a form of rebellion against God. It comes from losing sight of His promises and is an attack against His nature and character. If you forget the promises of God, the only thing you can look at is the problems of the present. Where are your eyes today?

📖 12:1–16

FROM DISSENSION TO TREASON

In Hebrews, the grammar of the opening verses of chapter 12 suggests that Miriam is the one leading the attack against Moses, but she is backed by her brother Aaron. This conflict is bigger than a family squabble. Miriam and Aaron have national religious positions of leadership, and they are challenging the leadership of Moses as sole mediator between God and Israel. Though the question seems to be about Moses' wife's ethnicity, it is really Moses' right to lead that is at the heart of the issue.

Critical Observation

Ethnic purity was an important issue in ancient Israel, but only in the protection of religious purity. This is evidenced in the instructions of Ezra to his countrymen to separate themselves from their pagan foreign wives before they could lead their husbands into idolatry.

Throughout the law of the Old Testament, however, there are explicit instructions that there is one code of law for the native Israelites and the sojourning foreigners in the land. In Numbers 9:14, aliens living among the Israelites could celebrate the Passover if they do so according to the statutes. So while Miriam and Aaron's charge against Moses has some foundation, it isn't entirely valid.

The gravity of Miriam and Aaron's objections is amplified in the last words of verse 2—God heard. Verse 3 interjects a kind of character witness on behalf of Moses.

In verses 4–8, all three siblings are summoned to come out to the tabernacle, a central locale that offers a reminder of the presence of the Lord. In verses 6–8, the Lord affirms Moses' unique commission as a prophet of God, a man who stands above the others among the Israelites, such as the recently endowed seventy elders, as well as above Miriam and Aaron. He is also the mediator of the covenant, hearing from God directly. Since this is the case, how could Miriam and Aaron dare to speak against him? To speak against God's servant is tantamount to speaking against God Himself.

The immediate response of the Lord to Miriam is one of anger, followed by withdrawal (12:9–13). The charges against Moses are dismissed and judgment meted out. When the cloud of God's presence withdraws, Moses and Aaron witness their sister's skin disease that requires her separation from the tabernacle and from the community itself.

Critical Observation

That Miriam rather than Aaron is plagued by the disease reinforces the idea that Miriam is the chief instigator of the dispute. Whatever the skin disease Miriam contracted, she would become an outcast from society, forced to live outside the holy camp. The laws regarding various skin diseases required the afflicted to live on the outskirts of the camp or town so as to not defile the purity of the community (Leviticus 13:45–46).

Aaron immediately apologizes to Moses, addressing him as lord and submissively confessing his sin of rebellion. This may have been an attempt to lighten the potential judgment against himself in the face of Miriam's judgment. But out of concern for his sister, he begs Moses for her healing, and Moses begs God for the same (12:11–13).

Moses' request is that she be given the kind of punishment she would have experienced if her father had spat on her face in contempt—seven days. This is also the standard period for the purification process for a leper (Leviticus 14:1–32).

Israel will not disembark on the next stage of the journey until the Lord leads them by the cloud. The rebellion of Miriam has consequences for the entire community as they wait for her purification.

Verse 16 marks the departure from Hazeroth toward the Desert of Paran in the modern southern Negev, or northeast Sinai region. The Paran wilderness is the goal of the first phase of the journey (10:11), and from that area the spies are to be sent to explore Canaan (13:3).

NUMBERS 13:1–21:35

ISRAEL DELAYED AT KADESH AND THE JOURNEY TO MOAB

Setting Up the Section

The events recorded here took place while Israel was camped at Kadesh. The sending of the spies and all that came from this event became engraved on the corporate memory of God's people. Later writers refer back to these incidents with a sense of painful disappointment (see Deuteronomy 1:26–46; Psalm 95:10–11).

📖 13:1–14:45

FROM TREASON TO REJECTION TO REBELLION

This account records one of the biggest mistakes made by the nation of Israel. At the heart is the question of whether circumstances can outpower God's plan.

In Exodus 3:8, Moses had been told by God that Canaan would be spacious and have an abundance of food. Here in Numbers, Moses chooses twelve leaders from the tribes of Israel to explore Canaan (13:1–16). While these leaders were chosen from the tribes, they weren't the tribal leaders. These spies were to evaluate the people, the land, and the cities (13:17–20). The twelve spies travel from the south (wilderness of Zin) to the north (Rehob) and return after forty days with their report (13:21–24).

Except for Caleb, the spies report that although the land is rich, it also is inhabited by mighty people who could outpower them (13:25–33). Ten of the spies report that in relation to these giants, the people of Israel look like grasshoppers. The spies who make the majority report only saw the giants, whereas Joshua and Caleb saw victory.

Demystifying Numbers

The descendants of Anak, the giants, are noted for their great size and strength (13:28). They are described as being related to the Nephilim (13:33), who lived on the earth before the flood (Genesis 6:4). Since the Nephilim would have been wiped out by the flood, however, these descendants of Anak were only associated with the Nephilim because of their great size.

The people responded to the spies' report with despair, prompting Moses and Aaron to prostrate themselves in the presence of God (14:1–10). The people's despair is a rejection of faith. When God is rejected, people become disillusioned and turn toward their past bondage.

Take It Home

To Caleb and Joshua, God is bigger than their enemies (14:6–9). These two see the land through the eyes of faith. To the other ten spies, the problems seem bigger than God. They minimize the greatest resource they have—the fact that God has already promised them the land. When a person acknowledges the power of God, he or she will not minimize the divine resources available.

After Joshua and Caleb stand against the majority, the people want to stone them. Then God appears. The Israelites' actions are actually a rebellion against God Himself—more than a rejection of the two men.

When God speaks of destroying the people, Moses intercedes on the basis of God's character (14:11–19). He reasons that the nations will hear about this destruction and it would impugn God's character. Moses declares God's glory and seeks to protect it.

The people are pardoned, but because of their sin, the generation from age twenty and older (except for Caleb and Joshua) would wander for forty years (one year for every day of the spies' investigation) and die in the wilderness (14:20–35). These people had treated God with contempt. Although He provided them with proof over and over again that He is their deliverer, they still refused to believe Him.

After the plague that attacks the spies, only Joshua and Caleb remain of the group that had investigated Canaan (14:36–45). Taking matters from bad to worse, the people continue to demonstrate their rebellion by entering the land against all instruction from Moses (14:39–45). This is an attempt to reverse their consequences, but of course they are soundly defeated by the Amalekites and Canaanites. Only through God's strength do they find victory.

Take It Home

From a spiritual point of view, the value of sending in the spies was not to determine if the conquest was possible, but to show Israel what God was going to give His people. This was not intended to be a joint decision, but a time of excitement and revelation. They were to see all that God was providing for them. Instead, they looked at the land through faithless eyes and sent the nation into a tailspin. Their story reminds us to notice how we are viewing the promises God has made in our lives. Do we believe or do we question?

📖 15:1–41

RENEWING WORSHIP

Setting Up the Section

Though we often think of the book of Numbers as the Israelites' journey across the wilderness, Numbers 15 marks the beginning of the only five chapters of this book that provide narratives of that journey (15–19).

This chapter also marks the first set of instructions for the people who now know they will wander in this wilderness until their deaths. Notice that this section begins with the reaffirmation of worship. The first thing God does after the pronouncement of the consequences of Israel's sin is reestablish the worship He wants from His people.

When the Israelites enter Canaan, they are to provide meal, oil, and wine as their thanksgiving offering (15:1–16). Today, we offer money because that is the fruit of our labors. In the case of these Israelites, who would eventually settle into farming and cultivating vineyards, these offerings were a gift of their labors.

Verses 3–10 describe a number of different styles of sacrifices and offerings. Leviticus 1–7 provides the guidelines for these rituals.

Just as the foreigners living among the Israelites are able to take part in the Passover, verses 14–16 include these foreigners in worship. While the Israelites are considered the people of God, their God accepts worship from anyone who is willing to be in right relationship with Him.

When the Israelites enter Canaan, they are to offer from the food of the land the first of their dough throughout their generations (15:17–21). This is an expression of gratitude for the harvest of grain.

The next instructions, listed in verses 22–29, change gears to deal with unintentional sins—sins of omission rather than commission. When the nation or an individual (native or alien) inadvertently sins against the commands of God, they are to make a sin offering.

On the other hand, if one sins defiantly, it is considered blasphemy, a capital crime. Verses 32–36 give an example of a man who is found gathering wood on the Sabbath. He is brought before Moses and Aaron, and then stoned by the congregation outside of the camp as God commands. While this is an extreme and uncomfortable example for the contemporary mind, it is the full knowledge with which the man committed the sin, rather than the details, that prompted his judgment.

In verses 37–41, God commands Moses to tell the Israelites to put tassels on the corners of their garments with a cord of blue through each. These tassels are to be constant reminders, not of one particular law, but of the relationship they solidified with God by their obedience. The color blue is related to both heaven and royalty in the minds of the Israelites.

THE REBELLION OF KORAH

This chapter marks the fifth complaint of the Israelites in the desert, this time against the authority of Aaron and his priestly line. In verses 1–3, the chief rebel is Korah, who descended from Levi through his son Kohath. As a Kohathite, he has high duties at the tabernacle—but he isn't a priest. Just as Korah wants more power, so do Dathan, Abiram, and On (who is not mentioned again). The rebels rise up against Moses and Aaron with 250 leaders of the community. The heart of their accusation is Moses' arrogance in claiming a special relationship with God. These rebels want the same privilege.

When the leaders accuse Moses and Aaron of exalting themselves in verses 4–7, Moses does not try to convince the rebels of his calling. Although it's clear that he's angry, he will let God defend him, if God so chooses.

Critical Observation

The test described here involves offering incense because this was one of the most holy responsibilities of the priests. The fatal disaster of Nadab and Abihu, priests who died by offering strange fire, seems to confirm this (Leviticus 10:1–3).

In Numbers 16:8–11, Moses also rebukes the Levites under Korah and his company, making it clear that their rebellion is against God, because they want to exalt themselves rather than wait for Him to exalt them. In verses 12–15, Moses summons Dathan and Abiram to come to him, but they refuse.

In the confrontation recorded in verses 16–24, the glory of God appears with the intention to destroy the entire congregation, save Moses and Aaron. Moses quickly asks God to spare those who did not follow the sin of these men. In verses 25–35, Moses announces the severity of what will happen—the Lord opens the ground and swallows up the households of the rebels and the 250 men who were offering incense. This event leaves no question as to God's stance on the rebellion, nor do His orders to Eleazar, to use the censers of the rebels to plate the altar—an ongoing reminder.

Demystifying Numbers

There is much we still don't know about Korah's rebellion. We don't know exactly when it took place. It could have occurred soon after the spies returned, or sometime during the four decades of wandering in the desert. What kind of disaster ended the rebellion is also unclear. Some speculate that the rebels' tents were pitched on a mudflat, common to the area, that's hard on the surface but boggy underneath. If the crust breaks, anything on its surface can be swallowed up. Whatever the details of the event, its record here stands as a reminder of the importance of surrendering to God's plan.

Perhaps not surprisingly, the next day the people complain again, accusing Moses and Aaron of causing the death of Korah and his men. The truth, however, is that Moses and Aaron had asked for the survival of the same people who are continuing to complain against them (16:41). Thus follows a plague (16:43–49) that kills 14,700. The deaths only stop because of Aaron's intercession. We aren't given a lot of details about the nature of this plague or what Moses' actions may have been in the midst of it, but the account serves to set up a transition to the next passage regarding Aaron's leadership.

📖 17:1–13

AARON'S ROD—GOD'S AFFIRMATION OF HIS MEN

The story of Aaron's rod is the third in a series that demonstrates the divine sanction of the priestly leadership of Aaron and the Levites. This incident, though, is inverted in structure compared with the first two (Korah's rebellion and the plagues at the end of chapter 16). Rather than people's complaints precipitating the threat of destruction, here God seeks to prove Aaron's call once and for all, and the people end up crying out to God for fear of destruction.

Demystifying Numbers

Each of the twelve tribal leaders has a staff with the name of the current leader carved into the wooden rod. These staffs symbolize the tribe and the authority of the leader.

In verses 1–7, the staffs of the twelve tribal leaders are to be brought inside the inner-most holy chamber and placed before the throne of God. This placement demonstrates the gravity of the occasion. The staff that sprouts leaves, then, will represent the leader whom God has appointed to stand before Him. Only God can impart life to that which is dead, and this test will show the combined tribes of Israel that God has conferred a special blessing upon the tribe whom He chooses.

The following morning, Moses enters the inner Tent of the Testimony and finds that not only has Aaron's staff sprouted, but God has caused it to bud, blossom, and produce almonds (17:8–13).

Critical Observation

The almond is one of the earliest trees to bud and blossom in the spring, and the fruit ripens in early to mid summer. But for a dead limb to sprout, bud, blossom, and produce ripe almonds overnight is a remarkable wonder, a natural process made supernatural. The almond branch in Israelite art and literature was a symbol of life that derived from their Maker. The bud and flower were shaped so elegantly that the three golden bowls on each side of the tabernacle lampstand were patterned after them (Exodus 25:31–40).

Moses subsequently returns with the twelve staffs so that the Israelites can observe the results. The priority of the Aaronic priesthood is vindicated.

The unanswered question closing Numbers 17—Are we all going to die?—will be resolved in the following two chapters, which contain the instructions from God concerning a proper approach to a holy and just God.

📖 **18:1-32**

RENEWED COMMITMENT TO THE LEVITICAL ORDER

Israel's high priests (Aaron's family line) and the Levites in general, as guardians of the tabernacle, are called to a dangerous and crucial task. After affirming their position to the Israelites, God now spells out to Aaron the Levites' roles, responsibilities, regulations, and rewards.

Numbers 18:1-7 reiterates (and builds upon) certain aspects of the priestly roles outlined in Numbers 3-4 (also Leviticus 8-10). The most basic responsibility is to be accountable for any potential sacrilege against the innermost holy place in the tabernacle. The priests must monitor their own purity as well.

The priests are allowed to keep some of the offerings given by the people (Numbers 18:8-19). This priestly tribute is divided into two levels of sanctity, the *most holy* offerings and the generally *holy* offerings. The holiest of the offerings, which are to be consumed by the priests, are cereal offerings, sin (purification) offerings, and guilt (reparation) offerings. The cereal grain offering, as described in 2:1-13 and 6:14-23, is an unleavened mixture of fine flour, oil, and incense. A memorial portion is burned on the altar as a sweet aroma to God, and the remainder is eaten by the priests.

The second level of tribute consists of the variety of firstfruits and firstborn gifts. The first fruit from the trees and offspring from the womb (people and livestock) are treated as special gifts from God that are to be returned to Him. Verses 12-18 provide guidelines for these offerings.

Critical Observation

God has much to say about firstborn gifts. The firstborn are the first male from the womb of the mother, whether human or animal. Animals defined by Levitical law as clean—such as cattle, sheep, and goats—are to be offered as sacrifices. Since humans cannot be sacrificed (nor unclean animals), a redemption price is established to be given instead of the firstborn. The process of human and animal redemption has a teaching purpose, too. It reminds the Israelites of their redemption from Egypt.

Numbers 18:19 restates the fact that the tribute from Israel is a gift from God for the priestly families, both male and female. God calls it "an everlasting covenant of salt" (NIV). Though the origin of this covenant is unknown, the function of salt in ancient Near Eastern society included the concepts of preservation and permanence.

Though the Levites receive no land, God is their inheritance. This is not to say that the priests and Levites somehow owned God (18:20–24). Instead, what physically accrued to God from the territorial inheritance of the Israelites would belong to them. These gifts become the Levites' birthright instead of territorial grant.

Critical Observation

The tithe, or *tenth*, is the required percentage of the productivity of Israelite labors that is to be rendered to God at the tabernacle (18:21). The statutes on tithing and the relationship between the Levites and the other Israelites are expanded in Deuteronomy 12:17–19 and 14:22–29.

During the wilderness journey, the Levites camp immediately around the tabernacle, serving as a barrier between the tabernacle and the community at large. This responsibility was a perpetual one. The contributions of the Israelites to God are, in turn, His gifts to these Levites for their dedicated service.

The previous accounts involve rules and regulations found elsewhere in the Pentateuch. Starting in verse 25, however, a new law emerges (18:25–32). The Levites are responsible to tithe to God, and thus to the priesthood, out of the tithes they receive. Furthermore, they are to contribute, in this tithe of the tithe, the very best of what is bestowed upon them. The original tithe, designated as the Levite inheritance in exchange for their service in the tabernacle, is treated like income. Like the other Israelites, the Levites are to tithe on this income.

📖 19:1–1:22

PURIFICATION

Setting Up the Section

Numbers 19 offers the cleansing process for those who have been in contact with a dead body. This is an important ceremony for the Israelites, because the nation will encounter many deaths on a daily basis for several decades. Thus, they must be prepared as to how they are going to remain ceremonially clean after dealing with a dead body.

Verses 1–13 outline a ritual involving an unblemished red cow. The cow is to be brought to Eleazar, the priest, and slaughtered outside of the camp. Eleazar then is to sprinkle some of the cow's blood toward the front of the tabernacle before the cow is completely burned. After burning, its ashes are to be mixed with cedar wood, hyssop, and scarlet material, then it is to be used to clean those who have touched a corpse.

The animal designated for sacrifice is a young cow. The color red may symbolize blood, but that is uncertain. The exact age of the animal is not made clear by the Hebrew, but the fact that it is not to be allowed to pull the plow or do any other type of work suggests it may have just reached maturity.

Eleazar is the one who is to receive the animal. He is the second, or deputy, high priest, and he is selected for this duty because the job causes the participant to incur temporary defilement, which the high priest can not.

Some details that set this ritual apart from the sacrifices at the tabernacle are that the animal is led out of the camp rather than being slaughtered at the altar. Also, every part of the cow is consumed by fire except the blood used in sprinkling.

The ingredients mixed with the ashes are the same as those employed in the sprinkling of lepers (Leviticus 14:4-7). Numbers 19:14-22 explains the use for this mixture. Anyone who even enters the tent of a dead person needs to be sprinkled with this mixture of water and ashes from the red cow on the third and seventh days (after the contact with the dead body) in order to be cleansed. In addition, the one who performs the sprinkling, as well as all the things that the unclean person touches, will be considered unclean until evening. These rituals for dealing with the dead, though mysterious, helped preserve the sanitary conditions of the camp.

📖 20:1-29

A SAD DAY

Setting Up the Section

In Numbers 20, Moses faces a series of sad events, beginning with the death of his sister, Miriam. This chapter highlights the seriousness with which we must treat the Word of God. In addition, it shows how God is faithful to Israel, in allowing a next generation to emerge so that His work might continue.

When the Israelites come in the first month to the wilderness of Sin, or Zin in some translations, and stay at Kadesh, Miriam dies and is buried there (20:1). Miriam is the leading female character in the story of the Exodus. This account of her death sets the somber mood for the rest of the chapter.

At Kadesh, the people resume their murmuring about lack of water, and rebel against Moses and Aaron because of it. They again lose sight of the plan of God and are caught in the misery of the moment. God commands Moses to take the rod, gather the community, and speak to the rock; then it will bring forth water (20:2-13).

For unknown reasons, Moses instead takes the rod, gathers the community, speaks to them with a hasty and passionate voice, and then strikes the rock twice.

There are two things that Moses and Aaron get wrong: the first is their unbelief, and the second is their lack of obedience. Believing is not just mentally agreeing with God; it is actually doing what God says. The consequence of their actions is severe—they will be prevented from bringing the people into Canaan.

The waters are called *Meribah* because the meaning of this name reflects the fact that Israel contended with God, but God proved Himself holy among them. Naming locations like this is meant to teach future generations about the history of Israel, and about all that God did in that region.

Following the two great blows already described in chapter 20—Miriam's death and the conflict at Meribah—Moses has to deal with the Edomites, who will not allow them to pass to Canaan (20:14-21).

Moses makes a diplomatic request to go through the land of Edom, but the Edomites state they will attack Israel before letting them pass through. Moses counters: What if they only pass via the main roads? And if any of the livestock drinks any of their water, they will pay for it. Edom still refuses, and the Israelites find another way.

Critical Observation

The Edomites are descendants of Esau, who was the twin brother of Jacob, forefather to the Israelites. The story of these brothers, told in Genesis 25–27, is filled with conflict. Understanding the distant family history, generations past, adds to the conflict described here in Numbers 20.

Chapter 20 opens with the death of Miriam and closes with the death of Aaron (20:22–29). When the Israelites come to Mount Hor, near the border of Edom, Moses, in obedience to God, takes Aaron and his son, Eleazar, up the mountain. (Scholars are not certain where Mount Hor is located, despite an early tradition identifying it with Jebel Nebi Harun near Petra.) There he gives Aaron's garments to Eleazar, and Aaron dies. When Moses places Aaron's vestments on Eleazar's shoulders, he is also transferring his responsibilities as Israel's high priest, the supreme mediator between God and Israel. The people mourn for Aaron for thirty days.

This point in the lives of the Israelites seems to be the lowest so far. Yet, God is allowing the next generation to take over, to carry on the work. God is still working and preparing the next generation to live in Canaan.

📖 **21:1–35**

SO NEAR, YET SO FAR: LESSONS ALONG THE WAY

After Aaron's death, Moses alone leads the Israelites closer to Canaan. Moving northward, the king of Arad attacks them and takes captives (21:1–3). This is an important first battle because it establishes a pattern. God will do the winning. The Israelites acknowledge that unless God gives their foes into their hands, they will not have any success.

The Israelites vow that if God will give the Canaanites into their hands, they will obey Him by completely destroying the cities. After this battle, the location is called Hormah, which means "destruction." *Hormah* became an ancient town on the southernmost borders of Palestine, not far from Kadesh. Tell Arad marks the spot today.

Later, when the people are traveling from Mount Hor to the Red Sea, they begin to grumble again about their circumstances and food (21:4–9). Remember that they are on this longer road to the promised land because the king of Edom refused to allow them to travel through his land (10:14–21). Perhaps because this journey is long, morale sinks.

When one complains, he or she is essentially saying that God has not provided the way He should have. It is an attack. This is why God responds by sending fiery serpents. The desert near the head of the Gulf of Aqabah is known for being infested with venomous reptiles. In fact, there are lizards, that raise themselves in the air and swing themselves from branches, and scorpions, which are particularly dangerous because they lie hidden in the grass. The people now face a threat, and in humility, they admit their misstep and ask for help from Moses.

According to God's instructions, Moses fashions the brass serpent and elevates it in plain sight of everyone in the camp. Every bitten Israelite who looks to it will be healed. Why this method? It is not that the brass snake or the pole is magical; it is the people's opportunity to choose faith and obey. Thus salvation is brought to the nation for their sin.

This is the last recorded occasion in which Israel grumbles about the food and yearns for Egypt.

Critical Observation

This form and method of salvation—the brass snake raised high—has become a picture of Jesus, hung on the cross, able to save those who look upon Him in faith (John 3:14, 15; 2 Corinthians 5:21).

In verses 10–21, Israel moves to the eastern frontier of the Edomites, in the valley of Zared. Then they pitch their tents on the other side of Arnon (now called El-Mojib). This is a deep, broad, and rapid stream, dividing the land of the Moabites and Amorites. In both places, God provides camp space and water.

Demystifying Numbers

In addition to the Bible, other sources written from this era record the history of Israel. Two sources were *The Book of Jashar* (see Joshua 10:13; 2 Samuel 1:18) and *The Book of the Wars of God*, mentioned in Numbers 21:14. Based upon these three short mentions, these two books were collections of victory songs and stories of the powerful acts of God working through His leaders during the early formation of Israel. Unfortunately, neither book survived, but their mention shows some of the alternate ways that God worked in spreading the word of His mighty power in calling, forming, growing, and protecting the nation of Israel.

The song of the well in Numbers 21:17–18 may also have come from *The Book of the Wars* (mentioned in verse 14). For those living in the desert, finding water is the most essential act for survival. In this song it appears as if princes, using their official rods only, not spades, find a well that is concealed by the brushwood or the sand. This song is a song of praise for the great provision of God.

In the account of Sihon, king of the Amorites, Israelite messengers request permission to march through their land, promising not take anything and to leave the city and its supplies alone (21:21–32). In addition, they will stay on the king's highway, which is the ancient trade route used by many merchants. This request is rejected, and Sihon sends troops to fight Israel. Unlike the similar situation with the Edomites (20:14–21), Israel has no alternate route, so they must stand and fight. In this case, they are victorious.

It is meaningful to note Genesis 15:16 here: "In the fourth generation your descendants will come back here, for the sin of the Amorites has not yet reached its full measure" (NIV). This is a promise that the Israelites will be brought back to the land of the Amorites, and as a form of judgment, they will defeat the Amorites and take their land, just as it happens here.

Critical Observation

The song of Heshbon was an old Amorite taunt song in which the Amorites taunt the Moabites because they had lost in battle. In it, an earlier Amorite conquest was celebrated over the Moabites. According to this song, Chemosh, a Moabite god, did not deliver the Moabites from the hands of the Amorites. The Jews are using this as their own taunt song, thus giving praise to God.

The Israelites make their way through various villages, clearing out many of the Amorites. God then directs them to turn and go up by the way of Bashan, a hilly region east of the Jordan, lying between the mountains of Hermon on the north and those of Gilead on the south (21:33–35). There lies an intimidating foe, Og, who is a giant (see Deuteronomy 3:11). This likely describes the size of the inhabitants that scare the spies in Numbers 13. The Lord tells Moses not to fear this man and gives Og over to the Israelties. God clearly shows the Israelites that they need Him at every turn on this journey.

The idea here in verse 14 is that God is celebrated as being a great warrior who has settled on the edge of the promised land with strength, power, and victory. In short, the Israelites are worshiping God for His great power and strength as they sit on the edge of Canaan waiting to go in.

ISRAEL AT MOAB ANTICIPATING THE PROMISED LAND

Setting Up the Section

The deceptively simple but profound story of Balaam and his donkey begins a period in which the Israelites—poised on the border of the promised land—encamp for an apparently lengthy time at the foot of the mountains of Moab, not unlike their encampment four decades prior at Sinai.

These accounts are humorous as well as somber. Some characters are stupid and stubborn, and there is more spiritual awareness in the donkey than in the humans. Structurally, watch for threes: the donkey avoids the angel three times, Balaam arranges for three sets of sacrifices, he has three encounters with God, and so on. The narrative itself extends over six days, through Numbers 24.

22:1–24:25

BALAAM'S STORY

As this account begins, Israel is about four months away from the end of the forty years' desert exile. When the sons of Israel camp in the plain of Moab, Balak, son of the king, becomes afraid. He has heard about Israel's victory over the Amorites.

Balak comes up with a plan. He seeks to defeat Israel by having Balaam, a Mesopotamian prophet, proclaim a curse upon Israel. An ancient text, the *Tell Deir 'Allah*, suggests that Balaam is a soothsayer of great renown in this region. The local text of that region suggests that he sees visions and dreams. Thus, he is an obvious choice for Balak to turn to for spiritual help. Balak sends a message requesting help and a fee.

When Balaam seeks direction from God, it is clear that the children of Israel are a blessed people and that it would be wrong to put a curse upon them. Yet, Balak sends another, more impressive delegation with a promise of more money in payment for the curses. In the end Balaam goes, but with the determination to only speak God's words.

Verses 21–35 tell the story of Balaam's journey. As he begins to leave with the leaders of Balak, he is stopped by his donkey. An angel of the Lord is in the road with a sword in his hand. This signifies that if Balaam tries to go to Balak, he will be killed. Balaam's donkey saves his life by not walking, despite being beaten.

Three times the donkey tries to avoid the angel. Then the donkey is given the ability to speak and converses with Balaam. Finally, Balaam sees the angel, who reveals that the donkey saved his life and that Balaam must speak only God's words.

This is not to say that God tells Balaam to go and then gets mad at him for going. The account probably implies that Balaam was not planning to carry out what God had requested.

In verses 36–41, Balak comes to meet Balaam, a gesture of some import, because the son of the king could have waited until Balaam came to him. Balak is upset with Balaam for not coming when first invited. He may have wondered if Balaam didn't believe Balak could pay—"Am I not able to honor you?" (22:37 NET).

Balak holds a banquet for Balaam and takes him to the high place of Baal to see a portion of Israel, perhaps hoping that this will make Balaam's curses stronger.

Critical Observation

Some scholars portray Balaam as a saintly seer; others as a money-hungry heathen sham. In the beginning of the story, he appears positive, intent on listening to God. Other Bible passages aren't so flattering, for instance Deuteronomy 23:4–5; 2 Peter 2:15; Jude 11; and Revelation 2:14.

Each of Balaam's blessings concerning Israel reiterates and confirms one of the promises of the Abrahamic covenant. What is about to take place in the life of Israel is a part of the fulfillment of what was spoken to Abraham in Genesis 12.

- **The first oracle (23:7–10):** Israel will be multiplied like the dust of the earth.
- **The second oracle** (23:18–24): Balaam proclaims that with God as their strength, Israel is indestructible and mighty. God cannot change His promise.
- **The third oracle (24:3–9):** Israel will inherit the land, and nothing will stop this from happening. The fact that Agag, the Amalekite king, is mentioned confirms specifically that Canaan is in mind here. This blessing also states that Israel will devour hostile nations. This fulfills the promise that they will possess their enemies' cities. The last words of this blessing bring home a key point of the Abrahamic covenant: May those who bless you be blessed, and those who curse you be cursed!
- **The fourth oracle (24:15–19):** This vision promises a king in the distant future who will defeat Israel's enemies and crush the foreheads of Moab. This passage seems to anticipate King David's victories, and the promise of his throne: the promise of the Messiah whom the Gentiles will obey. By this point, Balaam knows that the curse is not coming to Israel but to Balak. This fourth oracle is actually a series development of the third one, explicitly describing the distant future.

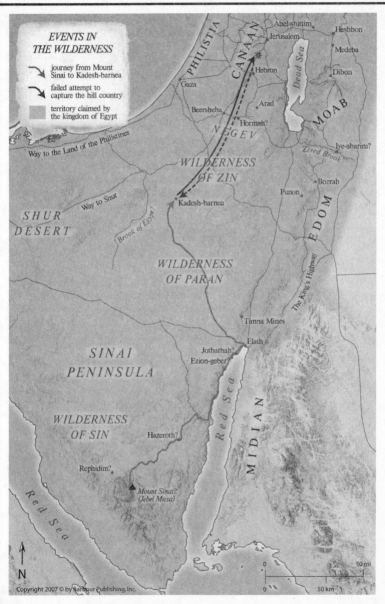

EVENTS IN
THE WILDERNESS

→ journey from Mount
Sinai to Kadesh-barnea

→ failed attempt to
capture the hill country

territory claimed by
the kingdom of Egypt

PHILISTIA

CANAAN

Abel-shittim

Heshbon

Jerusalem

Medeba

Hebron

Dibon

Gaza

Dead Sea

MOAB

Beersheba

Arad

Hormah?

Iye-abarim?

Way to the Land of the Philistines

NEGEV

Zered Brook

WILDERNESS
OF ZIN

Way to Shur

Kadesh-barnea

Bozrah

SHUR
DESERT

Brook of Egypt?

Punon

EDOM

WILDERNESS
OF PARAN

The King's Highway

Timna Mines

SINAI
PENINSULA

Elath

Jotbathah?
Ezion-geber?

Red Sea

WILDERNESS
OF SIN

Hazeroth?

MIDIAN

Rephidim?

Mount Sinai?
(Jebel Musa)

Red Sea

N

0   50 mi

0   50 km

Copyright 2007 © by Barbour Publishing, Inc.

221

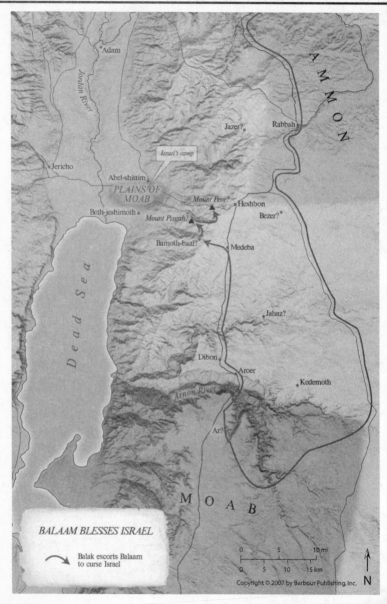

BALAAM BLESSES ISRAEL

→ Balak escorts Balaam
to curse Israel

0   5   10 mi

0   5   10   15 km

N

Copyright © 2007 by Barbour Publishing, Inc.

Finally, Balaam describes the future destruction of those leaders who are present: Amalek, Kain, Asshur, and Eber (24:20–24).

📖 25:1–18

THE THREAT FROM WITHIN

Setting Up the Section

After Balaam goes home, a new and more subtle assault on Israel spreads through the immense population. And, as we find out later (31:8, 16), Balaam is tied to it.

This strategy uses Moabite women—possible temple prostitutes—to seduce the men of Israel and lead the whole nation to ruin through idolatry. God hates sexual immorality, especially when it is tied to idol worship. Therefore, if Moab could not take down Israel through a curse from Balaam, it hoped to use the lust of the flesh.

While the Israelites are at Shittim, the region across the Jordan from Jericho, they are drawn into the worship of Moab's god, Baal of Peor, through Moabite women (25:1-3). Baal is a fertility god whose worship often involves sexual immorality. Israel would be drawn into sin with Baal more than once in its history.

The Lord commands Moses to slay all of the leaders of Israel so that He might turn His anger away from the entire people. Moses orders the judges to slay the men who have coupled themselves with Baal of Peor.

When one of the leaders of Israel blatantly brings a Midianite woman into the camp to have sexual relations with her, Phinehas, the grandson of Aaron through Eleazar, spears them both with one stroke. This stops the plague of apostasy and sexual immorality, which leads to the death of 24,000 Israelites—a number even larger than the 14,700 who died in Korah's rebellion (chapter 16). (There is some debate over whether 25:10 also refers to an actual plague.)

Critical Observation

How is Phinehas' slaying of the offending couple meritorious? The high priest represents God before the people. That's why God compares Phinehas' zeal to His own. The execution of the sinners illustrates in a brutal way just how much God hates sin.

In addition, the high priest represents the people before God. As such, Phinehas restores the covenant between God and Israel, which had been broken by worshiping false gods. That's why he is awarded the covenant of peace.

As a result, in verses 10–16, God affirms Phinehas, offering him a perpetual priesthood. Phinehas shows that he shares in God's jealousy for uprightness among the people. Therefore, the Lord proclaims that Phinehas has His covenant of peace. This means that he possesses a perpetual priesthood, having made atonement for the sons of Israel.

The Israelite who committed the sexual sin was Zimri, a leader of the Simeonites. The Midianite woman who participated was Cozbi, a daughter of Zur, who was a leader in Midian. Because this woman was a Midianite, the Lord commands Moses to be in perpetual war with the Midianites, who are closely associated with the Moabites. Moses is to attack them because they had been a part of this plot at Peor, to lead the Israelites away from God into idolatry and sexual immorality.

Take It Home

Right after the magnificent prophecies of Balaam comes this depravity, reflecting a common pattern of spiritual lows after high points. Think of the golden calf right after Moses is given the Ten Commandments, and the ordination of Aaron followed by the disobedience of his sons. Perhaps we are most vulnerable after a mountaintop experience. Israel's journey stands as a warning to seek consistent obedience in our walk with God.

26:1–65

PREPARATIONS BEGIN

Preparations are now beginning for the Israelites to take the land. The first thing that must take place is a census, in which men age twenty and older within each tribe are counted.

The counting of the people provides several things for the Israelites:

- It confirms the reality of God's promise of the land in Genesis 12:7. God makes good on His promises.
- It focuses the people on the step before them. They are going to get land that will be big enough for their clan, but they are going to have to fight for it. Thus, numbering the men for war makes that point abundantly clear.
- It reaffirms God's faithfulness to Israel. Even though people from every tribe rebelled against God, He did not wipe out every tribe. Therefore, this walk down memory lane reminds the people that God is trustworthy, just, kind, and reliable.

In Numbers 26:1–2, the Lord tells Moses and Eleazar to take a census. So, in verses 3–51, we see the results. On the plains of Moab by the Jordan, across from Jericho, Moses and Eleazar carry out the command. The census is to be of men twenty years and older who are able to go to war. It is important that a breakdown of the nation, its family distribution, and its military size be established.

The total amount numbers the men at 601,730 and the Levites at 23,000. Now that the census has been taken, the land can be distributed, and the leadership knows the size of the army.

Summary

- The families of Reuben number 43,730 men.

- The families of Simeon number 22,200 men.

- The families of Gad number 40,500 men.

- The families Judah number 76,500 men.

- The families of Issachar number 64,300 men.

- The families of Zebulun number 60,500 men.

- The sons of Joseph—Manasseh and Ephraim
  Manasseh: The families of Manasseh number 52,700 men.
  Ephraim: The families of Ephraim number 32,500 men.

- The families of Benjamin number 45,600 men.

- The families of Dan number 64,400 men.

- The families of Asher number 53,400 men.

- The families of Naphtali number 45,400 men.

In verses 52–56, the Lord commands Moses that the land is to be divided by lot. The larger inheritance is to go to the larger families; the smaller inheritance is to go to the smaller families. Because God is in charge of the outcome of the lots, there will be no fighting over who gets what land.

Demystifying Numbers

Many understand these lots to resemble a specially-made set of dice. The people could not control the way these dice fell, so it seemed to the people that God had room to lead.

Some consider these lots to be the Urim and Thummim (Exodus 28:30). According to the Jewish historian, Josephus, the Urim consisted of two stones, each contained in a pouch in the breastplate worn by the high priest. These stones would be thrown, and God would move them into certain combinations to make His will known. When decisions were made in this way, no one could argue that the decision was the result of politics, nepotism, or favoritism.

In the first census, the Levites are numbered separately because they are not to serve in the army. For the census described in verses 57–62, the Levites are omitted from the main census because they are neither going to serve in the army nor receive any land. Thus, we see a post-census count of the Levites. The Levites numbered 23,000 from a month old and upward.

In verses 63–65, with the exception of Moses, Joshua, and Caleb, there is no one left from the first census. The punishment on the people for their disbelief when they first faced the border was not entering the land (chapters 13–14). That original generation has died in the journey through the wilderness.

Compare the censuses of Numbers			
Tribe	Second Census	First Census	Change
Reuben	43,730	46,500	- 2,770
Simeon	22,200	59,300	-37,100 •
Gad	40,500	45,650	- 5,150
Judah	76,500	74,600	+ 1,900
Issachar	64,300	54,400	+ 9,900
Zebulun	60,500	57,400	+ 3,100
Ephraim	32,500	40,500	- 8,000
Manasseh	52,700	32,200	+20,500
Benjamin	45,600	35,400	+10,200
Dan	64,400	62,700	+ 1,700
Asher	53,400	41,500	+11,900
Naphtali	45,400	53,400	- 8,000

• Simeon's decimated population number may be attributable to its support for Dathan and Abiram, and to the recent catastrophic "affair of Peor," as Zimri (25:14) was a leader of a Simeonite family.

27:1–23

RESOLVING THE ISSUES

The first issue is one of inheritance among the daughters of Zelophehad (27:11). These five women approach the Tent of Meeting to implore Moses, an unprecedented act of courage and conviction.

Zelophehad had died without sons. Therefore, when the land distribution plan was set, his daughters would be left without land. Facing Moses, they want to know if it is fair for them to not have any land because they have no brothers. They also are concerned about the preservation of their father's name. Zelophehad apparently was one of the followers of the skeptical spies; therefore he died in the wilderness (14:10–12; 27:5).

Moses seeks the Lord (27:5–8), who commands him to allow the daughters to receive their father's inheritance. Then God prescribes a set of rules for the succession of the inheritance when other difficult cases arise: If a man dies without any sons, his inheritance is to be transferred to his daughter. If he has no daughter, then the inheritance goes to his brothers. If he has no brothers, the inheritance goes to his father's brothers. If his father has no brothers, the inheritance goes to his nearest relative in his own family to posses it. This ensures that everyone will get the land that was promised to Abraham.

In the second half of chapter 27, the Lord commands Moses to go up to the mountain of Abarim to see the land which He is giving to the nation of Israel (27:12–23). After

Moses views his final destination, he will die.

At Moses' request, God appoints Joshua as Moses' successor. Before all the people, Moses brings Joshua before Eleazar, the high priest, and transfers some of his authority to Joshua.

Joshua is to have the same leadership characteristics as Moses: faith in God, a heart of intercession for the people, strength to lead into battle, love for the children of God, and no fear to carry out God's plans for the nation.

📖 28:1–29:40

PATTERNS FOR WORSHIP

The Lord prescribes specific daily and yearly observances for the sons of Israel to keep when they enter into the land. The entire calendar for the nation is to be governed by worship.

The Lord commands Moses to be careful to present the various offerings at their appointed times, not as rote actions, but as prayers of dependence.

The Daily Offering (28:1–8): Two spotless male lambs are to be offered each day as burnt offerings to the Lord. One is to be offered in the morning and the other at twilight, with a grain offering and a drink offering.

The Sabbath Offering (28:9–10): In addition to the daily offering, two one-year-old male lambs without defect are to be offered to the Lord on the Sabbath. They are to be accompanied with a grain offering and a drink offering.

The New Moon (28:11–15): In addition to the daily offering, the nation is to offer two bulls, one ram, seven one-year-old male lambs without defect, and a male goat. These are for a sin offering, along with appropriate grain offerings and a drink offering at the beginning of each month.

The Passover (28:16–25): The Passover is to be celebrated on the fourteenth day of the first month. This is in association with the Feast of Unleavened Bread (Leviticus 23:4–8), which begins the next day and runs for the next seven days. On Passover, Israel is to rest and to present an offering of two bulls, one ram, and seven male, one-year-old lambs without defect along with their grain offering, and a male goat for a sin offering to make atonement for them in addition to the offerings above.

The Feast of Weeks (28:26–31): Fifty days after the Feast of Unleavened Bread, on the day of Firstfruits, the sons of Israel are to rest. In addition, they are to offer two young bulls, one ram, and seven one-year-old male lambs with their grain offerings and drink offerings, as well as one male goat to make atonement. This is to be done in addition to the offerings mentioned above.

The First Day of the Seventh Month (29:1–6): On this day, they are to rest as well as offer one bull, one ram, seven one-year-old male lambs without defect, the appropriate grain offerings, and one male goat as atonement for them. This is to be offered in addition to the other offerings and drink offerings.

The Day of Atonement (29:7–11): On the tenth day of the seventh month, they are to rest and offer one bull, a ram, seven one-year-old male lambs without defect, appropriate grain offerings, and a male goat for atonement, in addition to the other offerings and drink offerings.

The Feast of Tabernacles (29:12–38): This feast runs the fifteenth to the twenty-first of the seventh month. On the first day, they are to rest and offer thirteen bulls, two rams, fourteen one-year-old male lambs without defect, the appropriate grain offerings, and a male goat as atonement. These sacrifices are to be repeated on the second through seventh days, minus one bull each day.

The Eighth Day (29:35–8): On this day, they are to rest and offer one bull, one ram, seven one-year-old male lambs without defect, the appropriate grain offerings, and one male goat for a sin offering in addition to the regular offerings.

There is not a season, month, or week that goes by that does not have a time of worship associated with it. These offerings of worship are to be seen as prayers—prayers of dependence, repentance, salvation, and sanctification.

Take It Home

There are a few things that are important to observe in all of these sacrifices:

- Worship is to be seen as a part of daily life. There is not a moment or an experience that is to be divorced from worship.

- Excellence must be part of worship because God is worthy of it. All of these sacrifices and offerings are to be done with excellence. Only the best is to be given to God.

- God is pleased and honored with our obedience. When the children of Israel offer their sacrifice to God, it is a pleasing aroma to God. God loves obedience.

- God truly does pardon our iniquities. God put this system in place to provide a means for people to have their sins covered. This entire system anticipates the coming of the perfect sacrifice, Jesus Christ, who will take away the sins of the world (John 1:29).

- God planned for days of rest, which allow His children to have the rest they need. Every seventh day they rest. God provides for our needs because He loves us.

📖 **30:1–16**

VOWS

Setting Up the Section

Vows are commitments made to God that are over and above what is required by the law. Moses introduces the topic in 30:1–2, by reminding the leaders of Israel that vows obligate us to follow through

If a young woman makes a vow to the Lord while she is still at home under her father's authority, her father can undo the vow and release the girl from all responsibility. Girls only are mentioned in verses 3–5, but many theologians believe that all minors who reside under the parental roof are included.

If a woman who has taken a vow to the Lord marries, or binds herself with any form of obligation, there is still a way out. She is bound by the vow unless her husband hears of it and forbids it on the day that he learns of it. If this happens, the Lord will release her.

On the other hand, in verses 9–12, we learn that if a widow or divorced woman makes a vow to the Lord, she is bound by it. The only way she can get out of it is if she takes it in her husband's house, and he hears of it and forbids it on the day that he learns of it.

A husband may confirm or annul an oath of his wife, according to verses 13–15. If he does not annul the oath upon hearing it, the vow remains binding. If he does annul the vow some time after he has heard of it, he will be held responsible. In other words, he must not wait to annul it or he will be guilty before the Lord for breaking the vow.

Take It Home

The seriousness with which an oath is to be taken should motivate us to take a serious look at all our speech. The intent of this law is to teach us to watch what we say as unto the Lord. Whenever one considers oaths, pledges, and vows, he or she should not forget the words of Jesus on this issue, found in Matthew 5:33–37.

📖 31:1–54

GOD VINDICATED

Setting Up the Section

This chapter is a call to war. The Israelites are to go to war with the Midianites. The Midianites were the principle instigators of the wicked scheme of seduction in Numbers 25, in which they planned to entrap the Israelites into the double crime of idolatry and licentiousness. The Lord tells Moses that he is to treat the Midianites as enemies and to kill them. Now is the time for their destruction.

The Lord tells Moses exactly what to do in 31:1–16. Moses speaks the command of God to the people, and says prepare for war. They gather twelve thousand men (one thousand from each tribe), as well as Phinehas, the son of Eleazar, the priest with the holy vessels and trumpets, to fight against the Midianites. This war is to be fought in the manner that God prescribes because the offense was not against Israel but against God.

When the sons of Israel go to war against the Midianites, they gain an incredible victory (31:7-12). They

- kill every Midianite male;
- kill the five kings of Midian;
- kill Balaam, the son of Beor (from chapter 25);
- capture the women and children;
- plunder Midianite livestock;
- burn Midianite cities;
- take all the spoil and prey, which they present to Moses, Eleazar, and the entire Israelite camp at the plains of Moab.

In 31:13-24, the army returns to the sons of Israel; Moses is angry that they have returned with Midianite women. Earlier, the Midianite women had brought a plague upon Israel by leading the people into idolatry. Moses commands that all of the male children be killed, that only the virgin girls be allowed to live, and that the army purify itself (for contact with the dead) and wait seven days before they reenter the camp.

The judgment of God is very thorough. He does not take sin lightly, and the sin that drives the heart of this people brings about certain death to their city.

The Lord commands Moses, Eleazar, and the leaders of the tribes to divide the booty between the warriors and the congregation in verses 25-47. Moses also must issue a tax—one out of every five hundred captured persons and animals goes to the Lord. Half of the booty from the warriors goes to Eleazar, the high priest, and one out of fifty from the congregation going to the Levites. The priests and the Levites are not to go to war, and the only way that they will ever get any spoils is from taxation.

Booty	Total Amount	Half to Soldiers	Tithed to God	Half to Congregation	Tithed to Levites
Sheep	675,000	337,500	675	337,500	6,750
Cattle	72,000	36,000	72	36,000	720
Donkeys	61,000	30,500	61	30,500	610
People	32,000	16,000	32	16,000	320

Not one of the sons of Israel is found to be missing in action. As a result, in verses 48-54, the warriors provide a memorial offering of thanksgiving (6,700 ounces of gold) to the Lord. They want to celebrate God's goodness, as well as make atonement for all that they did in going to war.

Take It Home

When the Midianites sought to remove the blessing of the Lord from Israel, they joined those who cursed Israel and were, thus, cursed themselves. This chapter shows with great clarity the incredible seriousness with which God takes His people, His plan, and those who would try to stop Him. This should drive us to understand the importance of pursuing holiness, as well as the great value of taking God, His mission, and His plan seriously.

📖 32:1–42

AN INTERESTING TWIST

As the entire nation looks across the river to the promised land (32:1–5), there are two tribes, Reuben and Gad, who see that the land in the Transjordan region will be suitable for their numerous livestock. They request that they be allowed to settle in this region rather than going across the Jordan.

In verses 6–15, Moses severely rejects Reuben and Gad's proposal. He perceives it to be a sin like that of their fathers, who did not want to enter the promised land (chapters 13–14). He sees it as

- selfishness;
- discouragement to others;
- failure to learn from the sins of their forefathers;
- failure to walk in the path of obedience;
- failure to live for the will of the Lord.

The leaders of Gad and Reuben modify their request in 32:16–19. Even though they would like for their inheritance to be in the Transjordan, they will go and fight with the rest of the Israelites to help them acquire their inheritance. All they want is to be able to live in this spot after the land has been taken. Moses agrees to let them settle in the Transjordan if they will keep their word and go to war (32:20–27). If they do not fight, then they will be sinning against the Lord.

In verses 28–30, Moses tells Eleazar, Joshua, and the heads of the fathers' households that the sons of Gad and Reuben say they will fight with the sons of Israel in the promised land if they can be given the land of Gilead. Moses says that if they do not fight, they will be apportioned a possession in Canaan, and will have to accept what they are given. Moses puts in place a contingency for their disobedience, just in case they get too comfortable where they are.

The sons of Gad and Reuben agree to the plan (32:31–38). Moses gives to the sons of Gad, Reuben, *and* the half-tribe of Manasseh the kingdoms of Sihon, king of the Amorites, and Og, the king of Bashan, with all of its cities and territories. The first land is distributed to these families.

The sons of Machir, the son of Manasseh, take Gilead from the Amorites, and Moses gives the land to them. More land is being taken and these tribes are getting settled in their new home. The problem has been averted, obedience to God's plan is still going to be carried out, and the nation is about to experience what God promised to Abraham many years ago.

📖 33:1–56

A REVIEW OF GOD'S FAITHFULNESS

Before the Israelites take the promised land, Moses reviews the hand of God in leading the children of Israel out of Egypt to Canaan.

In the first four chapters of Numbers, we see how many of the generation that is entering the promised land were babies when the Lord delivered the Israelites from Egypt. They would not have remembered the great miracle of the Lord delivering them from their bondage, the most powerful event in the entire forty-year period. (Time and time again God refers to Himself as "I am the God who delivered you out of Egypt." One of the main ways God wants to be defined is as the God *who delivers.*)

Perhaps that's why God commands Moses to make this record, starting in 33:1–4. This new generation of followers needs to be reminded that God delivered them from Egypt and will deliver them from the enemies in the promised land. Their God is dependable.

The beginning of the journey, recorded in verses 5–15, following their deliverance from Egypt, is a time of intense testing.

As they travel from the Sinai Wilderness to Kadesh (33:16–36), the people are reminded of their grumbling against Moses and his leadership. It is here where the discontent of the people's heart is put on display—and as a result they reject God's will for entering the land and suffer a great consequence for their rebellion. The children entering the land need to be reminded of this colossal failure so that they will not make the same mistake as their parents.

Then, in the journey from Kadesh to Moab, even the leaders of Israel sin and suffer for their sin. Miriam, Aaron, and Moses all sin and face grave consequences in verses 37–49. None of them are allowed to enter into the promised land. Here we see that no one is exempt from following God in the manner and fashion that God determines.

Critical Observation

It would be horrible for the next generation to enter the promised land ignorant of their history and of the mistakes made before them. The power of God's hand of deliverance, the wildness of God's grace and mercy, the serious consequences of sin, and the extreme importance of obedience to God all must be embraced by the next generation.

The Lord speaks to Moses to tell the people to take the land (33:50–56). As they take the land they must drive the inhabitants out of the land and destroy all their false worship. If they do not do this, the current inhabitants will be a snare to the Israelites. In other words, the people who are in the land will draw them away from God.

After just receiving the history of their people, they must not take lightly this command found in verses 50–56. God calls His people to be separated from the world in order to be a light to the world about His great plan of salvation. Thus, the Israelites must be called out from these people, and they must ensure that the idolatry is cleared completely from the land. God makes it clear that He will do to Israel what He plans on doing to the idolaters if they do not drive them from the land. The consequences will be great if they fail to take God seriously.

When they take possession of the land, they must do it by lot, assigning to each tribe their portion as the Lord delineates. God is going to give each tribe what He determines they need. Even though the land is God's gift to the people, they still need to distribute the land according to lots so that there is impartial distribution. No doubt high levels of emotion would surface if they all have to pick their own land. God is going to give the land to the nation exactly in a manner that He wants so that all will be able to worship God for what He has provided.

Take It Home

Just as it is important that the next generation of Israelites not lose sight of the mighty hand of God in delivering them through such a journey, we, too, must remember how God has worked in our lives. When the work of God in the past is forgotten, then the character of God is overlooked in the present. The fallout of this is people who do not trust in God, live for God, and depend on God in the future.

📄 34:1–29

DISTRIBUTION OF THE LAND

Throughout Numbers, God has reiterated in multiple ways His promise that the people would reach Canaan (See 13:2; 14:8, 16, 23, 30; 15:2, 18; 27:12; 32:7, 9, 11). Now, the children of Israel are about to hear what portions of the land will be assigned to each tribe. This continues to affirm the certainty of this promise. God will distribute the land before they take it, because it is a sure thing that they will have the land.

The Israelites never occupy the entire land—they do not drive out all the inhabitants. One of the main enemies that emerges after Israel takes the land is the Philistines. They have strongholds in the western frontiers. This keeps the nation from enjoying all that God has provided for them.

The two and a half tribes of Gad, Reuben, and Manasseh would not be included in the apportionment of the land, since they already have their portion in the Transjordan (34:13–29). For the rest of the tribes, who divides the land? The job is given to Eleazer the priest, Joshua the son of Nun, and a chosen leader from each of the remaining nine and a half tribes.

Demystifying Numbers

Looking at the chosen leaders' names, it is important to read them with a method called *Theophoric naming*. Theophoric naming is a method of naming someone after God. In this list, the names given carry the idea of the greatness of God. Here's an example:

- Shemuel (heart of God)
- Hanniel (grace of God)
- Elidad (God loves)
- Kemuel (God establishes)
- Elizaphan (God protects)
- Paltiel (deliverance is God)
- Pedahel (God ransoms)

Naming people in this fashion was a way of declaring the greatness of God.

📖 35:1–34

SPECIAL LAND PROVISIONS

The Levites are to be given a portion of each tribe's inheritance (35:1–8). This is because the Levites are to devote their lives to the worship of God. The Levites are not to be given just one specific area of land; instead, they are allocated forty-eight towns with pastureland around them. The surrounding land extends around the city 500 yards (1,000 cubits) and extends 1,000 yards (2,000 cubits) around the city walls.

Six of the forty-eight Levites' towns are to be set apart as cities of refuge, to which a person who has killed someone may go for safety (35:9–34). The Lord is fully aware that there will be conflict between people. Thus, if someone kills another accidentally, he may flee to this place of refuge for protection until he can stand trial for his action.

To ensure that everyone understands what these cities are for, God explains in verses 16–21. A person who commits deliberate murder—if he strikes someone with an iron object, a stone, a wooden object, or his hand, by lying in wait or in enmity—is not allowed a place of refuge, but instead, the blood avenger is to put the murderer to death.

If a person commits involuntary manslaughter, if he pushes his victim suddenly without enmity, throws something at him without lying in wait, or strikes him with any deadly object without being his enemy or seeking his injury, then that person is allowed to have protection until a trial can be given.

Here is the way it works: If someone commits involuntary manslaughter, the congregation sends him to the city of refuge, where he is to stay until the death of the high priest. The victim's family is not allowed to hurt the person. If he leaves the city of refuge before the death of the high priest, the blood avenger is allowed to take the life of the one who committed the act.

Critical Observation

In Summary:

- First, if anyone is accused of a murder, two witnesses are to testify concerning the crime—no one is to be put to death on the basis of one witness.

- Second, the accused person is to surrender his life if he is convicted of murder.

- Third, the murdered person's kinsman is to be the avenger of the wrong, and thus they must carry out the execution.

- Fourth, there is no other penalty than the blood of another. Since murder is an attack on the very life that God gives, it is important that, if life is going to be held in regard, the person who takes the life must forfeit his life.

God takes life seriously. Therefore, the people must understand how to hold life in the same high esteem while allowing for accidents to occur.

📖 36:1–13

FUTURE OWNERSHIP OF THE LAND

In Numbers 27:1–11, there is land that is to be distributed to the daughters of Zelophehad, who had died without sons. The daughters want to know if they will get land since there are no men left in their family. God says they will. Now the question arises, what happens if these girls marry? Do they lose their land?

This brought up a question about marriage and land being inherited by other families. Could one family begin to marry women in another family, and thus begin to amass a giant amount of land? It would be a very natural way of thinking for individuals to become self-centered and try to acquire wealth and take from others, to their own detriment.

God speaks to this issue to ensure that there will be fairness. People must marry within their own tribe so that the land will remain distributed in the same fashion as it was first given. No inheritance is to pass from tribe to tribe. Land ownership is something that is very important to the nation. God does not want one family member to lose out on the inheritance, and He protects each family to ensure that each generation will have what their forefathers originally received.

This also highlights the significance of the family. God wants to ensure that each generation will be able to survive and not lose out due to land issues. It is important to note how Numbers ends. The daughters of Zelophehad do marry within their tribe: They obey the Word of the Lord. One of the great themes of the book of Numbers is the importance of obedience. God must be taken seriously, and obedience to Him must be more than a goal; it must be a lifestyle.

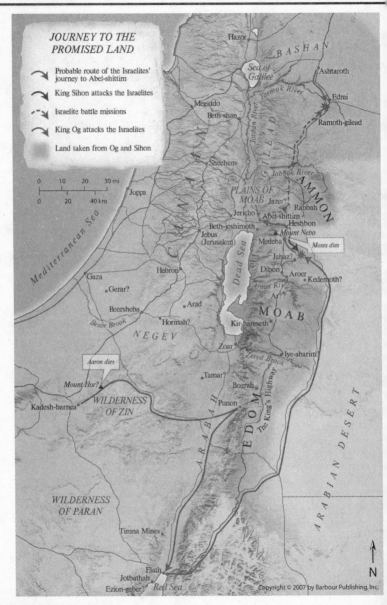

JOURNEY TO THE PROMISED LAND

Probable route of the Israelites'
journey to Abel-shittim

King Sihon attacks the Israelites

Israelite battle missions

King Og attacks the Israelites

Land taken from Og and Sihon

0   10   20   30 mi
0   20   40 km

Hazor

BASHAN

Sea of Galilee

Ashtaroth

Yarmuk River

Edrei

Megiddo

Beth-shan

Ramoth-gilead

GILEAD

Jordan River

Shechem

Jabbok River

AMMON

PLAINS OF MOAB

Jazer?

Rabbah

Joppa

Jericho

Abel-shittim

Heshbon

Beth-jeshimoth

Mount Nebo

Medeba

Moses dies

Jebus (Jerusalem)

Dead Sea

Jahaz?

Dibon

Aroer

Kedemoth?

Hebron

Arnon River

Gaza

Gerar?

Ari?

MOAB

Beersheba

Arad

Besor Brook

Hormah?

Kir-hareseth

NEGEV

Zoar

Iye-abarim?

Zered Brook

Aaron dies

Tamar?

Bozrah

Mount Hor?

Punon

The King's Highway

Kadesh-barnea

WILDERNESS OF ZIN

ARABAH

EDOM

ARABIAN DESERT

WILDERNESS OF PARAN

Timna Mines

DESERT

Elath

Jotbathah

Ezion-geber?

Red Sea

Copyright © 2007 by Barbour Publishing, Inc.

Mediterranean Sea

236

CONTRIBUTING EDITORS:

Robert L. Deffinbaugh, Th.M. graduated from Dallas Theological Seminary with his Th.M. in 1971. Bob is a teacher and elder at Community Bible Chapel in Richardson, Texas and a regular contributor to the online studies found at Bible.org.

Keith Krell, M.Div. has been the Senior Pastor at Emmanuel Bible Fellowship since December 2000. Prior to this position he served as Minister of Outreach and Care at Suburban Christian Church in Corvallis, Oregon (1996-2000), interned at New Heights Church in Vancouver, Washington (1993-95), and taught classes at Multnomah Bible College and Seminary (1994-95). He is a graduate of Multnomah (BA in Theology; Masters of Divinity). Possessing a passion for God's Word, Keith immerses himself in Bible study and research. He routinely writes articles and book reviews for various publications.

Dr. Stephen Leston is pastor of Kishwaukee Bible Church in DeKalb, Illinois. He is passionate about training people for ministry and has served as a pastor at Grace Church of DuPage (Warrenville, Illinois) and Petersburg Bible Church (Petersburg, Alaska).

CONSULTING EDITOR:

Dr. Tremper Longman is the Robert H. Gundry Professor of Biblical Studies at Westmont University. He has taught at Westmont since 1998 and taught before that for 18 years at the Westminster Theological Seminary in Philadelphia. Dr. Longman has degrees from Ohio Wesleyan University (B.A.), Westminster Theological Seminary (M.Div.), and Yale University (M.Phil.; Ph.D.). He has also been active in the area of Bible translation, in particular he serves on the central committee that produced and now monitors the New Living Translation.

WITH SPECIAL THANKS TO BIBLE.ORG

Bible.org is a nonprofit (501c3) Christian ministry headquartered in Dallas, Texas. In the last decade, bible.org has grown to serve millions of individuals around the world and provides thousands of trustworthy resources for Bible study including the new NET BIBLE® translation.

Bible.org offers thousands of free resources for:
- Spiritual formation and discipleship
- Men's ministry
- Women's ministry
- Pastoral helps
- Small group curriculum and much more

Bible.org can be accessed through www.bible.org.